THE
MANAGEMENT
CONTROL FUNCTION

by

ROBERT N. ANTHONY

Ross Graham Walker Professor of Management Control, Emeritus

Harvard Business School

The Harvard Business School Press

Boston, Massachusetts

92   91   90   89   5   4   3   2

Library of Congress Cataloging-in-Publication Data

Anthony, Robert Newton, 1916–
    The management control function / by Robert N. Anthony.

        p.   cm.
    Rev. ed. of: Planning and control systems. 1965.
    Bibliography: p. 187
    Includes index.
    ISBN 0-87584-184-8
    1. Industrial management. I. Anthony, Robert Newton, 1916–
Planning and control systems. II. Title.
HD31.A59 1988
658.4′01—dc19   88-16336
                CIP

The paper used in this publication meets the requirements of the American National
Standard for Permanence of Paper for Printed Library Materials Z39.49-1984.

CONTENTS

PREFACE

THIS book started out as a revision of my *Planning and Control Systems: A Framework for Analysis* (Boston: Division of Research, Harvard Business School, 1965). As it developed, however, the contents became sufficiently different to warrant a new and more descriptive title. The present book is partly a revision of the earlier one and partly a discussion of topics not contained in it.

In 1965, the function called "management control" was not generally recognized as a discrete activity; now it is. Much research on this function has taken place, and I have learned much from experience in businesses, in government and other nonprofit organizations, in the classroom, and in the courtroom. Although the new knowledge does not lead to a change in the broad outline of the conceptual framework, it does warrant more specific statements on certain topics that were discussed fuzzily, it suggests the addition of certain topics, such as project control, which were not mentioned, and it emphasizes the importance of a point that was only touched on in the earlier book, namely, that generalizations about management control should take into account differences in an organization's environment. As a minor matter, it suggests a few changes to make terms and their definitions more descriptive.

The sole purpose of the earlier book was to describe a useful conceptual framework. Management control is one topic in that framework. This book describes in some depth aspects of the management control environment and the management control process.

The preface to the 1965 book includes the following comment from a colleague:

> I am a patient man, I believe, but my tolerance of the sort of Medieval scholasticism that speculated on "angels per pin point" or on orders of classification is not great. I, frankly, couldn't care less. Go ahead and publish, but don't expect me to read it.

Such a comment was not encouraging. Nevertheless, I am mindful of the point that President James B. Conant of Harvard made so vividly in *On Understanding Science*, namely, that development of a framework or conceptual scheme often has led to progress, even though the framework turns out to be wrong.[1] Isolated experiences and discrete bits of knowledge are not very useful. When organized into some kind of pattern, however, the pieces often illuminate one another; the whole becomes greater than the sum of its parts.

The 1965 framework *has* proved to be useful. It, or a variation of it, has been used in a hundred or so books, monographs, doctoral dissertations, and articles. My hope is that the more specific statements in the present volume will turn out to be equally useful.

ROBERT N. ANTHONY

Waterville Valley, New Hampshire
March 1988

1. James B. Conant, *On Understanding Science: An Historical Approach* (New Haven: Yale University Press; London: Oxford University Press, 1947).

ACKNOWLEDGMENTS

A S is the case with thousands of his students, I owe much to Ross Graham Walker, a great teacher, who was the first person, so far as I know, to explain the principles of the management control function. Although he has been dead for many years, his influence persists.

Three of the research assistants who worked on the 1965 book have gone on to distinguished careers, and I continue to benefit from their comments: Dr. Robert Deming, Dr. James S. Hekimian, and Dr. Chei-min Paik.

Charles A. Anderson, Norton Bedford, John Dearden, James S. Reece, and David W. Young, my coauthors on other books, also contributed to my thinking on this one. Except for a few diagrams, I have not copied material from these books, but writing and revising them obviously helped develop the ideas contained herein.

Colleagues at the Harvard Business School who have provided helpful comments on drafts include William J. Bruns, Jr., Charles J. Christenson, Robin Cooper, J. Ronald Fox, the late Walter F. Frese, Paul R. Lawrence, Jay W. Lorsch, Kenneth A. Merchant, F. Warren McFarlan, Vijay Sathe, Robert L. Simons, and Richard F. Vancil.

Others who commented on my material or who furnished me useful material of theirs are Xavier F. Gilbert, IMEDE; V. Govindarajan, Tuck School of Dartmouth College; Donn B. Miller, O'Melveny & Myers; William Weekes, Deakin University, Australia; and Gordon Shillinglaw, Columbia University.

Secretarial and research help from the following is much appreciated: Nancy Anthony, Judy Grady, Emily Hood, Elizabeth Keyes, and Pat Lougee.

THE
MANAGEMENT
CONTROL FUNCTION

1
INTRODUCTION AND SUMMARY

NEED FOR A FRAMEWORK

IN order to be useful, information about any broad subject needs to be organized around a framework. If the topics and subtopics of the framework are well chosen, we can make generalizations about the subject that are generally applicable for one category but are not applicable for other categories. In contrast with anecdotes, which describe a single situation, these generalizations are useful because they summarize lessons drawn from many individual cases. They are most useful when their relationship to an overall framework is understood.

For example, most people would agree with the generalization that budgets are useful. In order to understand *why* budgets are useful and why some ways of preparing and using budgets are better than others, budgeting should be recognized as one part of a broader process that has to do with control in an organization. Furthermore, there are significant differences between the budgeting process and another process called "production control," even though both categories have to do with control. When budgeting and production control are recognized as belonging in quite different parts of a framework, it becomes clear that many generalizations that apply to one do not apply to the other. In short, progress in accumulating knowledge depends on the development of frameworks as the basis for arranging generalizations.

NATURE AND USES OF THE FRAMEWORK

A framework has both a vertical, or hierarchical, dimension and a horizontal dimension.

The lower one descends in the hierarchy, the more specific are the statements that can be made, but the more narrow are the events or objects to which they are applicable. Dogs and cats are mammals, and some general statements apply to both. More specific statements can be made about each subcategory: a dog barks; a cat meows. From these statements valid inferences can be drawn: if a mammal barks, it is more likely to be a dog than a cat.

Members of the categories on the same horizontal level of the framework have similarities as well as differences. Knowing how close these similarities are is often

3

important. For example, because the hearts of dogs are similar to the hearts of humans, certain experimental heart operations can be done on dogs before they are tried out on humans, but because dog hearts are not identical with human hearts, the results of such experiments must be used with appropriate caution.

This book proposes a framework for the broad subject area of the planning and control functions in organizations. It has two hierarchical levels. On the higher level, these functions are divided into three classes. On the lower level, one of these classes, the management control function, is described in terms of the environment in which it takes place and the processes involved in it.

Uses of the Framework

My objective is strictly pragmatic. The framework was not developed as an exercise in taxonomy, but rather with the goal of providing something useful—useful to those who do research on the management control function, to those who teach and learn about this function, to those who design and install management control systems, and to those who use these systems.

> CAUTION: *Although this book is intended to be practical, I believe that there should be no difference between good practice and sound theory. If a difference exists, either the theory is wrong or the practice is unsound.*

Use In Research

Researchers need a classification of topics and subtopics that indicates the limits within which their findings are relevant; that is, they want to make statements about each main topic that are valid for that topic but not necessarily valid for other main topics. They want to make statements about each subtopic that are consistent with the generalizations about the main topic and that are valid for that subtopic but not necessarily for other subtopics.

If the statements are in fact valid, they can be applied to new information obtained as the result of research, by deciding where the information fits into the framework. The statements made about the appropriate subtopic, plus those made about the appropriate main topic, will be relevant to the new information if it is classified properly. The foregoing statement is, of course, only approximately correct, for however carefully the topics are defined, there will be many borderline situations for which the precise classification is in doubt.

The other side of this coin is that researchers who report on a study of a specific subtopic have a difficult job unless there exists an accepted framework to which they can relate it. Either they must work out de novo the relevant statements for the main topic of which their subtopic is a part, or they must assume that readers agree with their perception of the generalizations applicable to the broad area, which is unlikely to be the case.

The job of authors and researchers who deal with some aspect of a subject is made much easier if they can assume that readers understand the framework and where material on a given subtopic fits into the framework. Unless readers have this familiarity, authors and researchers must include within each article they write a discussion of the whole area, which is a waste of effort and also tends to obscure the topic on which they want to focus.

Use in Education

For similar reasons, instructors need a framework to establish boundary lines between courses. With good boundaries, a curriculum can be designed with some confidence that, on the one hand, all relevant topics are covered in some course, and, on the other hand, there is not an unwarranted duplication of topics in several courses. Within a given course, a framework permits an orderly arrangement of topics so that students can fit new material in its proper place in the overall structure. Without a way of organizing new information, the learning process is inefficient. Textbooks provide such a framework for most subject areas; the more highly developed the subject area, the better organized are its textbooks.

Use for Systems Design

Systems designers also need a framework. As new ideas come to their attention they need some way of organizing them and of comparing them to, or contrasting them with, ideas they have previously accepted. If such an analysis leads them to accept a new idea, they need to know the limits of its applicability. Scientists study the human body because a better understanding of how it functions leads to generalizations about how to stay healthy and how to cure illness. However, few of the basic functions of the human body are subject to change. The heart pumps blood at a certain rate, and even a pacemaker can't do much to change the rate. By contrast, a study of management control systems in organizations can lead to changes in the systems themselves that will significantly improve the way the organization functions.

Use by Managers

Managers in an organization, of course, need to understand how to act effectively. From education, from reading, from discussion, and, most important, from experience, they develop an intuitive, personal framework consisting of generalizations about the most effective way to behave. This personal framework affects their behavior, either consciously or unconsciously. If managers accept an explicit framework, the generalizations that they develop from various sources are easier to organize, and this permits them to use these generalizations in a more efficient way. Ultimately, this is the most important purpose of a framework.

FOCUS OF THE STUDY

The study focuses on the management control function in organizations. The principal terms in the preceding sentence are explained below.

Organization

An organization is a group of persons working together for one or more purposes. Three points about this definition are important.

1. An organization has purposes or goals. It exists to accomplish something.
2. An organization consists of human beings. A factory with its machines is not an organization; the persons who work in the factory constitute its organization.
3. In an organization, the human beings work together.

People are one of the organization's resources, but organizations also use material, capital, energy, services, and other resources. They are in this sense "economic" organizations.[1]

The analysis here is not limited to a particular type of organization. Much of my experience has been with profit-oriented companies, but my work with government agencies and other nonbusiness organizations convinces me that the suggested framework and accompanying generalizations are relevant for both business and nonbusiness groups.

Management

An organization has one or more leaders. Except in extremely rare circumstances, members of an organization will not—indeed, they cannot—work together to accomplish the goals of the organization unless they are led. In business organizations, the leaders are called managers and, collectively, the management.

The goals of an organization are established by its board of directors, by someone who owns or controls it, or by an outside agency, such as the Congress. Managers select strategies for achieving these goals; they decide the tasks that are to be performed in order to carry out the strategies and the resources that are to be used for these tasks; they communicate the strategies and tasks to members of the organization; they see to it that the activities of the various parts of the organization are coordinated; they match individuals to tasks for which they are suited and try to establish amicable relationships among them; they motivate the individuals to carry out their assignments; they evaluate how well the individuals are performing; and they take corrective action when the need arises.

A manager is a person who is responsible for obtaining results through the actions of other people. Managers make decisions and persuade others to implement the decisions; other professionals make decisions and implement the decisions personally. I do not attempt to draw a precise line between managers and nonmanagers. In general, as used here, management excludes first-line supervisors because, although they may fit the description given above, they do not participate in many of the management control functions that will be described in later chapters. As a military analogy, managers roughly correspond to officers, and first-line supervisors to sergeants.

> CAUTION: *Physicians, lawyers, engineers, public accountants, professors, editors, and other professionals are not managers per se even though their work is important and even though they may supervise one or a few nurses, secretaries, or other assistants. They accomplish results primarily by their professional skills. When professionals spend much of their time in obtaining results through other people, as is the case with the managing partner of a law firm or the dean of a college, they are managers.*

Control

Control is used in the sense of assuring implementation of strategies. The management control function includes making the plans that are necessary to assure that strategies are implemented. Although "planning" and "control" are sometimes described as discrete processes, both these processes occur in the management control function.

> CAUTION: *Control does not necessarily mean assuring adherence to plans. A budget is a plan, but, with appropriate approval, managers should depart from the budget if they can devise better ways of implementing strategies than those assumed in the budget.*

The nature of the control process is described in books and articles on general systems theory. It is a process that is applicable to all systems, and its essentials are as shown in Exhibit 1-1. A system can be described at two levels: (1) the flow of energy and matter, which can be thought of as the *reality*, and (2) the flow of *information* about that reality. The function of information is to keep the real process in control.

Exhibit 1–1
The Control Process

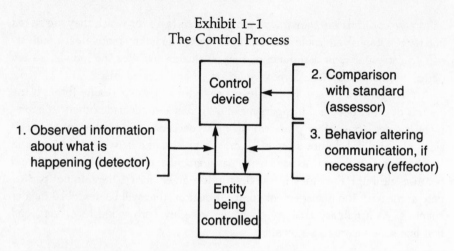

The control process consists of four steps. First, a standard of desired perform-ance is specified. Second, there is a means of sensing what is happening in the organization and communicating this information to a control unit. Third, the control unit compares this information with the standard. Fourth, if what is actually happening does not conform to the standard, the control unit directs that correc-tive action be taken, and the directive is conveyed as information back to the entity. This step is often called "feedback."

The Thermostat Analogy

The example commonly used in describing this process is the thermostat. The thermostat has a preset standard for the desired temperature in a room. It receives information about the actual temperature. If the actual temperature differs from the standard temperature, the thermostat directs the heating unit or the cooling unit to turn itself on. When new information indicates that the actual temperature has reached the desired state, the thermostat directs the unit to turn itself off. Note that no planning activity occurs after the first step in this process. The planning was completed when someone set the thermostat at the desired standard. From then on, the process was strictly one of control.

The thermostat analogy is often used to explain the control process in an organization. The "standard" is said to be the budget; actual performance is com-pared with the standard, and corrective action is taken if there is a variance. It is obvious, however, that this analogy is flawed. In an organization, a difference between actual and standard is not an *automatic* signal that corrective action is needed. If a machine breaks down, it is repaired even though the budget does not contain an allowance for such repairs.

Applicability to an Organization

If the model of the control process in Exhibit 1-1 is supposed to be widely applicable, how can this apparent difference be explained?

The answer to this question, I suggest, is that the principal control process in an organization is not a matter of comparing actual performance against a budget. If we accept as valid the idea that control involves comparison of actual with standard, then the defect of the thermostat analogy must be that the budget is not the relevant standard. This is clearly the case. Senior management does not necessarily want the organization to conform to the budget.

What does senior management want? Essentially, it wants subordinate managers to take actions to implement the organization's strategies, whether or not these actions conform to the budget. In cybernetic terms, the standard is not the budget; it is the organization's strategies. In the example of the machine breakdown, management wants production continued even though the cost of the breakdown is not allowed for in the budget.

Viewed in this way, the control process in an organization corresponds to the model in Exhibit 1-1 and is in all respects analogous to other control processes such as thermostats. This is because in the broad sense control has the purpose of conforming the behavior of some person or thing to a desired state of affairs. If the desired state is the implementation of the organization's strategies, then control does include certain types of planning, because planning is necessary in order to achieve the desired state.

This model also resolves the semantic problem posed by the fact that planning and control in an organization are closely related. In order to implement strategies, managers must plan. This planning is *a part of* the control process. The whole process involves all the actions that managers take to implement strategies, and many of these actions involve making plans.

The following sections summarize the discussion in the next six chapters.

BOUNDARIES OF MANAGEMENT CONTROL (Chapter 2)

Management control is one of three types of planning and control activities that occur in an organization. The other types are strategic planning and task control. In order to understand the management control function, it must be clearly distinguished from the other types.

Management Control

My definition of the management control function is implicit in the preceding discussion:

> *Management control is the process by which managers influence other members of the organization to implement the organization's strategies.*

The definition does not imply a value judgment about how good the management control process is in a given organization. Its purpose is to keep the organization "under control" in the sense of implementing its strategies so as to achieve its goals. Individual control systems succeed or fail in achieving this purpose in varying degrees. A certain thermostat may not be sufficiently precise to control temperature within desired limits, or it may be defective and not achieve control at all. The management control process in an organization is vastly more complicated than a thermostat, both because the work of the organization is more complicated than the work of a furnace or air conditioner and because the process involves the reaction of human beings, whose behavior is much more difficult to predict than the behavior of a heating or cooling unit. A management control system may be ineffective, or it even may be counterproductive. Nevertheless, its purpose is as defined above.

CAUTION: *The process governed by the thermostat is said to be "out of control" if the thermostat is defective. In management control, the term "out of control" is rarely appropriate. Management control in some organizations is better than in others, but the difference is one of degree.*

Strategic Planning

Management control is one type of planning and control activity that goes on in an organization. However, many planning and control activities are not encompassed by the definition of management control. For one thing, the definition assumes the existence of goals and strategies for the organization, but these do not come into being automatically. One important goal of a business is to earn satisfactory profits, but there are innumerable ways in which this goal may be sought. Just as someone must decide on the appropriate temperature and then set the thermostat, so someone must decide what the goals and strategies of the organization should be and communicate these to the managers who are to implement them. The development of appropriate goals and strategies is primarily a planning process.[2] I label this process "strategic planning" and define it as follows:

> *Strategic planning is the process of deciding on the goals of the organization and the strategies for attaining these goals.*

Strategies are guidelines for deciding the appropriate actions for attaining the organization's goals. They are big plans having major consequences. Some students of management restrict the word "strategy" to those plans that are made in response to a competitor's action or in anticipation of its probable reaction. There appears to be no particular reason for such a restriction, and the word is not used here in that limited sense.

The essential difference between strategic planning and management control is that the strategic planning process is unsystematic. The need for a strategic decision can arise at any time, either in response to a perceived threat or to take advantage of a perceived opportunity. Such threats and opportunities are not discovered systematically or at regular intervals.

Although a company may hire a consulting firm to review its strategies and make recommendations, such a review is made whenever management decides it is needed (or when management has been sold on the need), not every three years or five years, or at some other regular interval. The consulting firm probably has developed a systematic approach for making such a review; however, the review cannot be carried out by following a routine. The success of the review process depends primarily on the skill that the consultants bring to the job, not on a cookbook set of rules for doing strategic planning.

In many types of nonbusiness organizations, particularly governments, strategy formulation is especially unsystematic and difficult because leaders have differing opinions about what the entity's goals should be, and there is no rational way of resolving these differences.

Thus, although both strategic planning and management control involve the mental activity of planning, the nature of the planning activity involved in one is quite different from that involved in the other. Strategic planning is done by top management; it is done irregularly whenever opportunities arise or threats are perceived; it focuses on one aspect of the organization rather than on the organization as a whole, and it involves a large amount of judgment but a relatively small amount of personal interaction. Management control is a systematic process. It is done by managers at all levels; it is done on a regular basis; it involves the whole organization; and it involves a large amount of personal interaction and relatively less judgment. These and other differences will be discussed in depth in Chapter 2.

Strategic planning sets the boundaries within which management control takes place. The strategies of an organization provide guidelines that are useful in the management control process because they provide a basis for deciding on proposed courses of action. Of all the available alternatives, the one that is most consistent with the strategies is the one that should be adopted.

Most strategic planning takes place in organizations that already exist and are pursuing a certain set of strategies. In such organizations, strategic planning may result in a basic change in some aspect of the organization's direction, but it rarely results in a change in the total of all strategies.

Task Control

As the term suggests, the management control process focuses on managers. An essential characteristic of the process is that the "standard" against which actual performance is measured is consistent with the organization's strategies. A great many control activities are not carried out directly by managers, and the relevant standards are not directly related to strategies. Individuals involved in these activities may not even be aware of the organization's strategies. They have specific tasks to perform, and control consists of comparing actual performance with the standards for these tasks and taking appropriate action if there is a significant variance. I label this process "task control" with the following definition:

Task control is the process of ensuring that specific tasks are carried out effectively and efficiently.

Task control is distinguished from management control in the following ways.

- The management control system is basically similar throughout the organization; such similarity is essential so that the revenues and expenses of individual pieces can be aggregated. Each type of task requires a different task control system. A production control system is quite different from a research/ development system.
- In management control, managers interact with other managers; in task control either humans are not involved at all (as is the case with some automated production processes), or the interaction is between a manager and a nonmanager.
- In management control the focus is on organizational units called responsibility centers; in task control the focus is on specific tasks (for example, manufacturing Job No. 5687 or ordering 500 units of Item 84261).
- Management control relates to activities that are not specified, and management decides what is to be done within the general constraints of the strategic plans; task control relates to specified tasks and for most tasks little or no judgment is required as to what is to be done.
- In management control the focus is equally on planning and on execution; in task control it is primarily on execution.

These and other differences will be discussed in more depth in Chapter 2.

Relation to Management

Three planning and control processes having been identified, the question arises as to whether, in my enthusiasm for the subject, I have made the definitions so broad that they encompass the whole of management. Are any management functions excluded from the framework? If we take Henri Fayol's classification, the superficial answer is yes, for in addition to planning and control, Fayol includes organizing, commanding, and coordinating as management functions. It can be argued, however, that coordinating is actually a type of planning and that commanding is a part of control. This leaves organizing (which some call "staffing"), which essentially means decisions relating to personnel, and it could be said that putting the right person in the right job is an essential part of the management control process.

Although this view has merit, I have excluded most personnel activities of staffing from this analysis: the selection, placement, review, promotion, reassignment, termination, compensation, training, and development of employees. These obviously are important management functions. I exclude them primarily because the personnel system tends to be operated by human resources executives, rather than by controllers, and, as will be seen, I focus on the activities of the controller. I do include considerations relating to the rewards and motivation of personnel.

Moreover, in addition to the job of managing in the literal sense, managers have specialized expertise. The production manager knows about production; the marketing manager knows about marketing. These areas of expertise are clearly outside the boundaries of this analysis.

In this study, strategic planning and task control are described only for the purpose of drawing boundaries around management control. This permits generalizations to be made that, I hope, are valid for management control but not necessarily for the other processes.

A function, or activity, can be described in terms of (1) the environment in which it occurs and (2) its process, or how it works.

MANAGEMENT CONTROL ENVIRONMENT (Chapter 3)

The environment has two principal aspects: (a) the way in which the entity is organized, and (b) environmental influences that affect the behavior of people in the organization.

Organization Structure

Management control focuses on the activities of responsibility centers. A responsibility center is an organization unit headed by a manager who is responsible for its activities. It receives inputs (materials and services) from the environment, and it processes these inputs to produce outputs. The amount of inputs is usually measured as costs. If the amount of outputs is measured in money, the amount is revenue. Responsibility centers can be classified as expense centers if only their costs are measured, as profit centers if both costs and revenues are measured, and as investment centers if both profit and the investment used to generate that profit are measured.

A system that measures profit encompasses more elements of performance than one that measures only costs. Therefore, if measurement of both revenues and costs is feasible, the profit center or investment center is usually the preferred form of organization. Profit centers require more record keeping than expense centers, however, and they may induce a lack of cooperation with other responsibility centers that is harmful to the overall goals of the organization.

Environmental Influences

An organization has a set of rules, practices, guidelines, job descriptions, customs, and standard operating procedures, and a code of ethics, all of which influence the behavior of its members. These rules are timeless; they exist until they are changed. Management control is also influenced by the organization's culture, or climate. The most significant aspect of climate is the attitude of top management toward control. This attitude permeates down through the organization. The culture is also affected by factors inherent in the nature of the work the responsibility center does.

Behavioral Considerations

The purpose of the management control process is to ensure that the organization's strategies are implemented and consequently that its goals are attained. The process is primarily behavioral. Since managers have personal goals, the central problem is to induce them to act so that when they seek their personal goals, they are also achieving organizational goals; this is called "goal congruence."

Complete congruence between personal goals and organization goals cannot be attained; the aim is to work toward congruence to the extent feasible. For example, most managers have the personal goal of obtaining as much compensation as they can, whereas the organization's goals require that the amounts paid to managers be limited.

MANAGEMENT CONTROL OF OPERATING ACTIVITIES
(Chapter 4)

There are two somewhat different types of management control activities. One relates to the control of ongoing operations and the other to the control of projects. Management control of operations is discussed in Chapter 4, and management control of projects in Chapter 5.

The management control of operating activities consists of the following steps that take place sequentially: (1) programming, (2) budget preparation, (3) execution, and (4) evaluation.

Programming

Programming is the process of deciding on the major programs that the organization will undertake and the approximate amount of resources that will be allocated to each. In a business, programs are product lines plus research/development and similar activities. In a nonbusiness organization, programs are the principal types of services that the organization plans to provide. The programs are intended to implement the organization's strategies. A long-range plan (also called a master plan or a program, or a five-year plan) summarizes the individual programs and shows what is expected to happen for several years in the future, based on decisions made at the time it was prepared and on estimates of future environmental conditions. Although most organizations do some thinking about their future directions, many of them do not have, and do not need, a formal programming process.

Preparation of a long-range plan usually involves two cycles. In the first cycle, rough guidelines and general assumptions about the future are agreed to, and in the second cycle these are used to prepare the long-range plan. Usually, managers of lower-level responsibility centers are not involved in the programming process. Much of the work is done by staff people, and decisions are made by division managers and senior management.

Budget Preparation

A budget is a plan, usually expressed in monetary terms and usually for one future year. Almost all organizations have a budget. If the organization has a formal long-range plan, the budget is prepared within its constraints. Budget preparation essentially consists of fine tuning the first year of the long-range plan. An important difference between the long-range plan and the budget is that the budget is structured by responsibility centers rather than by programs. In budgeting, therefore, the programs are rearranged to conform to the responsibility centers that are responsible for executing them.

Managers participate fully in the process of budget preparation. The approved budget for a responsibility center represents a bilateral commitment between its manager and his or her superior. The manager commits to the performance stated in the budget, and the superior commits to acknowledging that the results will be satisfactory if the performance is attained. Both commitments are subject to change if the circumstances assumed in the budget change.

Execution

The budget is a guide to operations, but for many reasons departures from this guide may be warranted. The responsibility center's fundamental purpose is to implement the organization's strategies effectively and efficiently, and if the manager discovers a better way of doing this than is assumed in the budget, it should be acted upon. Conformance to the budget is not necessarily good, and a departure from it is not necessarily bad.

Managers act on the basis of information, some of which they receive informally by observation and conversation and some of which comes from formal reports. The primary purpose of this information is to alert the manager to the possible need for corrective action. Reports therefore should focus on critical success factors, should identify possible unsatisfactory conditions, and should be prepared frequently enough and promptly enough so that needed corrective action can be taken. Most management control reports are summaries of information collected in the task control system.

Evaluation

No management control system can provide a perfect measure of a manager's performance. Reports necessarily focus on the current period, whereas results in the current period are influenced by decisions made in earlier periods. More important, the consequences of many decisions made in the current period will not be known until some future period. Despite these limitations, evaluation is necessary. A fundamental requirement of reports used for evaluation is that the manager regards the way they are prepared and used as being fair. Essentially, the manager wants the limitations of the reported performance to be adequately allowed for in the evaluation process.

MANAGEMENT CONTROL OF PROJECTS (Chapter 5)

A project is a set of activities intended to accomplish a specified end result of sufficient importance to be of interest to management. Construction projects, research/development projects, and motion picture productions are examples. The special characteristic of a project is that when its product is delivered, the project ends. By contrast, operating activities continue indefinitely, with no discernible end point. In a project, the focus of control is on the project itself, rather than on activities in a given time period in individual responsibility centers, as is the case with the management control of ongoing operations. For this reason, a project control system differs from the system used in the management control of ongoing operations.

A project organization is temporary. A team is assembled, and it is disbanded when the job is done. If team members have permanent assignments elsewhere in the organization, they have two bosses while working on the project: the project manager and the manager of their "home" responsibility center. Such an organization is called a *matrix* organization. The dual responsibility and authority in a matrix organization complicate the management control problem.

In a project, and in each of its components, the focus is on three aspects: (1) its scope (that is, the specifications for the end product), (2) its schedule (that is, the time required), and (3) its cost. Measurement of performance requires that the project be divided into work packages, and that both the planned and actual scope, schedule, and cost of each be measured. A special problem of project management is that trade-offs among the three dimensions are often desirable. The schedule can be shortened by incurring overtime costs. Costs can be reduced by narrowing the scope of the project.

Project planning combines both programming and the budget preparation activities as these terms are used in the management control of ongoing operations. Usually, several iterations of the plans are made as better information becomes available. The final budget is prepared as close to the inception of the project as feasible, in order to incorporate the latest available information.

In actual operations, project managers engage in both planning activities and control activities. They plan when they anticipate possible causes of trouble and decide how to reduce or eliminate them. They control when they act to improve effectiveness and efficiency. This is another illustration of the futility of describing the planning and control processes separately.

Since many projects are unique, evaluation of project performance is usually more difficult than the evaluation of ongoing operations in which reliable standards based on past performance can be developed for many activities. There is also the temptation to use hindsight, that is, to base judgments on what might have been done differently if circumstances that became apparent later had been known at the time when a decision had to be made.

INFORMATION SYSTEMS (Chapter 6)

The management control function is supported by an information system. The system does not, by itself, provide control; it assists managers in their planning and control activities.

The management control system should be a unified, total system because its separate pieces will be aggregated into information about the entity as a whole. This requires that it be built around a financial core because money provides a common denominator that permits this aggregation. It should be an internally consistent system, with terms being defined in the same way throughout. In particular, the budget information should be consistent with the actual data, which seems obvious but which is not the case in some systems, including that of the federal government. The benefits of the information reported in the system should exceed the cost of collecting and using it.

Although the exact nature of developments cannot now be foreseen, managers undoubtedly will increasingly use decision support systems. As the name suggests, these systems support the decision-making process; they do not actually make decisions. These systems will reduce the number of people required for a given activity. Since the number of managers is in part a function of the number of people, the number of managers will also be reduced. The reduction will not be proportional because some of the manager's time will in future be devoted to making better decisions.

Designing and installing a revised management control system is a complicated, time-consuming process. The primary criterion for assuring its success is the support of senior management. It is also important that the effort not be too ambitious. Tackling individual pieces one after another is usually preferable to making a grandiose attempt to install a complete new system.

VARIATIONS IN MANAGEMENT CONTROL PRACTICES (Chapter 7)

The description in the preceding sections focused on what I believe to be a "typical" organization. There are variations from this typical situation for at least three sets of reasons: (1) external environmental influences, (2) factors internal to the organization, and (3) industry-specific factors.

The external environmental influences have the common characteristic that they affect uncertainty. At the extreme of a high degree of uncertainty are newly developed products, differentiated products, aggressive competition, uncertain sources of inputs, and an uncertain political environment. At the extreme of relative certainty are mature products, commodity products, price competition only, few sourcing problems, and few political uncertainties. Organizations in a highly uncertain environment tend to pay much attention to programming, to make only broad budget estimates, to revise the budget frequently, to set ceilings on discretionary costs, to permit much management latitude, to insist on a rapid flow of information, to evaluate performance subjectively and in terms of results rather than process, and to have the compensation package consist of a high percentage of bonus. Organizations in a relatively certain environment do the opposites.

Internal factors are the organization's strategies, whether causal input/output relationships can be identified, internal consistency of organization units, the interdependence among these units, key variables, and, perhaps most important, management style. Each of these has implications for management control.

Industry-specific factors are characteristics of certain industries that affect the management control process. They include service industries, financial institutions, professional organizations, nonprofit organizations, government organizations, regulated industries, and multinational companies.

SUMMARY OF THE FRAMEWORK

Exhibit 1-2 diagrams the framework. The topics and their relationships are as follows.

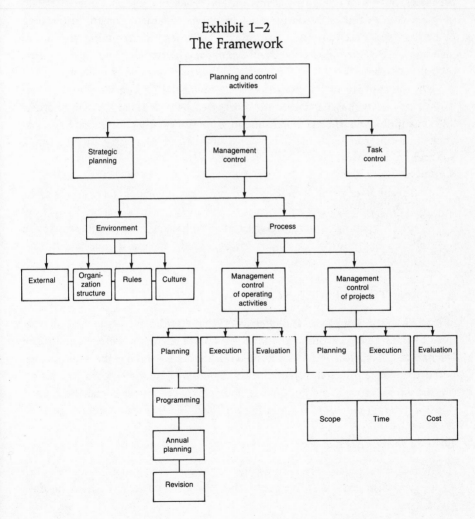

Exhibit 1–2
The Framework

There are three classes of planning and control activities: strategic planning, management control, and task control. The three types constitute an approximate hierarchy in the sense that task control takes place according to decision rules arrived at in management control, and management control exists to achieve the goals and strategies decided on in strategic planning.

This book focuses on management control. Management control can be described in terms of the environment in which it occurs, and of a process. The environmental influences are partly external to the organization. Within the organization, they consist of an organization structure; a set of rules, guidelines, procedures, and the like, and a culture. There are two types of management control processes, one for ongoing operations and the other for projects. Both have planning, execution, and evaluation phases. In the management control of ongoing operations, there are two types of planning activities: programming and annual planning, or budget preparation; the budget may be revised. In project control, control focuses on the scope, the time, and the cost dimensions of each project.

As is the case with all such diagrams, it should not be inferred that a precise distinction can be drawn between the categories, because there are many borderline situations. Nevertheless, the distinctions are sufficiently clear-cut so that valid generalizations can be made. They are summarized succinctly by William J. Sullivan:

> The captain of a ship is engaged, we might say, in management control. The architect who designs a new ship, or the analyst who develops a new concept of shipping is involved in strategic planning. The engine man who adjusts fuel rate to sea conditions and load tonnage is involved in task control.[3]

ALTERNATIVE FRAMEWORKS AND CONCEPTS

It would be presumptuous for me to assert that there are no satisfactory alternatives to the framework outlined above. Of course there are. Peter Lorange and Michael S. Scott Morton have a framework that is essentially the same as that outlined above, but includes an additional dimension.[4] Kenneth A. Merchant uses specific action controls, results controls, and personnel controls as main headings;[5] this is a different way of looking at the problem, and leads to useful insights.

Other Frameworks

The following paragraphs contrast my suggested conceptual framework with some of those proposed by others, not to be critical, but rather to sharpen the ideas given here.

The futility of trying to construct a framework in which planning and control are the two main classes has been mentioned.

Another classification is by "strategy" and "tactics." Although derived from military usage, this approach misinterprets how the military uses these terms. In military usage, "strategy" and "tactics" both relate to operations with a defined objective. They therefore correspond to project control, rather than to the control of ongoing operations. A tactical operation is a short project; strategic considerations apply to longer, more complicated projects. The military uses the term "grand strategy" for what I here call a strategic plan.

Some frameworks use levels in the organization—senior management, divisional management, departmental management—as the basis for classification. I do not think this is satisfactory. For example, senior management engages in both strategic planning and management control, but the two processes are quite different.

Several authors lump together the separate activities of strategic planning and programming under a single heading, either strategic planning system or long-range planning system. I believe this is unsound. Strategic planning, as I use the term, is basically unsystematic and an attempt to force it into a "system" can stifle the creativity that is its essential ingredient. Programming, by contrast, is systematic. It has prescribed procedures, and generalizations about how they should be done can be stated.

Terminology

Writers in the behavioral sciences for some reason like to think up new terms.[6] In some cases, the reason may be pride of authorship, but in others it results from a genuine feeling that the terms used by another author don't quite fit. If there were a standard-setting body to develop a common glossary and obtain adherence to it (as there is in financial accounting and many other professions), most of these apparent differences would disappear. However, it is unlikely that such a body will be created.

Partial Models

A control system has behavioral aspects, it has decision-making aspects, and it has information-processing aspects. Control takes place in an organization, and it can be described in both economic and behavioral terms. An individual author is likely to select one of these alternative points of view. This does not mean that he or she rejects or does not know about other points of view. It simply means that the other views need not be described for the points that the author is trying to make. Unfortunately, this approach tells only part of the story.

For example, task control is primarily rational. Operations researchers can develop valid models for task control that disregard behavioral considerations. If, however, these researchers disregard behavior in models intended for management control, their models are unrealistic. Similarly, generalizations about management control based strictly on the principles of economics are likely to be unrealistic. This happens, for example, in some articles on transfer pricing where the assumption is made that individual managers have full information on marginal costs and marginal revenues, or, even worse, that managers base decisions strictly on information reported in a management control system without considering the reactions of others or discussing possible decisions with others. Management control is a blend of rational and behavioral considerations, and neglecting either type leads to erroneous generalizations.

LIMITATIONS OF THE STUDY

For reasons given in the Appendix, the generalizations described in this study are not based on hard evidence. They are based on such information as I can obtain from the literature, from conversations, and from experience. Moreover, the generalizations are not intended to apply to all situations. Their limitations are described in the following paragraphs.

Organization Size

Small organizations are excluded. The management control function exists, at least in rudimentary form, in any organization that has a manager and a subordinate. Nevertheless, the management control function in small organizations—especially those so small that there is only a single manager—is so different from that in larger organizations that many of the generalizations that apply to large organizations do not apply to them.

Western Environment

Although I have had some experience in other environments, most of my work has been in the United States, a "Western," "well-developed" environment. Certain generalizations may not be relevant to organizations in other cultures. Although there is little positive evidence that such is the case, I am mindful of the disastrous results that have sometimes occurred when an American practice was transferred without modification to another culture.[7]

Informal Control Systems

Although it would be shortsighted to overlook the practical importance of the informal ways in which things get done in an organization, this study is mostly concerned with formal systems. By definition, one does not *design* an informal system; it develops without design (although managers can nurture and otherwise influence it). Since a basic reason for our interest in the management control function is to design better systems, I shall emphasize formal systems—those whose structure is visible and whose operation has explicit authorization. However, the ways in which informal systems impinge on formal systems and thereby affect the planning and control processes are discussed.

Information versus Decisions

The information flowing through a system is used to make decisions. I describe the information, rather than the principles of decision making. Thus, I describe a process called "budget preparation," but not the principles for deciding whether a given item in the budget is optimum. With the exception of task control, the system itself does not make decisions. People make decisions. A good information system should lead to better decisions, but in the last analysis the soundness of a decision is largely influenced by the ability of the people who make it. The systems should be designed so as to take into account the different ways that people use information.

Well-Managed Organizations

I shall describe management control practices in what I believe are well-managed organizations. My opinion of what constitutes a well-managed organization is of course subjective; there is no objective way of defining one.

CONCLUSION

Essentially this study seeks to reduce the diversity of statements about management control that are found in the dozens of books and hundreds of articles about control in organizations. I suggest that many of these differences are unimportant, and that if writers understood one another they would agree—or at least not disagree—on almost all the points.

A review of my *Planning and Control Systems* concluded with this paragraph:

> All this may sound like words, words, words. But words are an important tool of management. Acceptance of this framework as a common language would obviate much of the existing confusion, not only among researchers but also among working systems men. As Professor J. B. Haldane once pointed out: "Mechanics became a science when physicists had decided what they meant by such words as weight, velocity, and force, but not till then. Only in this way can management, too, become a science."[8]

2
BOUNDARIES OF
MANAGEMENT CONTROL

CHAPTER 1 summarized the reasons for developing a conceptual framework for any subject, described the characteristics of a useful framework, proposed a framework for the general subject of planning and control in an organization, and explained why certain alternative frameworks were less useful than the one proposed. Chapter 2 makes the framework more specific by describing the principal characteristics of the three planning and control processes: strategic planning, management control, and task control. Its purpose is to distinguish management control from the other two processes. If distinctions among the processes are not made properly, generalizations may not be valid.

The characteristics described here do not constitute a complete description of the processes. I focus on those characteristics that help to distinguish the processes from one another.

BASIC CONCEPTS

As background for this analysis, I describe briefly two relevant concepts: (1) systems, and (2) management functions.

Systems

The word "system" has many meanings.[1] It is perhaps most precisely defined in the discipline called "general systems theory." This discipline makes generalizations about systems of all types.[2] One category consists of living systems, which are arranged in a hierarchy: cells, organs, individual persons, families, organizations, nations, and supranational organizations. Organizations, the subject of this study, are fairly high in this hierarchy. Some central ideas from general systems theory follow.

A system can be described in terms of its *environment* (that is, the nature of its elements and the forces affecting them at one moment of time) and its *flows* (the interactions through time among the elements and between the system and its environment). The behavior of the system is determined by these two aspects, taken jointly.

Environment

A system has an internal environment and an external environment. The internal environment consists of the elements in which the system operates. In an organization, these would be the people in the organization, the rules and customs that help determine how these people behave, and the physical facilities. The external environment consists of forces that affect the organization. These forces also affect how the individuals in the organization behave.

Flows

There are two types of flows. First, there are *physical flows*, which consist basically of material things and energy. A company, for example, receives inputs of material, labor services, and other resources from its external environment, works with them, and furnishes completed goods or services to the external environment. Since all matter can be described in terms of energy equivalents ($E = mc^2$), general systems theory refers to these flows as energy flows. The second type of flow is the *flow of information*. What actually happens in a system is the flow of energy. Information *describes* what is happening, what has happened in the past, or what may happen in the future.

Confusion arises when a clear distinction is not made between these two types of flows. The word "system," as it is used by practical systems designers, obviously refers to the flow of information, not to the flow of energy itself. An accounting system or a production control system deals with the flow of information, not the flow of physical resources, although one must understand the flow of physical resources in order to understand the system. I shall usually use the word "system" to refer to the flow of information.

> Caution: *I tend to use "system" in the sense of "systematic": that is, activities that are carried on by step-by-step procedures. This is much narrower than the idea described above, but it is useful in distinguishing between structured and unstructured activities.*

Management Functions

Several functions are involved in the management or administration of an organization.[3] Management texts have lists, all of which include "planning" and "control," and most include a closely related function called "directing" or "coorinating." The planning, coordinating, and control functions are what is meant by the "system" in an organization, using system in the sense described above.

Relation to the Totality of Management

The planning and control functions do not comprise the whole of management. An important function of the manager is to make judgments about people: what their abilities and potentials are, what their responsibilities are, who should report to whom, whether A can work effectively with B, who should fill a given slot, and so on. This function is variously called "staffing," "organizing," or the "personnel function." As a generalization, the success of an organization depends to a greater extent on how well this function is performed than it does on the performance of any other management function.

Managers also spend much time on activities that are not management functions. Although the management function is limited literally to the process of obtaining results through the actions of others, managers nevertheless often obtain results directly, by their own actions. The sales manager, or even the chief executive officer, closes an important sale, and the production manager gets dirty hands when a serious malfunction occurs. Managers need the knowledge and skills relevant to the functions they manage. The production manager needs to know the technology of the manufacturing process; the marketing manager needs to understand the factors that influence the success of the marketing effort. This specialized knowledge is excluded from the analysis.

"Planning" and "Control" as Classes

Some authors divide the activities that are the subject of this book into two main classes: (1) *planning* (roughly, deciding what to do), and (2) *control* (roughly, assuring that desired results are obtained). In many cases, these activities are described as occurring at every management level in the organization. Some refer to the "assignment of these activities to various executives," as if they were separable functions.

I do not believe that this is the most useful classification scheme. Although planning and control are definable abstractions and are easily understood as calling for different types of *mental* activity, they do not relate to major categories of activities actually carried on in an organization, either at different times, or by different people, or for different situations.[4]

Most people in an organization engage in *planning*, from the salesman who decides which customer to call on next, to the chief executive officer who is thinking about the acquisition of a new subsidiary. But the planning done by the salesman is so different in its purpose and nature from that done by the CEO that few generalizations can be made that apply to both, and those generalizations that are valid for both are so vague and broad that they are of little help in solving practical problems.

With respect to the process called *control*, the type of control that is involved in assuring that a direct production worker's performance is satisfactory differs in important respects from the control exercised over, or by, the manager of a division, department, or other responsibility center. Therefore, if control were to be a major division, few generalizations could be made that would apply to all aspects of the process.

Furthermore, many authors describe the control process as involving decision making, whereas decision making is also clearly the essence of the planning process. Although conceptually, the control process can be divided into its purely control element and its purely planning element, such a breakdown is often confusing, since in practice a person may be responsible for aspects of both planning and control, and indeed an individual action may have aspects of both.

For example, consider the recurring cycle of activities that are generally understood to be included in the process called "budgetary control." The cycle starts with the preparation and approval of a budget, which clearly is a planning activity. But the approved budget is used as a basis for control; indeed, budget preparation and approval are principal means of achieving control. During the budget year, many activities occur that fit the definition of control, but at the same time the manager may decide to make a change in the way operations are being conducted, which is planning. In short, planning and control activities are so closely intertwined in the budgeting process that to describe each of them separately is not only difficult but also pointless because those concerned with the process usually are involved with both its planning aspect and its control aspect.

Moreover, "planning" and "control" do not have consistent meanings in the literature. For example, the function that some companies call "production planning," others call "production control."

Although it is not useful in structuring the framework that is the subject of this book, I agree with those who find the distinction between planning and control useful in thinking about what managers do. Some activities are planning; others are control.

Alternative Distinctions

Although, conceptually, the cerebral activities that relate to planning can be described and distinguished from the cerebral activities that relate to control, this distinction is not, I believe, a useful way of constructing a framework. In my attempts to find a more satisfactory framework, two main considerations emerged.

First, in the management literature a fundamental distinction is made between the process of policy formulation and the process of policy execution. Furthermore, using the hierarchy described in general systems theory, the policy formulation process is not found in lower-level systems such as cells, organs, and lower mammals; it is found to only a limited extent in humans, and it is primarily an activity of organizations, which are high up on the systems hierarchy. The goals of lower-level systems and the general way of achieving these goals are innate; the system itself cannot set or modify them. Most generalizations from general systems theory do not apply to the policy formulation process.

Second, although organizations do have several types of systems that fit the definition of control used in general systems theory, these systems differ from one another in fundamental respects. Consider, for example, the system appropriate for the control of a profit center, contrasted with that appropriate for the control of inventory levels. In the former, behavioral considerations are important; in the latter, the reaction of human beings is normally unimportant. In the former, decisions involve considerable subjective judgment; in the latter, decisions are normally made in accordance with well-accepted rules. In the former, information needed for control is incomplete and ambiguous; in the latter, information is often as good as that furnished by the thermostat to the furnace.

Thus, neither "planning" nor "control" provides a meaningful basis for a conceptual framework. A better approach is a taxonomy based on activities that include *both* planning and control, but that differ from one another in important respects. In order to make useful generalizations, each main category in this taxonomy should include activities that are essentially similar to one another.

The considerations stated above lead to three types of planning and control processes: strategic planning, management control, and task control. As indicated in Exhibit 2-1, each has aspects of both planning and control, but the relative

Exhibit 2–1
Relative Importance of Planning and Control

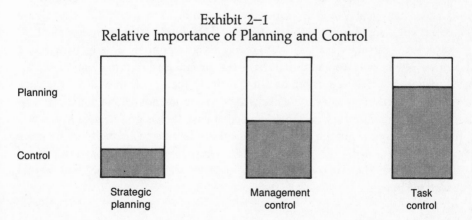

proportions differ. In the following sections, each process is defined and described in a general way. Then, management control, which is the topic on which I focus, is contrasted with the other two processes in order to draw boundary lines among them.

Boundaries not Sharp

It should be emphasized at the outset that the boundaries between each pair of these three processes are somewhat fuzzy. Although I shall describe the principal characteristics of each, it is easy to find processes in a given entity that have characteristics that fit partly into one category and partly into another. The descriptions are therefore generalizations applicable in many, but not all, situations. The borderline situations and exceptions are not so numerous that they negate the essential validity of the categories.

STRATEGIC PLANNING

Strategic planning is the process of deciding on the goals of the organization and the strategies for attaining these goals.[5]

Strategic planning has to do with goals and with strategies. By far the largest fraction of the strategic planning effort is devoted to strategies rather than to goals because goals tend to be unchanged for long periods of time.

Goals

I use the word *goal* to mean a broad, fairly timeless statement of what the organization wants to achieve, and the word *objective* for a more specific statement of a desired end result that is to be achieved within a specified time period.[6]

Every organization has one or more goals. In nearly all business organizations an important goal is to earn a satisfactory return on investment.[7] Other goals are to provide employment stability, to provide a good working environment, to serve the community and society, to reduce risks, to promote orderly growth, and so on. Nonbusiness organizations have the general goal of providing service.[8]

Few organizations spend much time defining their goals in writing, and such written descriptions as exist are likely to be vague and not helpful in the planning process. A municipality has goals, a general hospital has goals, and a liberal arts college has goals; but the goals of each and the differences among them are more likely to be a matter of general understanding of what municipalities, general hospitals, and liberal arts colleges actually do, rather than an explicit, meaningful written statement.

Strategies

Although most business organizations have approximately the same economic goal, the strategies of individual organizations differ in thousands of ways. Strategies are the courses of action that an organization has adopted as means of attaining its goals. They include the assignment of overall responsibility for implementation (often called *divisional charters*).

These strategies are classified in various ways.[9] One basic strategy answers the question: What business should we be in? There are also marketing strategies, financial strategies, organizational strategies, and research strategies. There are strategies for single industry companies, dominant industry companies, and conglomerates. There are strategies for new products, growth products, mature products, and declining products.

In military parlance "strategies," which relate to operations in a particular theater are distinguished from "grand strategies," which relate to worldwide, geopolitical goals. The "grand strategy" of the military corresponds to "strategy" as used in business. In the military, a strategy seeks to accomplish an objective in a particular theater, or even on a particular battlefield in that theater; it is therefore of relatively short duration. In business, strategies may exist for years without being changed.

At any given time an organization has a set of strategies. Although strategic planning is often described as strategy *formulation*, it is more accurately described as strategy *revision*: that is, it is a process of deciding on changes in existing strategies, rather than of formulating a complete set of strategies de novo.[10]

Strategies are big plans, important plans. They state in a general way the direction in which the organization is supposed to be headed. They do not have a time dimension: that is, they exist until they are changed. Strategic decisions are relatively unsystematic. The desirability of reconsidering strategies can be perceived at any time; there is no way of setting a timetable for the discovery process.

Sources of Strategic Ideas

Changes in strategies arise from two types of stimuli: threats or opportunities. Examples of threats are market inroads by competitors, a shift in consumer tastes, or new government regulations. Examples of opportunities are technological innovations, new perceptions of customer behavior, or ideas for improving organizational arrangements. A new chief executive officer usually has somewhat different perceptions of either threats or opportunities than his predecessor, and for this reason changes in strategies often occur when a new chief executive officer takes over.[11]

The steps involved in the strategic planning process have been described as (1) intelligence, (2) search, (3) evaluation, and (4) decision. "Intelligence" is the process of discovering a threat or an opportunity that may lead to a new strategy. "Search" is seeking alternative courses of action for solving the problem created by the threat or for capitalizing on the opportunity. "Evaluation" is estimating the consequences of each of these alternatives. "Decision" is selecting one of the alternatives (or, in many cases, deciding not to take any of them).

Ideas for new strategies can arise anywhere in the organization; anyone can have a "bright idea" or at least the germ of an idea that, after analysis and discussion, becomes a new strategy. There is no way of drawing an organization chart that assigns responsibility for strategy formulation, and no manual can be written that prescribes when and how strategic planning is done.[12] Some systematic aids to strategic planning exist, but they are at best general approaches that must be adapted to the requirements of the general situation.[13]

Strategies are decided at the top of the organization. Strategies for a whole corporation are decided at the top of the corporation; strategies for a division, at the top of that division. Divisional strategies and those for other lower levels are constrained by the overall strategies of the corporation.

A few organizations, usually large conglomerates, do have a staff that is constantly reviewing strategies, and to some extent a systematic method of conducting such a review exists. Such a system can be of some help, but it can also hamper the flow of new ideas if its importance is overemphasized.

Analysis of Proposed Strategies

There is little material in the literature of information systems or systems theory that has any relevance to strategic planning. None of the analogies with systems in lower-level organisms (including the functioning of the human body) is useful because these organisms do not engage in an activity that resembles strategic planning; basically, they can change the way they function only within narrow limits. Some techniques for analyzing proposed strategies in organizations do exist. Benefit/cost analyses, market research, forecasting, bargaining strategy, game theory, and other analytical techniques are useful. Staff members skilled in these techniques can make valuable contributions to such an analysis, but these techniques do not by any means guarantee that the optimum strategy, or even a good strategy, will be selected.[14] The decision is primarily a matter of judgment. The scientific method permits the analyst to arrive at a good solution to a problem in situations in which the relationships among the important variables are known. There is very little in science that aids in strategy formulation, however. If there were, the diversity of strategies that are found in businesses, even businesses in the same industry, would not exist. A few generalizations about optimum strategies have been made, and some of them have been validated, at least to a limited extent, by research.[15]

It is possible to develop a mathematical model that shows approximately how a given business operates, but it is not possible to develop a model that shows the optimum way the business *should* operate so as to achieve its goals. Informed, competent people can differ as to what is the best strategy.

Although improved analytical techniques are constantly being developed, they are, and are likely in the future to be, relatively unimportant. Strategic decisions are of great complexity; neither humans nor computers have the ability to cope with all the variables satisfactorily. Strategic decisions require information about what is likely to happen in the future, and such information is speculative. They depend on an estimate of a cause-and-effect relationship between a course of action and a desired outcome, and this relationship often cannot be predicted.[16]

For all these reasons, strategic planning is an art, not a science.

Organizational Considerations

Only a few studies of organizational behavior relate to the strategic planning process. Strategic planning does involve human interactions, so psychological considerations are relevant; but these are different from the considerations that affect the ongoing functioning of the organization. Although prejudices, perceptions of the ability of the proponent of a proposed strategy, and self-interest do influence strategic decisions, the general idea is to make the best possible judgment about the courses of action that the organization should follow, without regard to the effect of this decision on specific individuals.

The parties involved in the process are senior management (including senior management of divisions for divisional strategies) and staff. Line managers responsible for implementing a strategy may not be involved in its formulation (except to the extent that their acceptance of it is ascertained in advance). Operating managers tend to resist change; if they participate heavily in an analysis of a proposed strategy, they may succeed in killing it.

In the 1970s, many companies created corporate planning staffs, often sizable ones, whose task was to analyze possible new strategies. In the 1980s, there was a tendency to reduce these staffs and in some cases to eliminate them. The reasoning was that the planning staffs tended to stifle the acceptance of ideas that were generated elsewhere.[17]

Three types of persons are involved in the strategic planning process. First, there are the creative, innovative, entrepreneurial types who think up ideas. Second, there are the analytical types who have their feet on the ground and who subject ideas to hardheaded analysis. Third, there are the salespersons, people who sell a proposal to those who must approve it and, later, to those who must implement the approved strategy. An individual may have two of these characteristics, but rarely does one person have all three. Differences among these types can lead to friction, and senior management tries to maintain an appropriate balance among the disparate points of view.

Friction may also arise between the planning staff and operating managers. Staff people tend to ask questions that managers consider unanswerable. In the 1960s, the "whiz kids" assembled in the Department of Defense by Secretary Robert S. McNamara asked such questions as "Why do we need nuclear-powered aircraft carriers?" and "Why do we need aircraft carriers at all?"—questions that caused near apoplexy on the part of the admirals. William J. Sullivan of Princeton University wrote (in an unpublished paper): "The planner deals with what should be, rather than what is, an occupational interest he shares with all other revolutionaries." Line managers are unlikely to welcome revolutionaries.

In the federal government (where strategies are often called "missions" or "programs") special behavioral considerations are involved. In Washington a variety of interested parties push for their own programs, and the final strategy is usually a compromise. The process of compromise can be seen most clearly in the legislative branch; it is roughly accurate to say that the legislative branch is engaged in strategic planning and the executive branch in management control.

Although strategic revision is important, top management spends relatively little time in this activity. (A Cornell University study of how top managers spend their time reported that two percent is spent on formulating strategy.)

MANAGEMENT CONTROL

Management control is the process by which managers influence other members of the organization to implement the organization's strategies.[18]

The purpose of the management control process is to carry out the strategies arrived at in the strategic planning process and thereby to attain the organization's goals. The process involves the interaction of managers with other members of the organization, including other managers. Because these personal interactions are a crucial part of the management control process, behavioral considerations are important in understanding the process.

Efficiency and Effectiveness

The criteria for judging these management actions are efficiency and effectiveness. *Efficiency* is measured by the amount of output produced per unit of input. The most efficient engine is the engine that produces the most energy per unit of fuel consumed. (Efficiency is also expressed as the amount of input per unit of output.) *Effectiveness* is the relationship between the outputs of a responsibility center and the strategies of the organization. If a responsibility center makes the contribution to strategic goals that senior management thinks is attainable, it is effective. A responsibility center should be both efficient and effective.

Nature of Decisions

Within Strategic Constraints

Management control decisions are made within the guidance established by strategic planning. Without such guidance, the manager of a division might be inclined to accept any investment opportunity that is likely to improve the performance of the division. Senior management, however, may have a strategy that involves shrinking the size of the division, or it may prefer to use available funds in other divisions in which the profit opportunities are even greater. The management control process does not rely on general rules, such as "accept any investment proposal whose return is likely to exceed the cost of capital." Instead, the system provides guidance as to the particular circumstances in which investments should be undertaken. It is primarily for this reason that decisions about important proposed investments are made by senior management.

Partly Scientific

Many valid generalizations can be made about the management control process. At the most detailed level there are valid principles for preparing a budget. At a higher level there are valid, but more general, principles for reviewing a proposed budget for consistency with programs and for the appropriateness of the proposed amounts. At a still higher level, the decision to approve the budget becomes one of judgment, for which there are few valid rules. There is no way of demonstrating that a proposed budget is optimum. Also, there are no scientific principles, except in very crude form, that describe how a particular manager should interact with a particular colleague or subordinate so as to achieve the desired motivation.

Nature of Systems and Information

The management control process is systematic. As I will describe in Chapters 4 and 5, the process consists of a number of subprocesses that follow one another in a prescribed sequence, each of which can be described in a fairly specific way. These subprocesses are programming, budget preparation, execution, and evaluation. To a certain extent, the steps to be taken in each process can be set forth in written instructions, and standard forms for collecting and summarizing information are worthwhile.

The relevant information is of three general types: (1) information about the environment, (2) information about what is expected of the manager, and (3) information about what has happened.

A principal purpose of the system is to facilitate coordination. If the system is inadequate, individual managers are unlikely to take actions that are consistent with the organization's strategies for two reasons. First, individuals have personal goals, and these are not entirely congruent with the goals of the organization. A purpose of the management control process is to minimize the difference between individual goals and organizational goals. Second, individuals may not be well informed about the strategies of the organization, about the role of others in implementing these strategies, and about what actions are expected of them. Senior management attempts to ensure that subordinate managers are motivated to attain the organization's goals and that their individual plans fit into the overall plan of the organization, making a coherent whole.

Behavioral Considerations

Although systematic, the management control process is by no means mechanical. Since it involves human behavior, mechanical analogies, such as the thermostat, are not valid. The differences are essentially as follows:

1. The standard used by the thermostat is entirely preset; this corresponds to a planning decision as this term is used in management control. The thermostat does not make this decision; its only function is to take corrective action when the actual temperature deviates from the standard. The management control process includes *both* making planning decisions and taking action when actual performance deviates significantly from the standard stated in, or implied in, the plans. The planning process and the control process in an organization are closely connected, so closely that for many purposes they should be viewed as a single process.

2. Unlike the thermostat, the process does not operate automatically. Some of the devices for measuring and reporting what is happening in the organization can be mechanical, but important information is often detected through the manager's own eyes, ears, and other senses. Although in some cases there are mechanical ways of comparing actual performance with a standard, a determination of whether or not the difference between actual and standard is significant usually must be made by human beings, and the action taken to alter behavior also involves human beings. In order to effect change, a manager must interact with another person, and the result of such an interaction is influenced by the personal

relationship between the two. The term "black box" is used to describe an operation whose exact nature cannot be observed and that therefore cannot be described by mathematical symbols. A management control system is a black box; a thermostat is not.

3. The connection between the observed need for action and the behavior required to obtain the desired action in a management control system is by no means as clear-cut as it is in the case of the thermostat. Although an evaluator may judge that "costs are too high," there is no easy or automatic action that is guaranteed to bring costs down to what they should be.

4. Management control requires coordination. An organization consists of many parts, and the control system must ensure that the work of these parts is harmonious. This need does not exist in the case of the thermostat.

5. Control in an organization does not come about solely or even primarily as a result of actions taken by an external regulating device like the thermostat. Much control is *self*-control; managers act the way they do, not so much because they have been given specific orders, but rather because their own judgment suggests the actions they should take. This judgment is influenced not only by the formal system, but also by the informal environment, or culture, that exists in the organization.

6. The stated plans in a management control system are not necessarily those that should be followed. The plans were based on circumstances that, at the time when they were formulated, were believed to exist, both inside and outside the organization. If current anticipations differ from those assumed in the plan, the planned actions may no longer be appropriate. A thermostat responds to the actual temperature in a room. Management control, by contrast, should anticipate what conditions are going to be in advance of their actual occurrence.

TASK CONTROL

Task control is the process of assuring that specific tasks are carried out effectively and efficiently.[19]

Task control is transaction-oriented; that is, it involves the control of individual tasks. Rules to be followed in accomplishing these tasks are prescribed as part of the management control process; unless there are unforeseen circumstances, task control consists of seeing to it that the rules are followed. For many types of tasks, control can be achieved without the use of human beings. Numerically controlled machine tools, process control computers, and robots are task control devices. Human beings are used in the process if they are less expensive than computers or other control devices.[20] They are likely to be less expensive if the occurrence of unusual events is such that programming a computer with rules for dealing with such events is not worthwhile.

Although the preceding description applies to many types of tasks, there are important exceptions. Tasks performed by professionals—engineers, researchers, lawyers, physicians, teachers—do not fit the general description in important respects. In particular, they are not routine; they are not carried out by following a set of rules. Nevertheless, they tend to be repetitive, and there are general guidelines that are useful in performing the tasks.

Internal Auditing

Although there is some disagreement about this, I shall include the subject of internal auditing under the heading of task control. Internal auditing, it seems to me, is not a management control activity, but rather one that seeks to ensure that the control system itself is operating properly.[21]

Nature of Decisions

Many task control activities are scientific. The relationship between cause and effect, the action required to bring an out-of-control situation back to the desired state, the optimum decision to be made with respect to a given problem, are known within acceptable limits. Rules for economic order quantity determine the amount and timing of purchase orders; principles of probability determine when a process gets out of control. The rules are structured; the desired actions are clear-cut. Research in management science focuses principally on problems of task control. The analogy with the thermostat is valid for task control.

Task control is not entirely automatic, however. Unexpected or unprogrammed events occur, and human judgment is needed to deal with them. Also, professional tasks are not automatic. Although surgeons operate according to prescribed procedures, following the procedures does not necessarily ensure a successful operation. In all tasks involving professionals, the skill and judgment of the professional is important; otherwise there would be no reason for the profession to exist. Except for activities involving professionals, it is safe to say that in task control, a high percentage of the tasks is performed according to prescribed rules.

Nature of Systems and Information

Systems exist for various types of tasks, and they are structured to meet the requirements of those tasks. There are procurement systems, scheduling systems, inventory control systems, quality control systems, payroll systems, cost accounting systems, cash management systems, and many others. Through each system flows the detailed information needed to perform the task. In some cases the system itself may control the performance of the task, without human intervention.

Most of the information in an organization is the operating information needed for task control: What work is scheduled to be done today? What manpower, materials, equipment, and services are required? What operations should be performed? How many hours did each employee work, and how much did each earn? What amounts were disbursed, to whom, and for what purpose? Many task control systems are nonmonetary; the information is stated in physical quantities.

Although task control is systematic, the system is not necessarily simple. The switching gear used to connect the two parties in a telephone conversation costs billions of dollars and is extraordinarily complex. Nevertheless, developments in technology have made automatic switching gear less expensive than human telephone operators. Human beings are involved only if the system malfunctions or if a situation arises that cannot be handled electronically, such as the case of a calling party who does not know the correct telephone number (and even this function is now partly automated).

An entire steel mill can be controlled by electronic devices.[22] Each piece of equipment is controlled by a computer that instructs the equipment to carry out prescribed tasks. The computer senses the environment (for example, to find out the temperature of a steel ingot) and, if the environment is not at the desired state, initiates action to bring it to the desired state. If a variation from the desired state is something that cannot be corrected by that computer, the need for corrective action is referred to a computer at a higher level; that computer controls all the computers in one section of the mill. If necessary, this computer refers the problem to a coordinating computer for the mill as a whole. Computers at these higher levels then initiate the corrective action. This is a task control system even though it involves several levels of control, and these are similar to the several hierarchical levels in a human organization.

Systems for program trading and other types of decisions made by traders in the stock market are another example. They involve complicated decision rules and information about hundreds of stocks; many millions of dollars may be involved in a single decision. A highly paid expert may override the computer's recommendation, but the expert is acting as a professional trader, not as a manager. This is a task control system.

CAUTION: *Some task control systems, especially complex systems, are often labeled as management control systems, and this can cause confusion. For example, PERT (program evaluation and review technique) is a complicated, useful system for controlling the activities on a project; I classify it as a task control system, but some regard it as management control.*

Evolution of Task Control

As the preceding examples suggest, certain activities that were once performed by managers can be automated and hence become task control activities. The shift from management control to task control frees some of the manager's time for truly management activities (or, in some cases, it eliminates management positions).

Also, as tasks become more highly automated, fewer people—both line and staff—are needed to perform a given task. The number of people in the affected responsibility center therefore tends to decrease. Because the span of a single manager is limited to a certain number of individuals, a manager can thereafter manage more activities. Other things equal, the number of managers in an organization tends to decrease.

Behavioral Considerations

When employees are involved in the task control process, they act directly to perform the task. The inventory control clerk actually makes out the requisition that leads to a purchase order. The machine operator makes the necessary adjustments when the machine gets out of control. By contrast, in management control the action of managers is indirect. Managers (when they are acting as managers) do not themselves initiate the requisition or fix the machine; they see to it that this is done by the operators. The behavioral considerations involved in task control are therefore of a different character from those relating to management control. Job enrichment efforts and measures designed to improve productivity are behavioral and relate to individuals who are engaged in task control, but the principles behind these efforts are different from the principles that explain successful interactions among managers.

DISTINCTIONS BETWEEN THE PROCESSES

In the preceding section, I described the three planning and control processes separately. In order to clarify the boundaries between management control and strategic planning on the one hand and between management control and task control on the other, I now contrast them along several dimensions. These are grouped into four categories, and each is summarized in an exhibit, as follows:

The boundaries suggested here are not clear-cut. Planning and control activities lie along a continuum, and no sharp lines partition this continuum. For example, programming, which is one step in the management control process, involves the development of programs to implement strategies, and ideas for new strategies may emerge in the course of examining programs. Thus, programming may have aspects of both management control and strategic planning.

The generalizations given here are broad, and their validity varies with organizations of different types. For example, a stable organization that is relatively unaffected by perturbations in the environment may not need to invest much effort in thinking about changes in strategies, and the points made here about the strategic planning process will be of little interest to such an organization. By contrast, in the federal government much attention is given to strategies that will promote the general welfare. Moreover, the strategic planning process is described here as essentially a rational process in which top management seeks the best strategies for the organization, whereas in governments at all levels the process involves arriving at compromises among conflicting interests, rather than a single-minded effort to attain a fairly clear-cut goal. Forces that lead to variations in management control systems are discussed in Chapter 7.

NATURE OF PROBLEMS AND DECISIONS

Exhibit 2-2 outlines differences among the three types of processes with respect to the nature of the problems that typically are addressed in each process and the types of decisions that are relevant for these problems.

Focus

A management control system is a *total* system. The plans developed in the management control process cover the whole organization, and one important aspect of these plans is the coordination that ensures that the several parts of the organization are in balance. Sales programs must be balanced with manufacturing and warehousing capacity. Planned uses of funds must be balanced with the amount of money likely to be available, and so on.

The strategic planning process is much less likely to relate to the totality of the organization. A perceived opportunity or threat is likely to affect one product line,

Exhibit 2–2
Characteristics of Planning and Control Activities:
Nature of Problems and Decisions

	Strategic Planning	Management Control	Task Control
Focus	One aspect at a time	Whole organization	Each task distinct

Nature of problem	Difficult to identify
	Unstructured
	Many alternatives
	Causal relations
	  unclear
		Precedents exist
		Much repetition
		Alternatives limited
		Some parts pro-
		  grammed
			Prescribed rules
			Mathematical models

Criteria	Social and economic	Efficiency and effec- tiveness	Efficiency
Constraints	Sky is the limit	Generally stated in strategy	Tightly constrained
Planning horizon	As far as can be seen	Next few years Emphasis on one year	Immediate future

Decision process	Some formal analysis
	Mostly judgment
	Time for thorough-
	  ness
	Many iterations
	Irregular
		Much formal analysis
		
		Deadlines
		
		Few iterations
		Rhythmic
			Follow rules; judg-
			  ment if rules are
			  inadequate
			
			Repetitive

End product	Often one decision
	Goals, policies, strate-
	  gies, charters
		Comprehensive
		  plan for whole
		  entity
			Specific actions

Evaluation	Subjective and difficult Long interval	Less difficult At least annual	Usually clear-cut Immediate

one geographical area, one source of materials, one class of customers. The impact of the strategic decision on the whole company does need to be considered, but ordinarily the analysis focuses on only one part of the organization. If the proposed strategy is to enter overseas markets, the decision maker must consider only the relevant ramifications. If the domestic sales force, or the research laboratory, or the operations of certain plants or divisions are unaffected by the decision, no attention need be given to these areas.

The strategic planning process starts when trouble in some part of the organization is perceived or when someone gets an idea for doing something new, and the focus thereafter is on the trouble spot or the new idea, not on the organization as a whole.

> CAUTION: *Some people believe that senior management should be responsible for optimizing the whole organization, and that failure to consider the whole organization in every strategic decision leads to "suboptimization," which is said to be bad. Conceptually, it would be a fine thing if the whole organization were optimum all the time, but as a practical matter, complete optimization is probably beyond the ability of mortals to achieve.*

In exceptional situations the strategies of the whole organization may be reexamined. This can happen, for example, when a new management team takes over an organization that is in great difficulty. Also, certain organizations conduct activities that are sufficiently predictable so that strategic planning for the totality is feasible. An electric utility serving a defined geographical area and committed to a certain energy source can make overall plans for many years ahead with some assurance that the whole operation is optimum. These situations are rare, and, as in the case of an electrical utility confronted with an energy crisis, the need for changes in strategies may arise in unforeseen ways.

In task control, the focus is also on one part of the organization, such as control of inventory, or control of production.

Nature of Problems

Management control takes place within a functioning organization whose activities are limited by the nature and amount of available resources. An apparel manufacturer has resources for producing and marketing apparel, and it has staff units for finance, research/development, personnel, and other corporate functions. The design of the apparel will change, production methods will change, and other parts of the organization will change as better ways of doing things are discovered; but many activities will continue without change during the planning period, and decisions about these activities are similar to those made previously. Other activities will change, but the optimum type of change can be determined (these are "programmed" activities). Still others are subject to change, but only within limits that are fairly well understood; the range of alternatives is limited.

The strategic planning process also has to consider the organization as it currently exists, but by definition strategic decisions result in radical changes. The problem of recognizing a strategic problem is itself difficult, and, once the problem is identified, a wide range of alternatives for solving it usually exists. Selection of the best alternative is difficult because the cause-and-effect relationships of alternative courses of actions are usually not clear. The analyst must look a long way into the future. Setting a precedent is much more difficult than making a decision that is based partly on existing precedents.

Programmed and Nonprogrammed Activities

If the optimum relationship between inputs (that is, costs) and outputs (that is, results) of an activity can be estimated with reasonable accuracy, the activity is said to be a *programmed activity* because the relationships, at least conceptually, can be programmed for a computer. If an economic order quantity formula stating the optimum quantity of inventory to buy is valid, inventory control can be a programmed activity. Programmed activities usually are those in which task control is applicable. Management control is applicable to all nonprogrammed activities, including those that have a programmed component. The control of a division of a company is management control. The control of the accounting department within that division is management control. The control of the posting and check-writing sections of the accounting department is task control.

Criteria

In making strategic plans, the basic criterion is the extent to which an alternative strategy accomplishes the organization's goals. These goals are often not well defined; they include social as well as economic goals, and, particularly in nonbusiness organizations, there may be several conflicting goals. For these reasons the criteria are fuzzy.

In management control the basic purpose is to implement strategies, and these strategies are, or should be, reasonably well understood. The criteria for judging performance are efficiency and effectiveness, and these are more specific and more measurable than the criteria for judging performance in strategic planning.

In task control, the criterion is efficiency, that is, getting the job done on time and at the lowest possible cost. (This criterion includes quality considerations; the job is not done unless the quality of the output is acceptable.)

Constraints

In strategic planning, consideration must be given to the organization's current resources, including its reputation, its penetration in certain markets, and the expertise of its members. However, even the constraints suggested by these considerations can be overcome by acquisitions or other means.

The management control process takes place within policies and strategies arrived at in strategic planning. Also, decision makers accept many aspects of the human, physical, and financial resources available to the organization. In unusual circumstances, actions can be taken outside these boundaries, but they are exceptions and are treated as such.

The task control process is, of course, tightly constrained by the characteristics of the specific task.

Planning Horizon

Most strategies are followed until they are changed; they are timeless. In management control, the horizon is a few years in the future, with particular emphasis on the current year and the next year. In task control, the focus is on the time taken to accomplish the specified task.

The Decision Process

The management control process is *rhythmic*. Decisions are made according to procedures and timetables that are repeated year after year. As will be described in Chapter 4, the first step in the sequence is the process of the formulation of a program or long-range plan; next, one year of this program is translated into a budget; next, operations take place, and finally, actual results are compared with this budget, and corrective action is taken if necessary. The process is repeated annually, and each step must be completed by specified dates. These deadlines are such that there is not time to consider more than a few alternative solutions for a given problem. Many problems can be analyzed by formal methods, however (such as net present value analysis for equipment replacements), which adds to the assurance that the proposed solution is sound.

The strategic planning process is irregular. Except for the limited possibility of uncovering the need for planning through "environmental scanning," PIMS (Profit Impact of Market Strategy), 2 x 2 matrices, or similar techniques, problems and opportunities are addressed whenever they happen to come to management's attention. They do not arise according to a set timetable. After they are first perceived, they often must await analysis until staff time becomes available. There is no set date for completing the analysis. In a crisis, work may be rushed, but more likely the staff works on the problem until it is reasonably well satisfied with its analysis. After the staff work has been completed, discussion among management people may require much additional time. An operating budget is usually completed within three months; a strategic plan may take a year or two to formulate.

Because of the inability to estimate cause/effect relationships for the type of alternatives considered in strategic planning, formal analytical techniques are of little use. Indeed, attempts to rely on a systematic analytical approach may dampen the creativity that is of great importance. Each problem is sufficiently different from the preceding problem so that different approaches should be used.

A manual of strategic planning procedures, if it exists at all, contains only broad general statements—not timetables, checklists of steps to be taken, or analytical formulas.

> CAUTION: *In the classroom, strategic problems can be analyzed by* assuming *cause/effect relationships, but in the real world, knowledge of these relationships is likely to be so uncertain that use of sophisticated analytical tools is often not worth the effort.*

Deadlines are usually not as tight as in the management control process, and there is time to study various alternatives in considerable depth. The analysis of a proposed strategic decision can therefore be more thorough, even though less certain, than a management control decision.

These comments should not be taken as minimizing the importance of regular senior management strategy meetings. Such meetings can address the question "Where should we be heading?" and thereby generate ideas for new strategies. These meetings are held infrequently—perhaps once a year, or once every two years, except in times of crisis.

In a pure task control activity the action is simply to do what the rule says to do. In practice, however, events may occur that were not anticipated by the rules, and judgment in the application of the rules is then required. A production schedule may be laid out according to PERT, line-of-balance, or linear programming techniques; but receipt of a high-priority order, a breakdown in a piece of equipment, or failure of raw material to arrive on the factory floor at the proper time may require the use of judgment in rearranging the schedule. Nevertheless, such judgment is used in task control only in exceptional situations; in management control, judgment is necessary in almost all situations.

A roughly accurate way of distinguishing between management control and task control in this dimension is to note that management control controls *people* and task control controls *things.* Another roughly accurate distinction is that task control focuses on *actions* and management control focuses on *results.*

End Product

The end products of the strategic planning process are strategies, policies, and organization charters. Occasionally, the end product may be a change in goals. In some cases, the end product is a single decision: for example, we shall acquire

Company X. This decision, though, may have ramifications in many parts of the organization.

The end product of the planning phase of the management control process is a planned course of action within the boundaries set by these strategies and policies. The end product of the control phase of management control is the degree to which objectives have been attained.

The end product of task control is one specific action: for example, place a purchase order for 10,000 units of Item Y.

Evaluation

The soundness of strategies can be judged only after a long time has elapsed. Because outcomes are often affected by uncontrollable variables, they often cannot be evaluated at all. (Experts still disagree as to the soundness of strategies in the Civil War, which ended over a century ago.) The soundness of management control decisions can be judged sooner and with more confidence. The actions of senior managers are usually judged at least annually, and the actions of operating managers even more frequently. Although in some circumstances, an annual appraisal may be unfair, the time period cannot be much longer, if only because operating managers may stay in the same job for a relatively short period of time. The appraisal of the results of task control decisions is clear-cut and is made frequently.

NATURE OF SYSTEMS AND INFORMATION

Exhibit 2-3 outlines the differences among the three processes that are related to the nature of the systems and information applicable to each. Each topic is discussed in this section.

Structure

In management control, much of the information flows through a system. This system has a standard nomenclature. It is important, for example, that the term "labor cost" should have the same meaning throughout the organization. If some people think that it includes taxes and fringe benefits and other people think it includes only wages, misunderstandings with serious consequences can result. The system also has standard formats and regular schedules for the production of reports.

The system does not produce all the information. The manager also obtains information from newspapers, trade association publications, and other external sources and from internal sources such as conversations and telephone calls.[23]

Exhibit 2–3
Characteristics of Planning and Control Activities:
Nature of Systems and Information

	Strategic Planning	Management Control	Task Control
Structure	Essentially unsystematic Tailor-made	Both formal and informal	Primarily systematic Structured
Nature of information		Financial core	Much nonmonetary
	Mostly external environment	External and internal	Internal
	Future-oriented	Planned and actual	Actual
	Expected results	Expected and desired results	Model of the operation
Focus	Topic being studied Program	Both programs and responsibility centers	Specific transactions
	Not hierarchical	Hierarchical	Not hierarchical
Quantity	Much data in analysis, little to decision maker	Summaries Exceptions	Details
Accuracy	Rough	Fairly accurate	Accurate
Timeliness	Speed usually not crucial	Speed more important than accuracy	Real time
Stored data	Relatively unimportant	Important	Important

Strategic planning information is essentially unsystematic. Information is collected that is relevant to the problem being studied, and since each problem is different, the information needs are likely to be unique to that problem. Data collected in the organization's information system are often of some use in analyzing a proposed strategy, but analysts must work with the data that they find; the system cannot be designed so that it anticipates all the data needed for analysis of proposed strategies. The nature of strategic problems is that the information needed to analyze them usually cannot be foreseen.[24]

If the organization has a formal long-range plan or program, this serves as a benchmark or starting point in the analysis of proposed strategies. The long-range plan describes what is expected to happen over the next several years with currently approved strategies. This plan is developed as part of the management control process, not the strategic planning process.

Some organizations have developed a corporate model that shows the relationship of the main variables that influence the organization's economic performance. Although construction of such a model is usually a difficult task, many companies have devoted considerable resources to such an effort in recent years, with some success. Such a model may provide a starting point in a strategic analysis.

Task control information is, of course, relatively more highly structured and systematic.

Nature of Information

A management control system is built around a *financial core:* that is, plans and results are stated in monetary amounts. This is because the system is in part a coordinating device, and money is the only common denominator that can be used to measure, summarize, aggregate, and compare the heterogeneous quantitative measures of outputs and inputs (for example, hours of labor, pounds of material, units of product).

The system is by no means entirely financial; it includes such nonmonetary information as quantities of material, pounds of waste, hours worked, and many others. The nonmonetary information should be reconcilable with the monetary information (for example, data on the number of employees should be consistent with data on personnel costs). Nonquantitative data, such as reports on employee morale, customer complaints, and the like, are also included in the system. Nevertheless, the financial core is important in shaping the overall structure of the system. With only slight exaggeration it can be said that in a business the whole management control system is designed to focus on the "bottom line", that is, on net income, the return on assets employed, or the return on equity. The systems in nonprofit organizations have a similar focus on net income or its equivalent.

> CAUTION: *Although management control systems in nonprofit organizations are built around a financial core and although the "bottom line" is important in these organizations, financial reports of performance are not as important in nonprofit organizations as they are in business. The principal goals of a nonprofit organization are nonfinancial—basically providing services—and financial reports do not measure progress toward such goals. Indeed, measurement of performance in most nonprofit organizations is a difficult task, and the results are highly subjective.*

Strategic planning often, but not always, has a financial emphasis. Some studies of national energy strategy, for example, are done entirely in terms of "quads" of energy equivalents with no mention of monetary amounts.

The information in a management control system includes both external and internal information, and it includes information on planned performance, actual performance, and the difference between them. (Differences ideally are reported only when they are significant, in accordance with the "exception" principle.) Performance information may include nonfinancial as well as financial data. When the system incorporates nonfinancial objectives, it is said to be a "management by objectives" system, although logically a system that focuses on financial performance is also management by objectives, the objective being a satisfactory bottom line.

Information used for strategic planning is largely external, and it is almost entirely future-oriented.

Information in a task control system is largely internal; it is primarily actual rather than estimated, and quantitative rather than qualitative. It may or may not be monetary; for the operation of the system itself, nonmonetary information is often preferable (for example, the quantity of an inventory item rather than the dollar amount).

Desired versus Expected Results

Another subtle difference is that strategic planning information is intended to show the *expected* results of a strategy, but a management control system may show both the expected results and the *desired* results. As a way of motivating the division manager, the profit shown on a division's budget may be higher than the best estimate of the profit that the division will earn. When desired results differ from expected results, there must be a reconciliation at some level in the system; otherwise, incorrect judgments may be made about such matters as the amount of additional financing that is needed.

In designing a management control system, a relevant question is how tight the budget should be. Should it be set so high that only an outstanding manager can attain the objective? At what level does frustration inhibit a manager's best efforts? Should a manager's own estimate be accepted even though it is judged to be optimistic? Although questions such as these are relevant in management control, they make no sense at all in the strategic planning process. In that process, the objective is to make the best possible estimate of the results, nothing more. Psychological considerations are irrelevant. The data are impersonal.

Focus

The focus of strategic planning information is on the topic being analyzed, and the focus of task control information is on the specific task.

The focus of a management control system is much more complex. A management control system has two somewhat different dimensions: programs and responsibility centers. For making decisions about the programs that are to be undertaken, information is structured by programs; this information may not be related to the organization units that are responsible for executing the programs. (In a business, programs are product lines, research/development, and various staff activities.) In preparing annual budgets, for coordination of activities and for day-to-day management, the focus is often on responsibility centers, that is, on organization units headed by responsible managers. In a *matrix* organization, the focus is both on programs and on responsibility centers, which leads to an especially complex management control system.

An organization has a hierarchy of responsibility centers—departments consisting of sections, divisions consisting of departments, groups consisting of divisions—and the responsibility part of the system is also hierarchical, with information at higher levels consisting of summaries of information used at lower levels. Typically, neither strategic planning nor task control information is hierarchical.

Quantity of Information

In strategic planning, a large quantity of information may be used by the analysts. Simulations, which are of some help in certain types of problems, may involve several hours of computer time. An environmental impact study required in connection with certain strategic proposals may consist of a stack of paper three feet high. When the proposal is submitted to the decision maker, however, only highly summarized information is included.

In management control, the reports also consist almost entirely of summaries, although a great quantity of detailed information may be flowing through the system.

In task control, the data of most interest are those for individual tasks or transactions, not summaries.

Accuracy

In strategic planning, the information is necessarily imprecise. Basically, it reflects an attempt to predict the future, and no one can make such predictions accurately.

In management control, although estimates of the future are involved, the time span of an estimate is shorter than that in strategic planning, and accuracy is correspondingly better.

In task control, the information should be highly accurate.

In any system, of course, the data may be inaccurate because of deficiencies in the internal controls.

Timeliness

In strategic planning, the speed with which information is made available to those who work with it is, within limits, not of primary importance. Unless there is a crisis, a delay of days or weeks for the collection of certain data can be tolerated; the analyst, meanwhile, works on aspects of the problem for which data are available.

In management control, if a report is due on the fifth working day of the month, it should be published on that day. Accuracy is often sacrificed in the interests of timeliness.

In task control, the information is produced in what is essentially real time, at least in computer-based systems.

Stored Data

An information system includes data that are stored in its database. Strategic planners make some use of this information, but because of the unique nature of the problem being analyzed, the information is often not quite in the form desired and must be rearranged (that is, "massaged") in order to be relevant for the situation being analyzed. If the proposed strategy involves discontinuing a certain product line, historical information on the costs and profitability of that product line that have been collected for management control purposes are probably not directly relevant. They may, however, be of some use if restructured and adjusted to take account of the assumptions made in connection with the proposal.

Management control and task control make extensive use of stored data. Information on what costs have been, for example, provides an excellent starting point in estimating what costs are going to be in the future. Information on decision rules and on current status (for example, the quantity of an inventory item on hand) are essential for task control.

BEHAVIORAL CONSIDERATIONS

Exhibit 2-4 outlines the differences among the three processes that are related to behavioral factors. Each topic is discussed in this section.

Persons Involved

Senior management is involved in both strategic planning and management control.[25] Other managers are involved primarily in management control; they usually are not major participants in the strategic planning process and sometimes are not even aware that a plan is being considered. In part this reflects the distinction between "thinkers" and "doers." Operating managers are doers; by tem-

Exhibit 2–4
Characteristics of Planning and Control Activities: Behavioral Aspects

	Strategic Planning	Management Control	Task Control
Persons involved	Top management, staff Few in number	All managers Hierarchical	Individuals (or none)
Mental activity	Innovative Entrepreneurial Some analytical	Leadership Persuasive	Follow instructions
Coordination and communication	Relatively easy Small group	Difficult Whole organization	Inherently easy
Responsibility	Planner not responsible for results	Manager responsible for both plans and results	Supervisor responsible for results
Reward criteria	Entirely subjective	Partly objective Compensation based on results	Objective

perament they tend to be not very good at the thought processes involved in strategic planning. Furthermore, the pressures of current activities usually prevent them from devoting much time to strategic matters. Also, they tend to be familiar primarily with their own part of the organization, and they lack the broader knowledge required for strategic planning.

In task control the focus is on the doers. In automated tasks, no human beings are involved unless something goes wrong.

Staff people have an important role in strategic planning. A new idea may originate with anyone, but if it is considered worth pursuing, staff people are heavily involved in the analysis. They may work with the originator in the development of the idea, or they may work pretty much on their own. When the analysis has been completed, discussion and decision involve senior management. The process may require several iterations ("send it back to the drawing board") before a final decision is made.

In management control, staff people are much less important. The principal actors are line managers. Staff people may assist in the mechanics of budget preparation or in making a preliminary analysis of reports of actual performance, but the decisions and actions are those of the line managers, not the staff.

Strategic planning and management control activities may conflict with one another. The time that management spends thinking about strategy is time that otherwise could have been spent in controlling current operations, and in this sense strategic planning can hamper the management of current activities. The reverse situation is likely to be more serious: some senior managers are so preoccupied with current problems that they do not devote enough time to developing strategies.

Relatively few people are involved in strategic planning. In even a large organization, the planning staff is usually one of the smaller staff units. All managers are of course involved in management control.

Mental Activity

As noted earlier, three types of personalities are involved in the strategic planning process: the idea generator, the analyst, and the salesperson.

Those involved in the management control process are leaders. They know how to achieve results by working with other people. They use persuasion. They mediate differences between conflicting points of view. They inspire. They teach. And at appropriate times they criticize or "chew people out."

The strategic planning process is fairly rational (except in government, where it is essentially political), whereas in management control, decisions are often arrived at through negotiation or persuasion, which means they are affected by behavioral considerations. The basic reason why behavioral considerations are important is that the personal goals of individual managers are not necessarily consistent with organization goals. An important part of the management control process is to minimize the discrepancy between these two sets of goals, that is, to promote goal congruence. The management control system sets up rewards and negative incentives that are intended to induce a desired course of action.

The emphasis on rationality in strategic planning is only a matter of degree. During the discussion of proposed strategies, the parties advocate their point of view with every persuasive device they can think of.

In pure task control, the mental activity is primarily to follow instructions. In tasks involving professional expertise, the knowledge and skill relevant to the profession are, of course, important.

Coordination and Communication

An important distinction among the three processes is in the ease of communicating information. In strategic planning, this is a fairly simple matter since relatively few people are involved. Each problem is explored in depth, and the parties involved usually have a common understanding of what the numbers mean (although this is not always the case). In management control, the communication problem is much more difficult. Numbers in huge quantities circulate through the information system. Each is identified with a brief title such as "direct labor cost," or "overhead." Although the meaning of each label may be described in a manual, managers do not have the time or the inclination to consult the manual to the degree that its preparers intended. Misunderstandings are therefore common, and many discussions about reports get bogged down because the parties implicitly attach different meanings to the numbers.

Managers quickly learn the meaning of the numbers in the reports for their own sphere of responsibility, so there is unlikely to be a problem at that level (although there are instances in which a manager has for years assumed that an item such as "overhead" included elements different from what actually was the case). The problem arises when managers attempt to understand reports that they do not receive routinely or when senior management reads reports from a variety of sources prepared according to differing definitions. Those who have not experienced these misunderstandings find it difficult to accept the fact that they are widespread and that they are annoying. By hindsight, when the differences are brought to light, they are perfectly obvious.[26]

Even if the message communicated to a manager is reasonably clear, its influence on his or her behavior is affected by the peculiarities of the human information-processing system. Before information is acted upon, it passes through the process called "cognitive filtering." In this process, the brain disregards information believed to be unimportant and changes the meaning of other information according to its past associations and its preconceptions. Furthermore, the brain can process relatively few pieces of information simultaneously. There is evidence that not more than seven different pieces of information can be dealt with at once.[27] Books have been written about the problems of communicating accurately to human beings.

In task control, the task is repetitive, and operators should learn fairly quickly the exact meaning of the terms used in their job. This does require training, however, and if there is rapid operator turnover, misunderstandings may arise.

Responsibility

A key characteristic of management control is that managers are responsible both for plans and for actual performance. As the culmination of the budget preparation process, the manager agrees that the plan set forth in the budget is attainable and commits to attaining it. Reports prepared after the fact show what he or she has done to meet this commitment. In task control, the individual's responsibility for carrying out the task is even more apparent.

By contrast, the people involved in strategic planning may not be the people who are responsible for implementing the plan. Moreover, the soundness of the plan may not be known for years after the planners have finished their work.

Reward Criteria

In management control, much attention is given to the best way of rewarding managers for good performance. The basis for reward is partly objective (for example, surpassing budgeted performance) and partly subjective, that is, the judgment of superiors and peers. The control system incorporates and indeed focuses as a basis for reward on those aspects of performance that are objectively measured.

Strategic planners are also rewarded, but since the excellence of their plans cannot be measured until they have been implemented, and often not even then, the basis of the reward is necessarily subjective. Occasionally, stock options in a newly organized subsidiary may provide an objective basis for reward.

In many task control situations the rewards can be based on objective evidence of performance.

OTHER CHARACTERISTICS

Exhibit 2-5 summarizes certain other distinctions among the three processes. Its purpose is solely to facilitate the drawing of boundaries that separate the processes, and it is not intended to be an exhaustive list.

Exhibit 2–5
Characteristics of Planning and Control Activities:
Other Characteristics

	Strategic Planning	Management Control	Task Control
Balance between planning and control	Planning dominant, some control	Planning and control	Control dominant, some planning
Source disciplines	Economics	Economics Social psychology Systems theory	Management science Operations research Physical sciences
System design	Unsystematic	Industry-specific Analyze management needs Personal	Problem-specific Analyze process Impersonal

Balance between Planning and Control

I said in Chapter 1 that all three processes involve both planning activities and control activities, even though their titles suggest otherwise. In strategic planning, planning is, of course, dominant; a control system is needed only to assure that the planning process is proceeding satisfactorily. Such a system may be properly considered a task control system; the task is to analyze a proposed strategy.

In management control, planning activities and control activities are of about equal importance. Also, a given manager participates in both the planning activities and the control activities that relate to his or her sphere of responsibility. I cannot generalize about the relative amount of time devoted to each because this varies with different organizations and different individuals.

In task control, control activities are dominant, but the decisions of operators to take specified actions are, by definition, plans. Formulation of the rules that govern task control are a part of the management control process, however.

Source Disciplines

In strategic planning, the relevant discipline is economics (and also political science, if the organization is a government entity). Economists describe how business policies and strategies should be arrived at. They tend to assume that these policies and strategies will be implemented rationally and efficiently, and they do not pay much, if any, attention to the behavioral problems that are actually involved in implementation.

Economics is also a source discipline for management control, but social psychology is equally important. Those schooled in only one of these disciplines are likely to have a distorted view of what is really going on. Economists tend to write about an organization as if it were an impersonal economic engine, whereas social psychologists tend to overlook the importance of economic principles as explanations of what is happening and what should happen.

Findings of general systems theory are also relevant to management control, but only those findings that relate to high order systems. The simple model of a mechanical system, such as a thermostat, is inadequate. Even a cybernetics model is only roughly applicable. Such a model states that a standard exists, that actual performance is measured and compared with the standard (this is called "feedback"), and that if there is a significant difference, corrective or adaptive action is initiated. This model omits the behavioral considerations and therefore does not portray what is actually going on in an organization. Dangerously misleading conclusions can be drawn by those who think that this model does represent reality.

The cybernetics model does not allow for the following real-life factors: (a) the standard of desirable performance is often not known; (b) even if it was known at one time, subsequent circumstances may have led to new standards; (c) actual results often are not accurately measured; (d) the actions required to correct an unfavorable deviation may not be known, or, if known, may involve human beings, whose behavior cannot be predicted.[28]

In task control, general systems theory works well. To the extent that they are valid and useful, the principles of management science and operations research relate almost exclusively to task control topics. Some principles from the physical sciences help solve optimization problems, and hence are relevant for task control.

Systems Design

Strategic planning is essentially unsystematic. Consulting firms have developed general approaches to strategic planning, but they are at best a beginning for the analysis.

A task control system is essentially problem-specific. The basic features of a model for inventory control are applicable in a wide variety of businesses and also in nonbusiness organizations. The systems designer does study the process carefully to allow for the peculiarities of a specific situation, but this requires only adaptation of the basic model. Production scheduling models, queuing models, linear programming models, and others can be applied basically in a variety of environments. Systems designers find ways to improve the model, and improvements developed in one organization are widely adopted in other organizations for use in the same task.

By contrast, a management control model is, at best, industry-specific, and a single model has wide application only within similar organizations in a given industry. The proprietor of a drugstore can safely buy a system designed for drugstores in general and, with little or no adaptation, use it as a management control system in the drugstore. Trade associations, public accounting firms, and consulting firms have developed management control systems, or the rudiments of such systems, that, with appropriate modifications, are the basis for an acceptable system in motels, banks, real estate firms, construction firms, law firms, and many others. An all-purpose management control system does not exist, however.

The "canned" systems, at most, work in simple situations. In an organization of some complexity, the systems designer must learn, by on-the-spot observation, what information is needed in the particular organization and design the system to meet those needs. Furthermore, a management control system is affected by the personal preferences and personal style of managers, particularly those of the chief executive officer, and these factors must be taken into account in designing the system.

Exhibit 2–6
Examples of Decisions

Strategic Planning	Management Control	Task Control
Acquire unrelated business	New product or brand within product line	Order entry
Add product line	Expand a plant	Production scheduling
Add direct-mail selling	Advertising budget	Book TV commercials
Change debt/equity ratio	Issue new debt	Cash management
Adopt affirmative action policy	Implement minority recruit-ment program	Personnel record keeping
Inventory speculation policy	Decide inventory levels	Reorder an item
Magnitude and direction of research	Control of research organi-zation	Individual research project

EXAMPLES

As another way of explaining the differences among the three processes, Exhibit 2-6 gives some examples of activities associated with each.

3

THE MANAGEMENT
CONTROL ENVIRONMENT

CHAPTER 2 drew rough boundaries that separate the management control function from the strategic planning function on one side, and from the task control function on the other side. Chapters 3–7 describe generalizations about the management control function, which is the set of activities that occur within these boundaries.

There are two aspects to any function. First, there is the environment in which it takes place. Second, there is the process, how it works.

In Chapter 3 I describe general characteristics of an entity's environment that are important in understanding management control. The topics are arranged under the following headings: organization structure; behavioral considerations; rules, procedures, and guidelines; and the organization's culture.

The environment differs among entities in ways that affect the management control process. These differences relate both to factors in its external environment and to factors inherent in the nature of the work that it does. Management control in an entity with relatively certain revenues and standardized production operations is considerably different from management control in an entity whose markets are uncertain and whose production operations are built around craftsmen. The effect of these differences is discussed in Chapter 7.

ORGANIZATION STRUCTURE

An organization is a group of people who work together to attain one or more goals. Organization structure refers to the relationships among the participants in an entity. An entity has both a formal and an informal organization structure. The latter is unwritten, and perhaps unintended, but the web of informal relationships does have obvious implications for management. However, because it is unwritten it is difficult to identify and describe. This description therefore focuses on the formal structure.

Responsibility Centers

An organization does its work through subunits called "responsibility centers."[1] *A responsibility center is an organization unit that is headed by a manager who is responsible for its activities.* Responsibility centers are arranged in a hierarchy. At the lowest level in the organization there are responsibility centers for sections, work shifts, or other small organization units. At the next higher level there are departments or divisions that consist of several of these units plus overall departmental or divisional staff and management people; these larger units are also responsibility centers. From the viewpoint of senior management and the board of directors, the whole entity is a responsibility center. Although even these large units fit the definition of responsibility center, the term is used to refer primarily to lower-level units within the organization.

Exhibit 3–1
Nature of a Responsibility Center

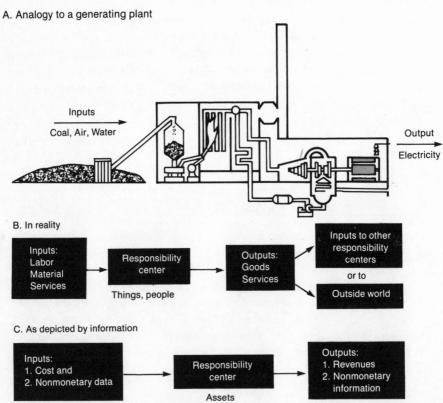

A. Analogy to a generating plant

Inputs
Coal, Air, Water

Output
Electricity

B. In reality

Inputs:
Labor
Material
Services

Responsibility
center

Things, people

Outputs:
Goods
Services

Inputs to other
responsibility
centers

or to

Outside world

C. As depicted by information

Inputs:
1. Cost and
2. Nonmonetary data

Responsibility
center

Assets

Outputs:
1. Revenues
2. Nonmonetary
information

Source: Exhibit 23-2 from Robert N. Anthony and James S. Reece, *Accounting Principles* (Homewood, Ill.: Irwin, 1983), p. 540. Used by permission.

A responsibility center exists to accomplish one or more purposes; these purposes are its *objectives*. Presumably, the objectives of an individual responsibility center are intended to help implement the strategies of the whole organization. Exhibit 3–1 is a schematic diagram showing the essence of any responsibility center. A responsibility center uses inputs, which are physical quantities of material, hours of various types of labor, and a variety of other services. Money provides a common denominator that permits the amounts of individual resources to be aggregated in the records. The monetary amount is ordinarily obtained by multiplying the physical quantity by a price per unit of quantity (for example, hours of labor times a rate per hour). This amount is the *cost* of the resources used. *Cost is a monetary measure of the amount of resources used by a responsibility center.* The inputs of a responsibility center are ordinarily expressed as costs.

The responsibility center works with these resources, and it usually requires working capital, equipment, and other assets to do this work. The results of this work are its *outputs*. Outputs are either goods, if they are tangible, or services, if they are intangible. Presumably, these outputs are consistent with the organization's objectives, but this is not necessarily so. For example, a manufacturing center may produce more goods than the marketing department can sell, or it may provide goods of inferior quality. These are outputs even though they are not consistent with the entity's overall objectives. Whatever a responsibility center produces, whether good or bad, desired or unwanted, constitutes its outputs.

The goods and services produced by a responsibility center may be furnished either to other responsibility centers or to the outside world. In the former case, they are inputs to the responsibility center that receives them; in the latter case, they are outputs of the whole organization. Revenues are the amounts earned from selling these outputs.

Exhibit 3–2
Types of Responsibility Centers

Type	Monetary Measurement	Example
Expense center	Cost (inputs)	Accounting department
Profit center	Profit (outputs minus inputs)	A division
Investment center	ROI (profit/investment)	A division

Types of Responsibility Centers

There are three types of responsibility centers, classified according to the way in which inputs and outputs are measured: expense centers, profit centers, and investment centers. In expense centers, only expenses are measured in monetary terms; in profit centers, both revenues and expenses are measured in monetary terms, and in investment centers, profits and also the amount of investment are measured in monetary terms.[2]

> CAUTION: *Although the inputs measured in an expense center are costs, the term "cost center" is not synonymous with "expense center." A cost center is a device for collecting costs for the purpose of allocating them to cost objects. Cost centers are not necessarily organizational units.*

Criteria for deciding which type of responsibility center is appropriate for a given type of activity are discussed at length in the management control literature. In general, an investment center provides the broadest basis for control, a profit center the next most broad, and an expense center provides a narrow basis.

Expense Centers

An expense center is a responsibility center whose inputs are measured in monetary terms, but whose outputs are not measured in monetary terms. There are two general types: engineered expense centers and discretionary expense centers. They correspond to two types of costs. *Engineered costs* are elements of cost for which the "right" or "proper" amount of costs that should be incurred can be estimated with a reasonable degree of validity. Direct material costs incurred in a production department are an example. *Discretionary costs* are those for which no such engineered estimate is feasible; the amount of costs incurred depends on management's judgment as to the amount that is appropriate under the circumstances. Even in highly automated production departments, the amount of indirect labor and of various services used can vary with management's discretion. Thus, the term "engineered expense center" refers to responsibility centers in which engineered costs predominate, but it does not imply that valid engineering estimates can be made for every cost item.

Profit Centers

A profit center is a responsibility center whose performance is measured as the difference between its revenues and its expenses or costs. A *strategic business unit* (SBU) is a profit center; an SBU often consists of a number of smaller profit centers. In some profit centers the amount of assets employed is also measured, and such a responsibility center is called an *investment center*. Although the term "profit center" suggests that they are found only in profit-oriented entities, many nonprofit organizations have profit centers. Any responsibility center that generates revenues by delivering priced goods or services to outside parties and/or other responsibility centers can be a profit center. The choice of whether a responsibility center should be a profit center depends on whether this facilitates management control, rather than on the usual definition of profit.

Criteria for Profit Centers

Many considerations are important in determining the best way to structure an entity's organization. They involve such questions as whether a functional organization is better than a divisional organization; which staff activities should be carried out by specialized staff units, and which should be carried out by line responsibility centers; and which decisions are made at or near the top of the organization, and which are delegated to lower levels. Some of these considerations are behavioral; that is, the entity is organized in part so as to take into account the skills and personality traits of individual managers. Most of these considerations are outside the scope of this book.

One set of considerations, however, is important to an understanding of management control systems. These have to do with the criteria for deciding what responsibility centers should be profit centers. (Many people classify investment centers as a special type of profit center. Unless otherwise indicated, I follow that practice in this book. With such a classification, the basic organizational issue is whether a given responsibility center should be an expense center or a profit center.)

Since in a profit center, both revenues and expenses are measured in monetary terms, the formal management control structure encompasses more elements of performance than is the case with an expense center. On the other hand, a profit center requires more record keeping than an expense center, and in some circumstances creation of a profit center may have dysfunctional consequences. The choice is strictly a management decision; there is no inherent reason or definition that requires that certain types of units be profit centers.

The manager of a profit center is motivated to do a good job of control, almost as if he or she were running a separate business. Divisions or other business units whose management is responsible both for producing and marketing a product line are almost always organized as profit centers. For other responsibility centers, the decision as to whether the unit should be a profit center is more difficult.[3] Some criteria are as follows.

1. *The manager of the responsibility center should be able to exert significant influence on both its revenues and its costs.* This does not mean that the manager must have complete control over outputs and inputs, for few, if any, managers of responsibility centers have such authority.

2. *The manager should perceive that the profit reported for the unit is fair, as a measure of its performance.* This does not mean that the amount of reported profit is accurate or that it encompasses all aspects of performance, for no profit measure does this. It means, roughly and with qualifications, that the higher the amount of profit reported, the better the profit center has performed.

3. *The competitive spirit that the profit center concept fosters should not have dysfunctional consequences to the organization.* If a unit is expected to cooperate closely with other responsibility centers, organizing it as a profit center may inhibit the desirable degree of cooperation. The manager of such a profit center may make decisions that add to the profit of his or her own unit, but that are detrimental to other units in the organization. For example, the manager may be reluctant to incur overtime costs even though the outputs may be badly needed by other responsibility centers. (Some of these possible dysfunctional consequences can be avoided or minimized by designing the management control system so that these actions do not adversely affect the profit center's reported performance.)

4. *Internal users of the responsibility center's services should be expected to pay for these services.* If senior management encourages operating units to use the services of certain staff units, these staff units perhaps should not be profit centers, at least until their clients are prepared to accept the value of their services. An internal audit organization, for example, usually provides services without charge and therefore should not be a profit center.

5. *A satisfactory quantitative, nonmonetary measure of the unit's output cannot be obtained.* If the unit produces a single product (for example, cement), a nonmonetary measure of its output may suffice for management control purposes. (However, pricing its outputs may be necessary as a basis for arriving at selling prices or for other reasons, and in these circumstances the incremental cost of creating a profit center may be small.)

6. *The benefits of the profit center concept should be clearly greater than the extra record keeping and other costs involved.* The cost of measuring the output of an accounting department is relatively large. In a small company or in a centralized large company, creating a profit center for the accounting department probably would not be worthwhile. In a bank, however, the accounting department is a significant element of cost; if the bank has branches, it may be worthwhile to charge the branches for the cost of the services furnished by the accounting department.

> CAUTION: *Some people believe that if a responsibility center does not sell a substantial percentage of its products to external customers, it cannot be a true profit center; it is, at most, a "pseudo" profit center. This term is an unwarranted aspersion. If the concept is properly understood, sales to other responsibility centers are just as real to the manager of the profit center as are sales to outside customers.*

Degree of Autonomy

Profit centers vary considerably as to the amount of autonomy that their managers have. A profit center may operate almost as if it were an independent company. (By definition, the manager cannot have as much autonomy as the chief executive officer of an independent company because all profit centers are part of a larger organization.) The managers of most profit centers have many limitations on their autonomy to make decisions.[4]

The management control system can communicate the restrictions on autonomy imposed by the organization as a whole. This is done in part by rules, which are discussed in the next section, and by budgets. No matter how carefully these formal communications are constructed, however, much depends on informal indications of which decisions are appropriately made by the profit center manager, which decisions require consultation with (but not necessarily the approval of) staff offices or higher line managers, and which decisions require approval of higher authority. Senior managers give more autonomy to subordinates they know well and whose judgment they trust than to new subordinates who have yet to prove themselves. Collectively, these informal attitudes constitute the "control climate," a topic discussed in a later section.

Criteria for Investment Centers

Creation of an investment center is worthwhile only if the manager has some control over the assets assigned to the unit, in addition to control over the elements that affect profit. In many investment centers, managers are responsible only for receivables and inventory, rather than for the total amount of assets employed by the unit, and in this case the investment is limited to these assets. Indeed, because the center's investment in fixed assets may be largely noncontrollable by its manager, incorporating all assets in the center's investment base may impede, rather than facilitate, control. There are ways of overcoming this problem, however, and unless the investment center comprises all assets that the center uses, comparison of performance with other investment centers or with outside companies may be difficult.[5]

An investment center is often regarded as a special type of profit center, rather than as a separate category. In this book, the discussion of profit centers usually is meant to include investment centers.

Transfer Prices

If a profit center provides goods or services to other units in the organization, prices for these products must be established. *A transfer price is a price used to measure the value of goods or services furnished by a profit center to other responsibility centers within the entity.* The behavior of managers of profit centers that provide goods or services and the behavior of managers of responsibility centers that receive these products are influenced by the way in which transfer prices are structured.

Although there is much disagreement in the literature about transfer price policies, I believe that a good general guide is: Use the same principle for transfer pricing that the company and its industry use for sales to outside customers. Some economics texts recommend the approach of drawing the same types of supply-and-demand curves that they say are relevant to arriving at outside selling prices. They fail to point out that few companies can draw a demand curve in which they have confidence. Other authors advocate the use of opportunity costs or variable costs, without pointing out that few companies use such cost constructions in arriving at outside selling prices.[6] In general, marketing texts are superior to economics texts in providing useful guidance on pricing. Evidence from practice suggests the following guidelines.

1. *If a valid market price for the product exists, it ordinarily should be the basis for the transfer price.* The market price may be adjusted to allow for differences between the external and the internal marketing environment; for example, for the fact that no bad debts are incurred on internal sales. If the market price is a distress price—that is, not the price at which market transactions ordinarily take place—it may not provide a satisfactory basis for the transfer price.

2. *If no valid market price exists, the transfer price should ordinarily be the product's standard full cost plus a normal return on capital employed.* This rule corresponds to general practice in arriving at normal selling prices to outside customers. The costs should be at standard, rather than at actual, so as to prevent the selling profit center from passing along inefficiencies to the buying profit center.

A variation of this general rule is to charge a fixed amount per month for the "rental" of the facilities, plus a variable amount per unit of product. This pricing method is similar to the "take-or-pay" contracts used by some industrial, public utility, and mining companies.

If the transfer price becomes a part of the cost of a cost-reimbursable contract, the detailed rules agreed to by the contracting parties are governing. For example, cost-reimbursement contracts of the Department of Defense and the National Aeronautical and Space Administration specify how costs, including interunit transfer costs, are to be calculated.

3. *In special circumstances the buying and selling units should be permitted to negotiate a different price.* When the selling unit is operating below capacity, it may be willing to take a lower price in order to make some contribution to overhead and profit.

CAUTION: *Many books and articles describe detailed, complicated, often esoteric rules for transfer pricing. The principles given above are adequate for most circumstances. The recommendation that most prices, including transfer prices, should be based on variable costs or opportunity costs is an unrealistic idea once held by some classical economists, but rarely found in practice.*

BEHAVIORAL FACTORS

Management control involves interactions among human beings. The behavior of people in organizations is therefore an important environmental factor. The process must take into account how individuals behave, as well as their knowledge, skills, and personality traits.

Personal Goals and Needs

People become participants—that is, they join an organization—because they believe that by doing so they can achieve their *personal* goals. Once they have joined, the nature of their contribution to the work of the organization is also based on their perception of what will help achieve their personal goals.

An individual's personal goals can be expressed as *needs*. Some of these needs are *material;* these can be satisfied by the money earned on the job. Other needs are *psychological.* People need to have their abilities and achievements recognized; they need social acceptance as members of a group; they need to feel a sense of personal worth; they need to feel secure; they need to be able to exercise discretion; they may need a feeling of power and achievement.[7]

Personal needs can also be classified as either extrinsic or intrinsic. *Extrinsic* needs are satisfied by the actions of others. Examples are money received from the organization and praise received from a superior. *Intrinsic* needs are satisfied by the opinions people have about themselves. Examples are feelings of achievement and of competence, or a clear conscience.

The relative importance of these needs varies with individuals, and their relative importance to a given individual varies at different times. For some people, earning a great deal of money is a dominant need; for others, monetary considerations are much less important. Only a relatively few individuals attach much importance to the need to exercise discretion or the need for achievement, but these persons tend to be the leaders of the organization.[8] The relative importance that people attach to their own needs is heavily influenced by the attitude of their colleagues and of their superiors.

Incentives

The *expectancy theory* model of motivation states that the motivation to engage in a given behavior is determined by (1) a person's beliefs or "expectancies" about what outcomes are likely to result from that behavior, and (2) how attractive these outcomes are, that is, their incentive for satisfying needs.[9]

Individuals are influenced both by positive incentives and by negative incentives. A *positive incentive*, or reward, is an outcome that is expected to result in increased need satisfaction. A *negative incentive*, or punishment, is the reverse.

Incentives need not be monetary. Praise for a job well done can be a powerful reward. Nevertheless, many people regard monetary rewards as extremely important. Such rewards may include a bonus based on a comparison between planned and actual results. Unless properly designed and administered, however, a bonus system can do more harm than good. (This point will be discussed further below and in Chapter 4.)

Goal Congruence

Because an organization does not have a mind of its own, the organization itself literally cannot have goals. "Organizational goals" are actually the goals of senior management. Senior management wants the organization to attain these goals, but subordinates have their own personal goals that *they* want to achieve. These personal goals are the satisfaction of their needs. In other words, participants act in their own self-interest.

> CAUTION: *Because people act in their own self-interest, it follows literally that they are selfish. This does not imply a cynical view of human nature, however. For most people, self-esteem is a need, and self-esteem requires that the person help other people, often at some sacrifice of personal pleasure or profit.*

The potential conflict between organizational goals and personal goals suggests a central purpose of the management control system. The system should be designed so that actions that it leads people to take in accordance with their perceived self-interest are actions that are also in the best interests of the organization; that is, the management control system should encourage *goal congruence*. It should be structured so that the goals of the participants, so far as is feasible, are consistent with the goals of the organization as a whole. If this condition exists, a decision that a manager regards as sound from a personal viewpoint will also be a sound decision for the organization as a whole. As Douglas McGregor states:

The essential task of management is to arrange organizational conditions and methods of operations so that people can achieve their own goals best by directing their own efforts towards organizational objectives.[10]

Perfect congruence between individual goals and organizational goals does not exist. One obvious reason is that individual participants usually want as much compensation as they can get, whereas from the organization's viewpoint there is an upper limit to salaries, beyond which profits would be adversely and unnecessarily affected. As a minimum, however, the system should not encourage individuals to act *against* the best interests of the organization. For example, if the management control system signals that the emphasis should be only on reducing costs, and if a manager responds by reducing costs at the expense of adequate quality or by reducing costs that cause a more than offsetting increase in costs in another responsibility center, then the manager has been motivated, but in the wrong direction. Two separate questions are therefore important when evaluating any practice used in a management control system:

1. What action does it motivate people to take in their own perceived self-interest?

2. Is this action in the best interest of the organization?

Cooperation and Conflict

The lines connecting the boxes on an organization chart imply that the way in which organizational objectives are attained is that senior management makes a decision, this decision is communicated down through the organizational hierarchy, and operating managers at lower levels then proceed to implement it. This is *not* the way an organization actually functions.

Actually, managers react to instructions from their superiors in accordance with how those instructions are perceived and how they affect the managers' personal needs. Moreover, interactions between managers affect what actually happens. Although the manager of the maintenance department may be responsible for maintenance work in all production departments, the maintenance work in a particular department may be slighted if there is friction between the maintenance manager and the manager of that department. Also, some actions that a manager may want to take to achieve personal goals have an adverse effect on other managers. Managers argue about which of them is to get the use of limited production capacity or other scarce resources, or about potential customers that both want to solicit. For these and many other reasons, conflict exists within organizations.

Nevertheless, the organization will not achieve its objectives unless managers work together with some degree of harmony. Thus, there is also cooperation in organizations. Participants realize that if cooperation is inadequate, the organization will dissolve, and they will then be unable to satisfy the needs that motivated them to join it.

An organization attempts to maintain an appropriate balance between the forces that create conflict and those that encourage cooperation. Some conflict is both inevitable and desirable. Conflict results in part from the competition between participants for promotion or other forms of need satisfaction; such competition is, within limits, healthy. A certain amount of cooperation obviously is also essential, but if undue emphasis is placed on fostering a cooperative attitude, the most able participants will be denied the opportunity of using their talents fully.[11]

RULES, PROCEDURES, AND GUIDELINES

Another aspect of the management control environment is the set of rules, practices, guidelines, job descriptions, customs, standard operating procedures, manuals, and codes of ethics that exist in any organization. For brevity, these are here lumped together as "rules." Unlike the directives or guidance implicit in budgeted amounts, which change from month to month, these rules are in force indefinitely; that is, they exist until they are modified. Typically, rules are changed infrequently. Some rules, such as those set forth in manuals, are formal; others, such as understandings about acceptable behavior, are informal. They relate to matters that range from the most trivial (for example, paper clips will be issued only on the basis of a signed requisition) to the most important (for example, capital expenditures of over $5 million must be approved by the board of directors).[12]

Types of Rules

Some rules are guides: that is, organization members are permitted, and indeed expected, to depart from them either under specified circumstances or if in the person's judgment a departure is in the best interests of the organization. For example, there may be a rule stating the criteria for extending credit to customers, but the credit manager may extend credit to a customer who currently does not meet these criteria if the customer has been especially valuable and may become so again.

Departures from the rules may or may not require the approval of higher authority. Some are literally rules; they should never be broken. A rule that prohibits payment of bribes and a rule that an airline pilot should never take off without permission of the air controller are examples. Some rules are prohibitions against unethical, illegal, or other undesired actions. Others are positive requirements that certain actions be taken (for example, fire drills at prescribed intervals). The distinction between prohibitions and positive requirements may not be apparent, and managers should be made aware of the distinction.

Some of the specific types are listed below.

Physical Controls

Security guards, locked storerooms, vaults, computer passwords, television surveillance, and other physical controls are part of the control structure. Most of them are associated with task control, rather than with management control.

Manuals

Much judgment is required in deciding which rules should be made formal (that is, put in a manual), which should be guidelines rather than fixed rules, what discretion should be allowed, and a variety of other matters. The literature does not contain anything other than obvious guidance on these matters. Bureaucratic organizations have more detailed manuals than other organizations; large organizations have more than small ones; centralized organizations have more than decentralized ones; and organizations with geographically dispersed units performing similar functions have more than single-site organizations.

With the passage of time, some formal rules become obsolete. Manuals and other sets of rules therefore need to be reexamined periodically to ensure that they are consistent with the desires of the current senior management. In the pressure of day-to-day problems, the need for reexamination often is overlooked; if so, the manuals are likely to contain rules for situations that no longer exist, or for practices that are obsolete. If these rules are permitted to remain, managers are likely to have an unfavorable impression of the whole manual.

System Safeguards

Various safeguards are built into the information processing system to ensure that the information flowing through the system is accurate and to prevent (or at least minimize) fraud and defalcation. They include cross-checks of totals with details, required signatures or other evidence that a transaction has been authorized, separation of duties, frequent counts of cash and other portable assets, and a number of other rules that are described in texts on auditing. They also include checks of the system that are made by the internal auditors and the external auditors.

Rewards

An important set of guidelines is the reward structure. The reward structure (including its obverse, penalties) is supposed to promote goal congruence. At the present state of our knowledge, few valid principles regarding the types of rewards that influence goal congruence are known.

Ideally, managers should be rewarded on the basis of their actual performance, compared with what their performance should have been under the prevailing circumstances. This ideal cannot be achieved, for two basic reasons. First, the performance of a responsibility center is influenced by many factors other than the actions of its manager, and the performance of the manager usually cannot be cleanly separated from the effect of these other variables. Second, managers are supposed to achieve both long- and short-run objectives, but the management control system focuses primarily, and necessarily, on the short run. The system can only report what has happened; it cannot report what will happen in the future as a consequence of the manager's current actions. Managers are therefore motivated to focus on achieving short-run goals.

With the increased analytical power made possible by computers, some mitigation of the first problem is possible. Although the second problem is well recognized, I don't know a good solution. One possibly promising approach is to separate expenses associated with current performance from those that are called "strategic expenditures"—expenses that are intended to improve future performance. Strategic expenditures include such items as research/development costs, start-up costs, and training costs. However, the line between operating expenses and strategic expenditures is difficult to draw in practice.

Because of the difficulty of measuring the degree to which actual performance was congruent with the organization's goals, the reward structure—salary, bonuses, stock options, promotions, and so on—should be governed as much by the judgment of the manager's superior as by any quantitative formula.

Our lack of knowledge about how best to measure a manager's performance is probably the most serious weakness in management control systems.

CULTURE

In 1983, the Aluminum Company of America faced a serious crisis. It had lost its aluminum monopoly; its earnings were practically zero; it was making its first major staff reduction since the 1930s. As one device for studying its strategy, Alcoa hired a group of historians to find lessons that could be learned from the past.[13] Among other things, the historians reported on the corporate culture. They did so under two headings: "enduring cultural strengths" and "embedded cultural restraints."

They defined enduring cultural strengths as "habits of thought and behavior and structural characteristics that have served and will continue to serve the company well, if they are not undermined by change." Examples of the characteristics they listed are that the company continued to provide a high sense of security and stability among employees, that Alcoa was a people-oriented company with an unusually good labor history and a remarkable flexibility.

They defined embedded cultural restraints as "those deeply held assumptions . . . that affect management judgments, patterns of behavior, and relationships . . . —aspects of the corporate culture that will, consciously or not, condition thinking about the future." Examples of the assumptions listed were a focus on domestic rather than international activities, and a preoccupation with research that had immediate, rather than fundamental, results.

Alcoa's attempt to identify specific aspects of its culture is unusual. It is a fact, however, that every organization has a culture: an atmosphere, a feeling for what attitudes are encouraged and what discouraged. Its cultural norms are derived in part from tradition, in part from external influences (such as its unions and the norms of the broader society), and in part from the attitude of its senior management and its directors.[14]

Culture is also referred to as an organization's climate. As defined by Kenneth R. Andrews:

> The term "climate" is used to designate the quality of the internal environment which conditions in turn the quality of cooperation, the development of individuals, the extent of members' dedication or commitment to organizational purpose, and the efficiency with which that purpose is translated into results. Climate is the atmosphere in which individuals help, judge, reward, constrain, and find out about each other. It influences morale—the attitude of the individual toward his work and his environment.[15]

The bestseller *In Search of Excellence* is primarily an attempt to describe the culture in several companies that were judged to be well managed. The failure of that book to provide an accurate description (as evidenced by the fact that several of these companies ran into serious trouble shortly after the book was published) illustrates the difficulty of explaining the influence of culture in a given situation.[16] Nevertheless, cultural norms are extremely important. They explain why each of two entities may have an excellent management control system but why one has much better actual control than the other.

An organization's culture is rarely stated in writing, and attempts to do so almost always result in platitudes.[17]

Resistance to Change

One aspect of culture that is important in the management control process is the tendency of members of the organization to resist change. Certain practices are "rituals"; they are carried on automatically because "this is the way things are done around here." Others are "taboos"; "we just don't do that here," even though no one remembers why. Attempts to change practices meet resistance, and the larger and more mature the organization, the greater the resistance is.[18]

The organization may have potent ways of reacting to stimuli. A cabinet officer in the federal government may find it impossible to create the desired control climate, no matter how hard he or she tries, because of the behavioral norms that the bureaucracy has long accepted and finds ways of perpetuating.

Management Attitude

Perhaps the aspect of culture that has the most important impact on management control is the attitude of a manager's superior toward control. Usually, the attitude of an immediate superior reflects in a general way his or her perception of the attitude of the chief executive officer, modified, of course, by the immediate superior's own attitude. This is another way of saying "an institution is the lengthened shadow of one man."[19]

The CEO's attitude may be expressed in any of a number of ways. If performance reports typically disappear into the executive suite and no response is forthcoming, managers soon perceive that the reports are not important. Conversely, if a report is discussed at length with the manager, the signal is that the report is important. Conversations may convey management's expectations about performance as powerfully as the formal budget.[20]

Other Aspects of Culture

Similarly, the control climate is affected by the attitudes of the manager's peers and by staff units. These also reflect to some extent the attitude of the chief executive officer.

Finally, the culture in the external environment affects the control climate within the organization. Some attitudes appear to be industrywide. Also, when times are tough, people tend to take the control process more seriously than when the economy is booming.

In short, management control is fundamentally behavioral; the various control tools are effective only as they influence behavior, and they will influence behavior only to the extent that the culture of the organization is conducive to doing so.

Exhibit 3-3 is an interesting way of summarizing these influences on the manager, in this case the manager of a profit center. It focuses on the perception of autonomy, that is, the decisions that the manager can make personally, as distinguished from those that require consultation with someone else. Corporate management has certain intentions about autonomy consistent with its philosophy and

Exhibit 3–3
Vancil's Conception of Decentralized Management

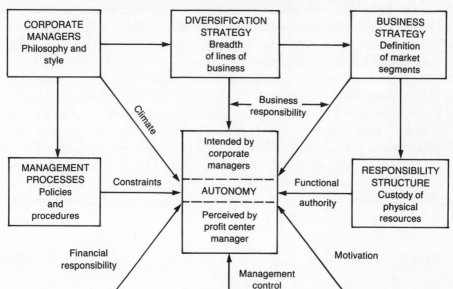

Source: R. F. Vancil, *Decentralization: Managerial Ambiguity by Design* (Homewood, Ill.: Dow Jones–Irwin, 1979), p. 128.

style and its strategies. It creates management policies and an organization structure whose purpose is to effectuate these intentions. The profit center manager has perceptions about autonomy, in part derived from the policies and procedures, in part from the way in which costs and assets are assigned to the profit center, and in part because of the nature of the organization's reward structure. Ideally, the intentions of corporate management coincide with the perceptions of the profit center manager, but this ideal is never achieved perfectly.

Role of the Controller

The person responsible for the operation of the management control system is here called the *controller*.[21] The controller organization is a staff unit, in contrast with the management control function itself, which is a line function. Its responsibility is similar to that of a telephone company in that it assures that messages flow through the system clearly, accurately, and promptly, but it is not responsible for the content of these messages or for acting on the information they contain. The CEO may delegate certain responsibilities to the controller, such as approving certain changes in the budget, but line officials have, or at least should have, the right of appeal from the controller's decisions.

An especially controversial problem is the proper relationship between the corporate controller and the controllers of divisions or other subordinate units. Some believe that divisional controllers should report primarily to the corporate controller, and have only a "dotted line" relationship with their division managers; others believe the opposite. Although I once concluded that the divisional controller who reported to the corporate controller would be unable to function effectively because of the perception that he or she was a spy, I now believe that either relationship appears to work, with its success depending primarily on what senior management wants.[22]

4

MANAGEMENT CONTROL OF OPERATING ACTIVITIES

O NE aspect of management control is the environment in which it takes place; this aspect was discussed in Chapter 3. The other aspect is the process. The management control process is discussed in Chapters 4 and 5. Chapter 4 focuses on the management control of ongoing operations. Chapter 5 focuses on the management control of projects.

INTRODUCTION

The management control process is primarily behavioral. It involves interactions among managers and between managers and their subordinates. Managers differ in their technical ability, their leadership style, their interpersonal skills, their experience, their approach to decision making, their attitude toward the entity, their liking for or dislike of numbers, and in other ways. This chapter focuses on what might be called a "typical" manager; variations that take some of the above differences into account are discussed in Chapter 7.

The formal management control system is basically the same throughout an organization; however, the way in which the system is used varies greatly, depending on the personal preferences of those who use it. For example, managers differ in their attitude toward the relative importance of cooperation and competition. As explained in Chapter 3, a certain amount of each is essential.

People other than managers are involved in the control process. Inspectors examine the quality of the work. In sizable organizations there is an internal audit staff. One of the primary functions of the internal auditors is to investigate how well the information system is functioning, suggest improvements in it, and call management's attention to failures to follow prescribed practices.

CAUTION: *From time to time new control devices are discussed. Managers must decide which are important and which are either ephemeral or are familiar practices packaged with new labels. In the 1970s, a gimmick was "zero-base budgeting," but by the late 1980s it had faded into oblivion.*

As shown in Exhibit 4-1, the management control process for operating activities has four phases: programming, budget preparation, execution, and evaluation. Each is described below.[1]

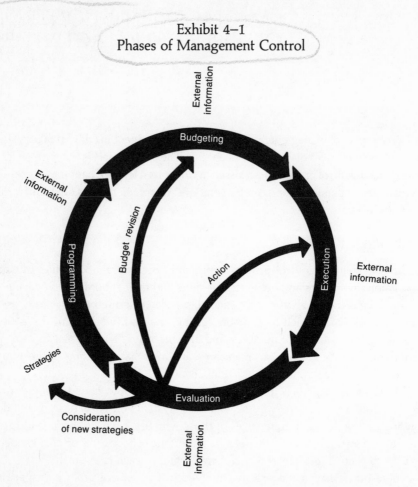

Exhibit 4–1
Phases of Management Control

PROGRAMMING

Most competent CEOs spend considerable time thinking about the future. The result may be an informal understanding among the senior management group of the future direction the entity is going to take, or it may be a formal statement of plans. The formal statement of plans is a program or long-range plan, and the process of preparing and revising this statement is called "programming" (also "long-range planning"). *Programming is the process of deciding on the programs that the organization will undertake and the approximate amount of resources that will be allocated to each program.*

> CAUTION: *As used here, "programming" is not related to what Herbert Simon calls "programmed decision." A programmed decision is repetitive and routine; programming has the opposite characteristics.*

Relation to Strategic Planning

In the 1965 book *Planning and Control Systems*, I waffled as to whether the programming process should be considered a part of strategic planning or a part of management control. I am now convinced that programming is part of management control. It is a systematic process, carried on at prescribed times and in a prescribed manner. In the classroom, the subject of business policy is usually divided into two parts: policy formulation and policy implementation. Strategic planning relates to the former; programming (as well as other aspects of management control) relates to the latter.[2]

In the strategic planning process, the entity's goals and the main strategies for achieving these goals are decided. In the programming process, these goals and strategies are basically accepted as givens (although occasionally a better strategy may be identified in the programming process). Program decisions are therefore intended to implement strategies.

> CAUTION: *Programming is not a substitute for strategic planning. Ideas for changes in strategy are not likely to emerge during the programming process. A possible strategic initiative may surface at any time and from anyone in the organization. If initially judged to be worth pursuing, it is analyzed immediately, without waiting to be fitted into a programming timetable.*

There is a close relationship between strategic planning and programming. The currently approved formal program is a starting point in the analysis of proposed new strategies, and the analysis of proposed programs may itself lead to a reexamination of strategies. Financial models developed during the programming process are useful in testing the implications of proposed strategies. Nevertheless, conceptually these two processes are distinct. In particular, strategic planning is relatively unsystematic, whereas programming is systematic.

Evolution of Programming

Thirty years ago the programming process in most organizations was unsystematic. Management did give some thought to long-range planning, but not in a systematic, coordinated way. (There were exceptions, not often recognized in the programming literature. Utilities projected their plant requirements for 20 years or more; forest product companies made plans over the 40-year cycle of timber growth; any company that built a new plant gave some thought to the likelihood of making profitable use of the new capacity over many future years.)

A few companies started formal programming systems in the late 1950s. Most of the first efforts were failures. They were minor adaptations of existing budget preparation systems; the required data were much more detailed than was appropriate; most of the work was done by staffs rather than by line management; and participants spent more time filling in forms than in thinking deeply about alternatives and selecting the best ones. Lessons were quickly learned, however: the objective should be to make difficult choices among alternative programs, not to extrapolate numbers in budgetary detail; much time should be spent on analysis and informal discussion, and relatively less time on paperwork; the focus should be on the programs themselves rather than on the responsibility centers that are to carry them out.

Currently, many organizations appreciate the advantages of making a plan for the next three to five years. The practice of stating this plan in a formal program document, or model, is widely, but by no means universally, accepted. The amount of detail has been greatly reduced.[3]

Program Structure and Content

In most industrial organizations, programs are products or product families plus research/development, planned acquisitions, or other important activities that do not fit into existing product lines. In IBM, for example, mainframe computers, desktop computers, and typewriters are programs. (By contrast, General Electric structures its programs in terms of profit centers.)

In service organizations, including government and other nonprofit organizations, programs tend to correspond to the types of services rendered by the entity. In a multiunit service organization, such as a hotel chain, each unit or each geographical region may constitute a program.

Programming also includes the process of analyzing proposed capital investments, other than investments for routine replacements (which are allowed for in the program by specifying an aggregate amount) and strategic investments (whose analysis is strategic planning).[4]

In many entities, programs are identified with specific profit centers or other discrete organization units. When this correspondence exists, programming is easier than when a program cannot be identified with a single responsible manager.

CAUTION: *A program structure that is at right angles to the entity's organization structure may indicate that changes should be made in one structure or the other.*

The formal long-range plan covers a period of approximately five future years. Five years is a long enough period to estimate the consequences of program decisions made currently. The consequences of a decision to develop and market a new product or to acquire a major new capital asset may not be fully felt in a shorter period. The horizon beyond five years is usually so murky that attempts to make a long-range plan for a longer period are not worthwhile. However, some relatively stable organizations, such as public utilities, prepare long-range plans that extend out as much as 20 years, and many organizations prepare very rough programs that extend beyond five years.

The dollar amounts for each program show the approximate magnitude of its revenues, expenses, and capital expenditures. Because of the relatively long time horizon, only rough estimates are feasible. Such estimates are satisfactory as a basis for indicating the organization's general direction. If the long-range plan is structured by divisions, the "charter," which specifies the boundaries within which the division is expected to operate, is also stated in the plan.

A few organizations prepare two long-range plans: one assuming normal operations and the other a "contingency plan" to be implemented in a crisis.

Nature of the Programming Process

Two Types of Long-Range Plans

In most programming systems, a new plan is prepared annually; but a few large entities have a continuously updated long-range plan; it is changed whenever a major decision is made. A continuously updated programming process will become more widely used as computers make its preparation easier. It increases the likelihood that program decisions will be properly incorporated in the plans. For example, if the acquisition of new equipment is justified on the grounds that it will reduce labor costs, the program is automatically adjusted to reflect this decision; that is, the labor costs affected by the decision are reduced, beginning as of the time when the equipment is scheduled to become operational.

A procedure for updating a plan whenever a new decision is made is complicated, and few organizations believe that this effort is worthwhile. However, current decisions do not necessarily wait until the next formal programming cycle, and unless the implications of these decisions are incorporated promptly, the long-range plan may become obsolete. The approved long-range plan is the benchmark used in analyzing proposed changes in strategies, and strategic plans may be considered at any time.

Persons Involved

The programming process involves senior management and the managers of divisions or other principal responsibility centers, assisted by their staffs. Managers of lower-level responsibility centers usually do not participate in the programming process. Although staff personnel participate fully in the process, decisions are made by line managers.

The final plan reflects the consequences of decisions concerning the direction the organization should take, particularly on how resources are to be used. These are essentially statements of the magnitude of resources to be devoted to each program and the anticipated results of these efforts. These statements are classified by programs rather than by responsibility centers. Indeed, there may be no mention of activities of lower-level responsibility centers such as individual departments in a factory or individual sales offices in a marketing organization. Such details are set forth in the operating budget that is prepared in the next step of the management control process.

Steps in the Programming Process

In many organizations, the programming process goes through two cycles. In the first cycle, rough guidelines and general assumptions about the future are agreed to, and in the second cycle these are used to prepare the plan itself. The first cycle may consist of nothing more than a meeting or "retreat" of senior management, often lasting for several days or a week and often held at a location away from the normal workplace. The second cycle involves preparation of the proposed program, discussion of it, and eventual agreement on it.

If the entity is on a calendar-year basis, the programming process for the following year starts in January or February. At that time, headquarters staff examines last year's program and revises it to incorporate the effect of recent strategic decisions. The assumptions contained in that program—inflation rates, wage rates, market shares, margins, and so on—are checked against current trends in the entity, its industry, and the whole economy. The implementations of strategies incorporated in the long-range plan are examined to see if they are working out as anticipated. This examination may lead to changes in the plan as it then stands.

Guidelines incorporating these assumptions and changes are then prepared. These guidelines, together with instructions for preparing next year's plan, are communicated to program managers (who may also be profit center managers).

In the spring, each program manager submits a tentative program to headquarters. The headquarters staff examines it for consistency with the guidelines and for internal consistency, and attempts to resolve inconsistencies by discussions with the program manager. The staff combines the separate programs into a long-range plan for the whole entity.

This first cut at the plan usually reveals a "planning gap." In a profit-oriented entity, "gap" means that the difference between revenues and expenses is not adequate to produce the desired return on investment, or that desired expenditures for capital items exceed the funds available, or both. In a nonprofit entity, the gap usually means that estimated expenses exceed estimated revenues and other sources of funds.

Discussions are then held for the purpose of closing the gap. In some entities (but not necessarily in every year), these discussions may take the place of the "retreat," mentioned above, that is held before the programming process begins. These discussions are between managers, not staffs.

By summer the approved program is completed.

Ongoing Program Reviews

The formal programming process takes place annually, and the resulting long-range plan relates to the organization as a whole. Apart from, but related to, this process is a periodic review of ongoing programs, particularly programs of staff and support units. Review of an individual program is conducted about once every five years. (Many states legislate such reviews by what are called "sunset laws." In this legislation, the dates for the reviews are specified.) The review is conducted by headquarters staff, by a task force created for the purpose, or by outside consultants. The purpose of the review is to assess the need for the program, the magnitude of the effort that is appropriate, and the manner in which it should be conducted. This activity is often called a *zero-base review*.[5]

> CAUTION: *The review should not be a self-examination. It should be conducted by a unit whose head is independent of the manager whose program or responsibility center is being reviewed.*[6]

The practice of conducting periodic program reviews is a relatively recent development. Historically, these reviews have been conducted only in response to a crisis, such as evidence of mismanagement or of obviously poor results. In a crisis situation, the tendency is to fire the management without calmly addressing the underlying problems. In the absence of a crisis, there is a tendency not to challenge the need for an existing program or the way in which it is conducted, particularly when the program has powerful supporters. (Powerful support is the reason why many government programs of dubious merit are permitted to continue.)

If the ongoing program review results in changes, these changes are incorporated in the formal long-range plan.

Other Programming Activities

In addition to these scheduled activities, people in the organization are on the lookout for ways of getting the job done more efficiently. When better ways of performing are discovered, they are implemented as soon as possible, without waiting for a prescribed date in a timetable.

Who Should Have a Formal Program

Programming is time-consuming and expensive. The most significant expense is the time devoted to it by management, but it also involves a special programming staff and considerable paperwork. A formal programming process is not worthwhile in some organizations. It is desirable in organizations that have the following characteristics.

1. Its top management is convinced that programming is important. Otherwise, programming is likely to be, or to become, a staff exercise that has little impact on actual decision making.[7]

2. It is relatively large and complex. In small, simple organizations, an informal understanding of the organization's future directions is adequate for making decisions about resource allocations, which is a principal purpose of preparing a program.

3. Considerable uncertainty about the future exists, but the organization has the flexibility to adjust to changed circumstances. In a relatively stable organization, a program may be unnecessary; the future is sufficiently like the past so that the program would be only an exercise in extrapolation. (If a stable organization foresees the possible need for a change in direction, such as a decline in its markets or drastic changes in the cost of materials, it prepares a contingency program showing the actions to be taken to meet these new conditions.) If the future is so uncertain that reasonably reliable estimates cannot be made, preparation of a formal program is a waste of time.

In summary, a formal programming process is not needed in small, relatively stable organizations, and it is not worthwhile in organizations that cannot make reliable estimates about the future or in organizations whose top management does not prefer to manage in this fashion.

BUDGET PREPARATION

Although an entity's operating activities go on without a visible break between calendar dates, almost all sizable entities prepare a formal financial plan, or budget, for each year. In profit-oriented entities, this is because of the importance of the *bottom line* on the annual income statement to investors, analysts, and owners. Nonprofit organizations, including governments, typically use annual budgets as the primary management control device.

A *budget is a plan, usually expressed in monetary terms and usually for a period of one future year.* Not all short-range plans conform to this definition. In particular, the technique called "management by objectives" is essentially nonfinancial, but is an integral part of the budgeting process if properly carried out.[8]

Nevertheless, the term "budget" is used as a general term for short-range plans of all types, because most such plans are built around budgets.[9] The budget, being monetary, is the most convenient way of expressing the magnitudes of the planned inputs and outputs. Monetary numbers can be aggregated; heterogeneous physical quantities cannot be aggregated.

The purposes of a budget and the budget preparation process are: (1) to motivate managers to make plans, (2) to inform managers what they are expected to do and what they are expected to accomplish, (3) to obtain a commitment from managers, (4) to coordinate the separate activities of the organization, and (5) to provide a standard to be used in judging actual performance.

If the entity has a formal long-range plan, budget preparation is essentially a fine-tuning of that plan and if necessary a reclassification of program data so as to show the revenues and costs of each responsibility center that is involved in implementing the plan. If the entity does not have a formal long-range plan, budget preparation may incorporate the programming process.

> CAUTION: *When companies attempt to prepare an annual budget and a long-range plan at the same time, they usually discover that most attention is given to the budget and relatively little to the long-range plan.*

Relation to Programming

Although some people lump budget preparation and programming together as a single process, there are important differences between them. Some of these are the following.

1. Programming involves senior managers; operating managers ordinarily are not involved. Budgeting involves operating managers as well as senior managers. Proposed budgets originate with operating managers, and they participate fully in subsequent budget discussions. Often, and particularly with respect to new programs, operating managers do not participate in program decisions.

2. Staff personnel have a considerable input to the programming process, but relatively less input to the budgeting process. In a large organization, the program-

ming staff is distinct from the budget staff. The program staff (perhaps called "planning staff" or "analysis staff") is skilled in analyzing proposed new programs; the budget staff is skilled in finding soft spots in proposed budgets.

3. The program structure consists of programs and major projects; it includes both capital expenditures and operating items; and it covers a period of several years. The budget is structured by responsibility centers (which may or may not cut across programs); the focus is on operating revenues and expenses; and it typically is for a single year.

4. For a fiscal year that begins January 1, the programming cycle begins in the preceding spring and is completed by early fall. The budget preparation cycle begins in the fall and is completed just prior to January 1. Budget preparation is done under greater time pressure and is more hectic than programming.

5. A program is a broad-brush sketch of the future. A budget has more detail, both because it is a fairly specific guide to operating decisions and also because it will be used subsequently to evaluate the performance of individual managers. Also, "management by objectives" objectives are incorporated in the budget, but not usually in the program.

6. Programming decisions can have consequences of great magnitude. Budgeting decisions are typically much less significant, because they are made within the context of the current level of operating activities, except as those activities will be affected by program decisions.

7. Behavioral considerations are much more important in the budget preparation process than in the programming process. As explained below, the approved budget is a bilateral commitment; the program is not a commitment. Because the budget will be used to evaluate performance, operating managers tend to be much more concerned with the numbers in the budget than with the numbers in the program.

Characteristics of the Budget

Following are the principal characteristics of the budget.

1. The budget usually covers a period of one year in the future and states revenues, costs, and other items for monthly or quarterly periods within the year. In a few entities (including some states), a budget covers two years; in a few others, the budget covers only six months, but these are minor exceptions to the general rule.

2. Budget preparation focuses on the operating budget. Ancillary budgets, such as a cash budget and a budgeted balance sheet, often are prepared also, but these are usually mechanical extrapolations based on decisions made during the preparation of the operating budget. The complete budget package also includes a capital

budget, but the major capital budget decisions were made during the programming process, and the annual capital budget is primarily a time phasing of disbursements for approved capital projects.

3. The information in the operating budget is arranged by responsibility centers. Coordination, motivation, and performance evaluation can be accomplished only if the budget is structured in this way.

4. If costs are expected to vary with changes in volume, the operating budget shows how costs are expected to change with changes in volume. Such a budget is called a *flexible budget*. It provides a basis both for planning the response to changes in volume and also for identifying variances caused by volume changes. The budget for the volume level expected for the period is called the *master budget*.

CAUTION: *The literature contains many references to the desirability of preparing a "probabilistic" budget, usually with three categories: best estimate, optimistic, and pessimistic (or some variation such as best estimate, plus 10 percent revenue, and minus 10 percent revenue.) These budgets are rarely found in practice. Managers spend almost all their time preparing the best estimate, and arrive at the other numbers by rough extrapolations.*[10]

Preparation of the Operating Budget

Budget preparation ordinarily takes the approved long-range plan as its starting point. In the absence of a long-range plan, the current level of spending is taken as the starting point. As those who experimented with "zero-base budgeting" quickly learned, the task of evaluating each budget amount from a base of zero requires more time than is available during the budget process. (See the Appendix for a discussion of this point.) Also, those who criticize the practice of starting with the current level of spending (known as "incrementalism") may not fully appreciate the practical time constraints.

Senior management also decides on a set of guidelines and assumptions that are to govern budget preparation, and these are distributed to operating managers.

Each manager then proposes a budget for his or her responsibility center. Presumably, this proposal is consistent with the long-range plan and with the guidelines and assumptions.

CAUTION: *Because of time constraints, it is unlikely that major decisions will be made during the process of preparing a budget. Major decisions are made during the programming process.*

This "first cut" at a budget is aggregated, and the resulting income statement for the whole entity is examined by headquarters staff to determine whether the indicated performance is satisfactory. If it is not, the guidelines may be changed and revisions in the proposed budget are made. The staff, at this stage and throughout the process, also examines whether the plans of the several units within the organization are consistent with one another. For example, does a manufacturing unit plan to make the number of units that a marketing unit plans to sell? Coordination of the various units is one important purpose of budgeting.

It is essential that managers at all levels participate in the budget preparation process. If budgets are imposed without such participation, managers feel no commitment to attain the objectives. Participation starts at the lowest level in the organization. Managers at this level discuss their proposed budgets with their superiors, and the parties negotiate an agreement. In these negotiations, attention is focused on items of *discretionary cost*, that is, costs whose optimum amount cannot be known and whose budgeted allowances are therefore matters of judgment; most production overhead items and nearly all research/development, selling, general, and administrative costs are discretionary. By contrast, little management attention is devoted to items of *engineered costs*, that is, items whose optimum amount can be estimated within relatively close limits; examples are direct labor and direct material costs of many manufactured products. Staff people can easily calculate the amounts for these items.

In preparing a budget, managers are tugged by two opposing forces. On the one hand, they want an "optimistic" budget in order to indicate to their superiors that they expect to turn in good results—better than last year, better than other managers, as good as anyone has a right to expect. On the other hand, they want a "pessimistic" budget so as to provide a low base against which their actual performance will be judged. In general, the tendency to make a pessimistic budget is stronger, especially in organizations whose managers are sophisticated.

> CAUTION: *The academic literature refers to "slack," which is the difference between a budgeted cost and the lower cost that theoretically is actually needed to accomplish the planned results. Slack does exist; however, it rarely can be measured. Even if slack is measurable, a budget is unrealistic if it does not allow for contingencies or for the fact that humans do not work at maximum efficiency.*

The agreement between a manager and his or her superior is a bilateral commitment: the superior agrees that performance in accordance with the budget represents satisfactory (or even excellent) performance; the subordinate agrees to achieve this performance and to be held accountable for doing so. Both commitments are subject to the implicit qualification, "unless actual conditions are different from those assumed in the budget." Put another way, the approved budget gives managers the *authority* to carry out the program and also makes them *responsible* for doing so within the stated amounts.

Presumably, both parties agree that the budget is "reasonably attainable." Experiments have shown that a budget with unrealistically high goals is disregarded. Conversely, a budget that implies low goals is not an adequate motivating device.

The amount of the commitment may differ from the best estimate of *expected* performance. If the superior believes that the budget amounts are too optimistic, a "budget reserve" is established for the difference between committed and expected performance. This reserve appears as a component of the overall budget for the organization, but it is not identified with individual responsibility centers. It is necessary so that decisions on financing, dividends, and the like can be based on expected performance.

The budgets negotiated at the lowest level are combined into a budget that is a basis for a discussion at the next higher level. The superior at that level becomes the advocate of the budget to the superior at the next higher level, and so on up the organization. The budget is eventually approved by the chief executive officer and the board of directors. The success of the budgeting activity depends to a great extent on the emphasis and support given to it by the chief executive officer.

EXECUTION

The budget preparation process lays the groundwork for the control of operations, often referred to as "program execution."

> CAUTION: *This process is sometimes referred to as* budget *execution, which is an unfortunate term. The organization's primary purpose is to carry out programs, not to conform to a budget.*

Its payoff is in its effect on actions taken as operations proceed. These actions are also affected by the information made available, by the rules, and by the organization climate, all as discussed in Chapter 3. The flow of information relating to operations and the evaluation of performance is diagrammed in Exhibit 4-2.

The principal control activity in the execution phase is task control. Managers, as distinguished from task supervisors, are involved in a variety of activities, some related to control and others not.

The manager's functions are to coordinate with other responsibility centers, to break bottlenecks, to resolve disputes within the responsibility center, to approve proposed actions that subordinates are not authorized to take on their own authority, to suggest solutions to problems, to suggest better ways of getting the work

Exhibit 4–2
Information Flow in the Control Process

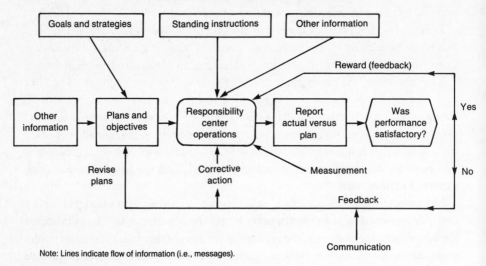

Note: Lines indicate flow of information (i.e., messages).

done, and, most important, to enhance the "control climate" by commending subordinates for good performance and constructively criticizing, educating, or taking other appropriate action for unsatisfactory performance. These activities are essentially unforeseen and unplanned. If work is proceeding satisfactorily, the manager is not even needed.[11]

> CAUTION: *Managers cannot literally "control costs." What managers do—or at least what they attempt to do—is to influence the actions of the people who are responsible for incurring costs.*

The budget, together with other plans, serves as a device for coordinating the activities of individual responsibility centers. It is also a guide for the manager of the responsibility center, but it is only a guide. If a better way of achieving objectives is discovered, or if conditions change from those assumed in the budget, the manager should depart from the budget. Nevertheless, there is a presumption that the manager will operate in accordance with the budget unless there is a good reason to do otherwise. (Certain types of departures, such as spending significantly more than the budgeted amount, require the approval of the manager's superior.) The manager's job is to achieve objectives; conformity to the budget is not desirable if the plan assumed in the budget turns out not to be the best way of achieving objectives. Adherence to the budget is not necessarily good, and departure from it is not necessarily bad.

Budget Revisions

If circumstances change, the budget may or may not be revised. Some managements believe that unless the budget is revised, it is no longer a statement of planned performance. Others believe that revision destroys the basis for an analysis of the differences between actual performance and the performance as agreed to in the approved budget. A middle ground is to preserve the original budget but periodically to prepare a "current estimate" showing the revised estimate of performance.

Guides, Ceilings, Floors

Operating managers should understand which budget amounts are guides, which are ceilings, and which are floors. Some budget amounts (for example, entertainment, advertising) mean that the manager is expected to spend not more than the amount stated without obtaining specific approval. Others mean that the manager should spend at least the expected amount (for example, training). Still other amounts are general guides in the sense that spending is expected to be approximately, but not exactly, the amount stated. These distinctions may not be explicitly stated in the budget, and managers should be made aware of them. For those items that are guides, managers should be aware of the tolerable variations from the amount stated.

Operating Information

In the course of operations, information is collected about what is going on. Much of this information is needed for task control. Most management control information is a summary of task control information.

The primary purpose of information about operating performance is to alert the manager about the possible need for corrective action. It follows that the manager must receive information promptly enough to be able to act and that the information should be structured so that the need for possible action is red-flagged.

Critical Success Factors

In addition to regular reports of actual performance compared with budget performance, there should be a means of promptly reporting events related to critical success factors. In every operation a few factors are especially important in determining the success of the operation. Reports should be constructed so that they emphasize these factors and provide information about them as promptly as possible. A critical success factor, or key variable, has these characteristics: (1) it is *important* in explaining the success or failure of the organization; (2) it is *volatile* (that is, it can change quickly, often for reasons that are not controllable by the manager); (3) *prompt action* is required when a significant change occurs; (4) the change is *not easy to predict*; (5) the variable can be *measured*, either directly or by a surrogate.[12]

Analysis of Variances

Many reports are designed to facilitate an analysis of the causes of variances between actual and budgeted performance. (Actually, the cause of the variance should be made known informally, prior to the issuance of formal reports. The report states the quantitative amount of each cause and confirms the informal message.) This suggests that controllable items should be separated from noncontrollable items, that the effect of changes in volume on revenues and costs should be ascertainable, and that, if feasible, changes in other circumstances should be stated. A technique for relieving the manager of responsibility for noncontrollable items is to make the "actual" amounts for these items equal to the budgeted amounts; hence, no variance is developed for them.

The reports should be structured so that summary information is backed up by detailed information; this facilitates the search for causes of variances in important items on the summary reports. For example, a summary report on sales volume may be backed up by detailed reports on sales by territory, by customer types, by channels of distribution, and so on.

Characteristics of Good Reports

The frequency with which reports of actual performance are prepared depends on the manager's ability to take corrective action if it is needed. In the majority of organizations, management performance reports are prepared monthly (in contrast with task reports, which may be prepared daily, hourly, or in real time). In those responsibility centers in which there is little latitude to make changes at short intervals, the reports are prepared quarterly. Reports on critical success factors may be prepared more frequently than other reports.

Performance reports are disseminated promptly after the end of the period they cover. The usefulness of information and the stimulus provided by information decreases rapidly with the passage of time.

If feasible, the format of reports is adapted to the preferences of the managers who use them. Some managers prefer graphs; others prefer numbers. Some like much detail; others do not. With manual information processing, custom-tailored reports were prohibitively expensive. With computers, and especially computer graphics, they are more feasible. In particular, reports for the chief executive officer should be designed to meet that person's preference.

EVALUATION

The final step in the management control process is the evaluation of the manager's performance. Since this occurs after the event, it cannot literally affect what has happened. Nevertheless, knowledge that performance is going to be evaluated can be a powerful stimulus. Performance evaluation also provides the basis for revising plans.

Sources of Information

Information about what has actually happened comes to the manager's attention both from formal reports and also from informal sources. The informal sources include conversations, memoranda, meetings, and personal observations. Since informal information is not governed by the disciplines that are built into a formal reporting system, its validity varies. Thus, the bias of the originator or other sources of inaccuracy needs to be taken into account. When this is done, informal information can be extremely important. Formal reports alone are an inadequate basis for control.

An important control principle is that the formal performance reports should contain no surprises. Important news should be conveyed to interested parties informally, as soon as feasible, and in any event prior to submission of formal reports.

Since a management control system is built around a financial budget, there is a natural tendency to structure performance reports so that they correspond to the budget and to emphasize the correspondence between actual and budget in evaluating performance. This may result in an overemphasis on the financial results. Because measures of nonfinancial, and especially nonquantitative, performance may be difficult to make, these aspects of performance may be given less weight than they should be. Overemphasis or misuse of these measures can have dysfunctional consequences.[13]

Most control reports focus on personal performance as contrasted with economic performance. "Personal performance" refers to the performance of the manager as a manager. "Economic performance" refers to the performance of the responsibility center as an economic entity, without regard to the ircumstances prevailing. For example, the report of a downtown department store may indicate that the manager is performing well, even though the store incurred a loss. The loss indicates poor economic performance, but this may be because shoppers have deserted the downtown area in favor of suburban shopping centers; it may not be a reflection on the manager's ability.

Use of Performance Information

The essential idea of evaluation is that actual performance is compared with what performance should have been under the circumstances prevailing. The measurement of actual costs incurred is relatively straightforward (although there are some problems). The measurement of actual output is also straightforward if output can be measured by revenues earned or by a good nonfinancial measure such as tons.

> CAUTION: *A simple quantitative measure, such as tonnage, may not reflect differences in the cost of various items that make up output. A good monetary measure incorporates these differences. Another alternative is to use weights that reflect the cost characteristics of various items.*

Except in the most straightforward production operations, there are problems in arriving at reliable measures of the quality and the quantity of actual output. The inherent inadequacies of these measurements need to be taken into account.

In measuring what performance should have been, the budget (supplemented by a statement of objectives in an MBO system) is the usual starting point because it represents a standard that presumably was agreed to by the manager and his or her superior. However, the budget was based on certain assumptions as to the conditions that would exist during the budget period, and to the extent that actual conditions differed from those assumed, the budget amounts theoretically should be adjusted for these differences. If standard costs are used, the noncontrollable variances between actual and standard costs, such as those caused by volume or input prices, provide an objective basis for such adjustment. In other respects, the allowances for changed circumstances are made subjectively by the evaluator.

Evaluators tend to hold subordinates accountable for some changes in assumed conditions that conceptually are not controllable. Their rationale is the "manager should accept responsibility for coping with changed circumstances, whatever they were; that's the manager's job." Within limits, this reasoning is defensible, but it cannot be applied, of course, to totally unforeseen events such as fires, uncontrollable accidents, or sharp increases in input prices.

The person being reported on has a natural tendency to pass the buck: that is, to attribute unfavorable performance to causes that are noncontrollable or that are the responsibility of someone else. Managers, and staff analysts on their behalf, make their own judgments as to the validity of these claims.

The noncontrollable causes having been identified, attention is focused on the amounts not explained by them. These amounts were presumably controllable. As a starting point, but only as a starting point, there is a presumption that if actual controllable costs were higher than budgeted costs or if actual controllable revenues were lower than budgeted, then the manager has not performed as well as expected. This is a rebuttable presumption; the subordinate may have good explanations for the apparently unfavorable variances.

Action

The purpose of a control report is to provide a basis for action, if action is necessary. In many cases, of course, the report indicates that performance was satisfactory, and the only action required is to compliment the subordinate on having done a good job. In other cases, the formal report merely confirms what the superior has learned from informal sources, and he or she may have already taken corrective action. Even if little or no action is necessary, managers regularly discuss performance reports with their subordinates. Unless the subordinate is convinced that the reports are important, the management control process built around the budget tends to be disregarded.

It is essential that managers perceive that judgments about their performance are fair. This perception has two aspects: (1) to the extent feasible, the performance report should measure fairly the performance of the manager in doing the job that was agreed to in the budget preparation process; and (2) in evaluation of the report, one should allow for its inevitable inadequacies. Inadequacies in the reported performance include changes in circumstances not allowed for in the report, inadequate allowance for noncontrollable factors, and inadequate allowance for justified departures from plans.

The performance reported for a given period rarely reflects the manager's actual performance in that period. Quite apart from the difficulty of measuring the performance of the responsibility center in a period, the performance report cannot allow for two factors that are relevant to the manager's performance: (1) performance in the period was affected by actions taken by managers in prior periods that influence both the resources available and also the control climate in the current period; and (2) in the current period, the manager takes actions that will affect performance in future periods, and the report cannot show the ultimate consequences of these actions. The first point is especially important if a different manager headed the responsibility center in the earlier period. The second point is an inherent limitation on all reports of current performance and is probably the greatest weakness in the whole management control process.

A few companies have attempted to take the second factor into account by the operating budget into two parts. One part relates to ongoing activities, and for this part actual spending is supposed to be not higher than budgeted spending. The other part is labeled "strategic funds," and for this part, the manager is expected to spend at least the amount budgeted.[14] As a practical matter, managers tend to defeat the purpose of this practice by recording borderline items as spending of strategic funds. Moreover, neither this nor any other device can measure the actual impact of the manager's current performance on future profitability. The future is unknowable. For example, an advertising campaign launched in the current period may eventually prove to be a huge success, but then again it may be a failure. Or a training program may produce a sizable group of graduates, but whether the increased productivity of these employees exceeds the cost of training them may not be known for some time. (Of course, the discovery or invention of a profitable idea can be identified, but these events are relatively rare.)

Much of the evaluation of a manager's performance is self-evaluation; the report influences his or her future conduct. This process is called "feedback."

> CAUTION: *Feedback in management control is inherently different from the analogous phenomenon of feedback in electrical circuits. For example, if the actual temperature deviates from the desired temperature, a thermostat causes an automatic response, and this changes the temperature in the desired direction. In management control, the response to reported information is by no means automatic. The response may not be what the person's superior wants, and indeed there may be no response at all.*

Rewards

If the manager is likely to perceive reported performance as being a reasonable approximation of actual performance, rewards (for example, bonus, stock option, stock appreciation rights) can be based on reported performance. In other circumstances, the reported performance should be modified by subjective judgment in arriving at the reward. In general, rewards based entirely on objective measures are appropriate only at low levels in the organization. At higher levels, an increasing fraction of the criteria used in determining the amount of the reward should be subjective. The method of arriving at rewards and the type of award (cash, stock options, special fringe benefits) are complicated subjects. The best experts are consulting firms who specialize in this topic; however, they do not publish their latest ideas because these are their stock-in-trade.[15]

> CAUTION: *For understandable reasons, managers tend to focus on those aspects of performance that are included in the reward system. In order to counteract this*

tendency, senior management attempts to emphasize the importance of judgment in weighing the unmeasured factors. Applying judgment is difficult, however, and it can lead to favoritism, or unwillingness to be tough-minded.

Evaluation of Programs

The preceding section has focused on evaluating and rewarding the performance of managers. In some circumstances, the evaluation of programs is also necessary. This task is especially difficult in the case of social programs carried on by government agencies or others. In recent years the Congress has required that certain programs be evaluated on a regular basis. A decade or two ago, techniques for doing this were crude indeed, but they have improved greatly in recent years.[16]

MANAGEMENT CONTROL
OF PROJECTS

THE discussion in Chapter 4 focused on management control in an organization that tends to carry on similar activities day after day. This chapter discusses the somewhat different process that is used for the management control of projects. After a discussion of the characteristics of projects and of how the control problem for projects differs from the control of ongoing operations, the main sections deal respectively with (a) the project control environment, and (b) the project control process.

NATURE OF PROJECTS

A project is a set of activities intended to accomplish a specified end result of sufficient importance to be of interest to management. Projects include construction projects, the production of a sizable unique product (such as a turbine), rearranging a plant, launching a new product, consulting engagements, audits, acquisitions and divestments, litigation, permanent financing or refunding, research/development work, development and installation of information systems, and many others.

The special characteristic of a project is that when its objective is accomplished (and in some cases, sooner), the project ends. An ongoing organization intends to operate indefinitely; a project team goes out of existence when its product is produced. A military campaign and a battle within a campaign are projects; the ongoing operation of the military establishment is not. The construction of a building and the renovation of a building are projects; the routine maintenance of the building is not. The development of the space shuttle and its test flights were projects; the regular flights of the space shuttle, although extraordinarily complicated, are ongoing operations. The production of a motion picture is a project; the production of a weekly television series is an ongoing operation.

The completion of a project may lead to an ongoing operation, as in the case of a successful development project. The transition from the project organization to the operating organization involves difficult management control problems, but these are not discussed here.[1]

Projects vary greatly. At one extreme, a project may involve one or a few persons working for a few days or weeks, performing work similar to that done many times previously, as with an annual audit of a medium-size company conducted by a public accounting firm. At the other extreme, a project may involve thousands of people working for several years, performing work unlike that ever done before, as was the case with the project to land the first men on the moon. The discussion here will not focus on either of these extremes. Rather, it focuses on projects that involve enough people so that a formal project organization is necessary and enough resources so that a formal management control system is necessary. Extremely complex, first-of-a-kind projects have more complicated control problems than those discussed here, although the general nature of these problems and of the appropriate control system is similar.[2]

Contrast with Ongoing Operations

This section describes characteristics of projects that make the management control of projects different from the management control of ongoing activities.

A project usually has a single objective; ongoing operations have multiple objectives. In addition to its responsibility for doing its current work, a responsibility center in an ongoing organization must also coordinate its work with that of other responsibility centers. Moreover, the decisions that the manager makes now are likely to affect operations for the indefinite future: new procedures are implemented; new techniques are developed; employees are trained for new positions. The project manager also makes decisions that affect the future, but the time horizon is the end of the project. Project performance can be judged in terms of the desired end product; operating performance should be judged in terms of all the results that the manager achieves, some of which are not known until a year or more in the future.

In many cases, the project organization is superimposed on an ongoing organization, and its management control system is superimposed on the management control system of that organization. This structure causes problems that do not exist in an ongoing organization. Satisfactory relationships must be established between the project organization and the ongoing functional organization. Many members of project organizations have dual responsibilities. They have a permanent "home" in a functional department of the ongoing organization and in that capacity are responsible to the manager of that department. They are also responsible to the project manager. This *matrix* organization creates problems that are described in a later section. Similarly, a special management control system must be developed for the project, and it must mesh at certain points with the system of the ongoing organization.

Project control focuses on the project; management control of ongoing organizations focuses on a designated period of time, such as a month. The objective of a project is to produce a satisfactory product, by a specified time, and at an optimum cost. These three aspects of control are referred to, respectively, as scope (or quality), schedule, and cost. By contrast, control in ongoing organizations focuses on the activities of a time period such as a month and on all the products worked on in that period. The primary focus of the management control of operating activities tends to be on cost, with quality and schedule being treated on an exception basis; that is, the formal system emphasizes cost performance, but special reports are prepared if quality and schedule are judged to be less than satisfactory.

Projects usually involve trade-offs among scope, schedule, and cost. Costs can be reduced by decreasing the scope of the project. The schedule can be shortened by incurring overtime costs. Similar trade-offs occur in ongoing organizations, but they are not typical of the day-to-day activities in such organizations.

Performance standards tend to be less reliable for projects than for ongoing organizations. Although the specifications of one project and the method of producing it may be similar to those for other projects, the design is literally used only once. It follows that standards against which actual performance is measured are unique to the project (although reasonably reliable standards may be derived from experience on similar projects).

Standards for repetitive activities are developed from past experience or from engineering analyses of the optimum time and costs. To the extent that the activities on a given project are similar to those on other projects, the experience on these projects can be used as a basis for estimating time and costs. If the project is the construction of a house, good historical information exists on the unit costs of building similar houses. (However, changes in materials, in the technology of house building, or in building codes may make this information unreliable as a guide to the cost of building a new house, and site-specific problems may also affect the actual cost of a given house.) By contrast, the typical project is sufficiently different so that historical information is not of much help, and allowances must be made for its unique characteristics. The cost estimate for constructing a house usually contains a contingency allowance, whereas such an allowance is not customary in calculating the standard cost of a mass-produced product.

Plans for projects tend to be changed frequently and drastically. Unforeseen environmental conditions in a construction project or unexpected facts uncovered during a consulting engagement may lead to changes in plans. The results of one phase of the investigation in a research/development project may completely alter the work originally planned for subsequent phases. Such changes tend to be less frequent in ongoing operations.

The rhythm of a project differs from that of ongoing operations. Most projects start small, build up to a peak activity, and then taper off as completion nears and only clean-up or report writing remains to be done. Ongoing activities tend to operate at the same level for a considerable time and then to change, in either direction, from that level to another.

Projects tend to be influenced more by the external environment than is the case with ongoing organizations. Production activities occur within a plant whose walls and roof protect them from the environment. Construction projects occur outdoors and are subject to climatic and other geographical conditions. If the project involves excavating, conditions beneath the earth's surface may cause unexpected problems, even for such a simple project as building a house. Consulting projects take place on the client's premises and involve "finding one's way around," both geographically and organizationally.

Resources for many projects are brought to the project site. Workers on a production line use material that is brought to them; workers on a construction project go to the project. A construction project has logistical problems that do not ordinarily occur with production operations.

These distinctions are not clear-cut. A job shop, such as a printing company, produces dissimilar end products; however, the focus of management control in such an organization is on the totality of its activities during a month or other specified period, not on individual jobs. Some project organizations are created for the purpose of carrying out the project, and its members are not associated with functional departments in an ongoing organization. Projects in a research laboratory are conducted on the premises rather than in outside facilities.[3]

THE CONTROL ENVIRONMENT

Project Organization Structure

A project organization is a temporary organization. A team is assembled for conducting the project, and the team is disbanded when the job is completed. Team members may be employees of the sponsoring organization; they may be hired for the purpose; or some or all of them may be engaged under contracts with outside organizations.

If the project is conducted in part by an outside contractor, project management must quickly establish satisfactory working arrangements with the contractors' personnel. These relationships are influenced by the terms of the contract, as will be discussed below. If the project is conducted within the sponsoring organization, some of the work may, in effect, be subcontracted to support units, and similar relationships must be established with them. For example, a central drafting unit in an architectural firm does drafting for all projects, and management control problems of such arrangements are similar to those of contracting with outside organizations.

Matrix Organizations

If members of the project team are drawn from the parent organization, team members have two bosses. This is the characteristic of a matrix organization. In overhauling a ship, for example, craftsmen (for example, electricians, sheet metal workers, pipe fitters) are drawn from various functional departments in the shipyard and work on the project when their skills are needed. Their basic loyalty is to their functional department. Whether or not they appear at the work site at the desired time depends in part on decisions made by the manager of their functional department, who considers the relative priorities of all projects requiring the resources that he or she controls. The project manager therefore has less authority over personnel than the manager of a production department whose employees have an undivided loyalty to that department.

Evolution of Organization Structure

Different types of management personnel and management methods may be appropriate at different stages of the project. In the planning phase, architects, engineers, schedulers, and cost analysts predominate. In the execution of the project, the emphasis is on production managers and, if the situation warrants, on troubleshooters. In the final stages, the work tapers off, and the principal task may be to obtain the sponsor's acceptance, with salesmanship skill being a principal requirement (especially in consulting projects). However, senior project management should continue throughout the whole project.

Contractual Relationships

If the project is conducted by a contractor, an additional level of project control is created. In addition to the control exercised by the contractor who does the work, the sponsoring organization has its own control responsibilities. This additional level of control complicates the management control process. The contractor usually brings its own control system to the project, and this system must be adapted so that it meshes with the sponsor's system, providing information that the sponsor needs. The sponsor reserves the right to revise the scope or schedule of the project under certain circumstances, and may put pressure on the contractor to improve performance. The management control system should facilitate the implementation of changes that have been agreed to.

The form of the contractual arrangement has an important impact on management control. Contracts are of two general types—fixed price and cost reimbursement—with many variations within each type.

Fixed-Price Contracts

In a fixed-price contract, the contractor agrees to complete the specified work by a specified date at a specified price. Usually, there are penalties if the work is not completed to specifications or if the scheduled date is not met. It would appear, therefore, that the contractor assumes all the risks and consequently has all the responsibility for management control; however, this is by no means the case. If the sponsor decides to change the scope of the project or if the contractor encounters conditions not contemplated by the contractual agreement, a change order is issued. The parties must agree on the scope, schedule, and cost implications of each change order. To the extent that change orders are agreed to, the consequences are borne by the sponsor. On some complex fixed-price projects, there are thousands of these change orders. In these circumstances, the final price of the work is by no means fixed in advance. Keeping track of the effect of these change orders can be a complicated matter.[4]

In a fixed-price contract the sponsor is responsible for auditing the *quality* of the work to ensure that it is done as specified. This may be as difficult a task as auditing the *cost* of the work under a cost-reimbursement contract.

> CAUTION: *The general public and many Congressmen tend to believe that most government contracts should be fixed-price. They are unaware of the problems mentioned above. Thus, public opposition to cost-reimbursement contracts should be anticipated, even in situations in which their use is well justified.*

Cost-Reimbursement Contracts

In a cost-reimbursement contract the sponsor agrees to pay reasonable costs plus a profit; therefore, the sponsor is responsible for the management control of costs.[5] Contractors refer to this as a "soft dollar" contract, and the term indicates their attitude toward cost control, as contrasted with their attitude toward a fixed-price, "hard dollar" contract. (Even so, a reputable contractor has some motivation against incurring unnecessary costs; it wants to maintain a good reputation.)

In these circumstances, the sponsor needs a management control system and associated control personnel comparable to those needed by the contractor with a fixed-price contract. A cost-reimbursement contract is appropriate when the scope, schedule, and cost of the project cannot be reliably estimated in advance.[6]

Information Structure

The focus of management control information in a management control system for an ongoing organization is on responsibility centers and on the work done and the costs incurred in those responsibility centers in a given period of time. In the project control system, the information is structured by elements of the project. For the project as a whole and for each of its elements, the focus is on three dimensions: (1) its *scope*, or specifications for the end product; (2) its *schedule*, or the time required; and (3) its *cost*.

Work Packages

The smallest units of the project with which these elements are associated are called *work packages*, and the way in which these packages are aggregated is called the *work breakdown structure.*[7]

A work package is a measurable increment of work, usually of fairly short duration (a month or so). It should have an identifiable starting point and completion point, so that there is an unambiguous way of knowing when a work package has been completed. The completion point is called a *milestone*. A work package should be the responsibility of a single manager.

If the project has similar work packages (for example, the electrical work on each floor of an office building), each should be defined in the same way as the others so that information about them can be compared with one another. If the industry has developed cost or time standards for the performance of certain types of work packages (as is the case in many branches of the construction industry), or if the project organization has developed such standards on the basis of prior work, definitions used in these standards should be followed, so that actual cost for a work package can be compared with these standard costs.

Other Accounts

In addition to work packages, cost accounts are established for overhead and support activities. Unlike the work packages, these activities have no definable output. Their costs are usually stated per unit of time, such as a month, just as the overhead costs of ongoing responsibility centers are stated.

The chart of accounts and the rules for charging costs to projects are also developed in advance. Which cost items will be charged directly to work packages? How, if at all, will indirect costs be allocated to work packages? What will be the lowest level of monetary cost aggregation? (Costs for small work packages might be expressed in terms of man days, rather than money, for example.)

If during the project it turns out that the work breakdown structure or the accounting system does not provide a useful way of finding out what is happening on the project, the structure may need to be revised. This may require recasting much of the information already collected and much of the information relating to future plans. Therefore, it is worthwhile to give considerable attention to the design of work packages in planning the project.

> CAUTION: *Revising the information structure in midstream is a difficult, time-consuming, frustrating job. In retrospect, managers sometimes regret that they had not called in the systems designers sooner.*

STRATEGIC PLANNING

I discuss the strategic planning process only to the extent necessary to distinguish it from the management control process. Strategic planning for a project is one aspect of the process of planning the strategy of the entity as a whole. As a part of the strategic planning process, a need may be identified for a new plant, a new direction for research, or something else that leads to a project. Of course, many projects do not involve a change in strategy; they are a more or less regular part of the organization's activities.

As is the case with strategic planning in general, the process of considering a proposed project usually starts in an unsystematic way.[8] Someone perceives an opportunity or a threat and has an idea for a project that will capitalize on the opportunity or meet the threat. The idea is kicked around informally for awhile. Alternatives for accomplishing the desired results are explored. The scope of the proposed project is expanded if the original idea turns out to have additional ramifications, or it is narrowed if management decides that not so much should be bitten off at one time.

> CAUTION: *For projects involving the installation of new information systems, there is a tendency to make the project unnecessarily broad. Tackling one division or function at a time may make the job more doable.*

Rough estimates of the cost and the time required are developed. The cost of a building may be estimated with no more precision than a general idea of the cost per square foot of similar buildings multiplied by a rough estimate of the number of square feet required. Similarly, the cost of a new airplane may be obtained by multiplying a cost per pound by the estimated weight, and the cost of a road by an estimate of a cost per lane-mile, multiplied by the number of lane miles. The estimated time required for doing the project may be similarly rough.

If the idea is not shot down (which many are), it eventually is reduced to a written proposal. This is discussed at various levels in the organization, modified, and eventually either approved or rejected by senior management or by the board of directors. The strategic planning process ends with this decision (although subsequent events can of course lead to a reconsideration).

At this stage, therefore, there is agreement on what is to be accomplished with the project and a rough estimate of its schedule and cost. Considerable evidence supports the conclusion that at this stage both the time required and the cost tend to be underestimated; this is probably because not all the future uncertainties are adequately allowed for. The approval is for *what* is to be done; there may not be agreement at this stage on *how* the work is to be done, that is, whether in-house, by contract, or by some combination of these.

MANAGEMENT CONTROL PROCESS

As is the case with the management of ongoing operations, the line between strategic planning and management control is fuzzy. In the above description, I assumed that strategic planning ended when there were both approval to proceed and agreement on what in general should be done. Some would have strategic planning end earlier, as soon as there is agreement to proceed with something. The question of where to draw the line is unimportant.

The management control process consists of the same activities as those described for the control of operations, except that the two separate activities, programming and budgeting, are combined into a single activity, planning.

PROJECT PLANNING

The persons who participated in the strategic planning process are unlikely to be responsible for carrying out the project. (If the project is someone's "baby," that person will often keep a close eye on developments and occasionally may become the project manager.) Similarly, in the early stages of the project planning process, the planners are not likely to be persons who will be involved in the execution of the project. Until the project team is organized or a contractor selected, those who will carry out the project have not been identified.

Although I do not separate programming and budget preparation, the early stages of the process are similar to programming in that the activity involves heavy staff participation and fairly rough estimates; and the later stages correspond to budget preparation, with more participation by those who will carry out the project and a fine-tuning of scope, schedule, and cost.

The planners take as a starting point the rough estimates used as the basis for the decision to go ahead. The planning process culminates with detailed specifications for the product, detailed schedules, and a cost budget. In the intervening period, various studies may be made, unit costs of similar work are collected and used to refine the estimates, a management control system and underlying task control systems are developed (or adapted from those already available), an organization chart is developed, and the boxes on this chart gradually are filled with the names of personnel who are to manage the work.

On a project of even moderate complexity, there is a "plan for planning," that is, a description of the tasks that must be done, who is to do them, when they should be completed, and the interrelationships among tasks. The planning process is itself a subproject within the overall project. There is also a control system to ensure that the planning activities are properly carried out. Thus, the planning process also involves control (and, as will be seen, the control of the work being done also involves planning, which is why management control is not separable into discrete "planning" and "control" functions).

As the planning progresses, changes are likely to be made in the scope of the project, and these impact on the schedule and on costs.

Nature of the Project Plan

The final plan consists of three related parts:

1. Scope

This consists of the specifications of each work package and the name of the person or organization unit responsible (unless the project is one in which specifications are nebulous, as is the case with many consulting and research/development projects).

2. Schedule

This is the estimated time for each work package and the interrelationship between work packages (for example, which work packages must be completed before others can be started). The set of these relationships is called a *network*. The schedule may be stated as a PERT, Line of Balance, or CPM chart.

> CAUTION: *Some people advocate that the cost of each work package should be included along with the schedule. This may be feasible for fairly simple projects, but maintaining an updated network that contains both schedule and cost information is usually more work than is worthwhile for projects of even moderate complexity.*

3. Cost

Costs are stated in the project budget, usually called the *control budget*.

In order to compare actual performance with the plan, these three dimensions must be carefully related to one another. The work package device is the basis for maintaining this relationship. The estimated time required and the estimated cost of each work package are associated with that work package. Both actual time and actual cost are measured in relation to the work accomplished.

CAUTION: *As noted above, measuring the monetary costs of work packages may not be worth the effort. Measuring quantities of resources used, such as hours of labor or yards of concrete, may be adequate for individual work packages.*

Preparing the Control Budget

The control budget is prepared close to the inception of the work, allowing just time enough for approval by decision makers before commitments of cost. Indeed, for a long project the initial control budget may be prepared in detail for only the first phase of the project, with fairly rough cost estimates for later phases. Detailed budgets for later phases are deferred until just prior to the beginning of work on these phases. Delaying preparation of the control budget until just prior to the start of work ensures that the control budget incorporates the most current information about scope and schedule, the results of cost analyses, and current data about wage rates, material prices, and other variables. Delaying the preparation of control budgets for later phases avoids doing work that is based on what turns out to be obsolete information.

The control budget is an important link between planning and performance. It represents the sponsor's expectations as to what the project will cost. If, as the project proceeds, it appears that there will be a significant budget overrun, the project may no longer be economically justified. In these circumstances the sponsor may reexamine the scope and the schedule, and perhaps modify them.

As is the case with the operating budget, the control budget for a project is a commitment by both the project manager and the sponsor. Because of the uncertainties inherent in most projects, however, it usually is a less firm commitment than that implied by an approved operating budget.

Other Planning Activities

During the planning phase, other activities are performed: material is ordered, permits are obtained, preliminary interviews are conducted, personnel are selected, and so on. Except for the fact that all these activities must be controlled and integrated into the overall effort, these activities are outside the scope of this description of the management control process.

One set of activities involves the selection and organization of personnel. After personnel come on board, they get to know one another, they find out where they fit in the project organization, they learn what to expect and what not to expect from other parts of the organization, and they learn what is expected of them. Information learned and expectations developed during this stage are a part of the control "climate," which can have a profound effect on the successful completion of the project.

Development of Systems

During the planning process, the control systems that are to be used during the project are developed, unless systems that have been successfully used on similar projects are available. These consist of both task control systems and the management control system. As is the case with the ongoing system described in Chapter 4, the information in the management control system is usually a summary of details obtained from the task control systems.

PROJECT EXECUTION

Project managers shift from control activities to planning activities on a daily, even hourly, basis. They see to it that today's work gets done properly, which is control; and they identify possible causes of trouble that lie ahead and take steps to anticipate and if possible reduce or eliminate them, which is planning.

Content of Reports

As a consequence of the planning process, there exist for most projects a specification of work packages, a schedule, and a budget. For each work package, the responsible manager is identified. The schedule shows the time required for each activity, and the budget shows estimated costs of each principal part of the project. As mentioned above, if resources planned to be used in detailed work packages are expressed in nonmonetary terms, such as the number of man days required, the control budget states monetary costs only for a sizable aggregation of individual work packages.

In the control process, data on actual cost, time, and accomplishment are compared with these estimates. The comparison may be made either when a designated milestone in the project is reached, or it may be made at specified time intervals, such as weekly or monthly.

Basically, the manager is concerned with these questions: (1) Is the project going to be finished by the scheduled completion date? (2) Is the completed work going to meet the approved specifications? (3) Is the work going to be done within the estimated cost? If at any time during the course of the project the answer to one of these questions is "no," the manager needs to know the reasons and what can be done to correct the situation.

These three questions are not considered separately from one another, for it is sometimes desirable to make trade-offs among time, quality, and cost. For example, overtime might be authorized in order to assure completion on time, but this would add to costs; or some of the specifications might be relaxed in order to reduce costs.

Nature of Information

Information used by management is essentially a summary of information collected in the task control systems. Although the nature of this information varies greatly depending on the type of project, task control systems may include such things as working drawings, bills of material, work schedules, time sheets, inventory records, purchase orders, and equipment records. In the design of these systems, their use as a source of management control information is one consideration.

Quantity of Reports

In order to make certain that all needs for information are satisfied, systems designers often create more than the optimum number of reports. An unnecessary report or extraneous information in a report requires extra costs in assembling and transmitting the information. More important, users may spend unnecessary time reading the report or they may overlook important information that is buried in the mass of detail. In the course of the project, therefore, a review of the set of reports is often desirable, and this may lead to the elimination of some reports and the simplification of others.

> CAUTION: *This paperwork problem (some call it "information overload") may not be serious. Competent managers learn which reports contain the information that is likely to be important to them, and they focus on these first. If, but only if, they identify possible problems from these summary reports, they refer to information in the more detailed reports. In these circumstances, the presence of reports that often are not read creates only the trivial problem of finding filing space.*

Percent Complete

Some work packages will be only partially completed as of the reporting date, and the percentage of completion of each such work package must be estimated as a basis for comparing actual time with scheduled time and actual costs with budgeted costs. If accomplishment can be measured in physical terms, such as yards of concrete poured, the percentage of completion for a given work package can be easily measured. If no quantitative measure is available, as in the case of many research/development and consulting projects, the percentage of completion is amorphous. Some companies compare actual labor hours with budgeted labor hours, but this assumes that labor effort accomplished as much as was planned, which may not be the case. Narrative reports of progress may be of some help, but these often are difficult to interpret. Usually the manager must rely on personal observation, meetings, and other informal sources as a basis for judgment.

Summarizing Progress

In addition to determining the percentage of completion of individual work packages, a summary of progress on the whole project is also needed. Progress payments often are made when specified completion points are reached. Thus, the system usually contains some method of weighting work packages or other ways of measuring accomplishment of specific tasks so as to develop an overall measure of accomplishment. A simple approach is to use the ratio of man hours on a work package to total man hours, but this is reliable only if the project is labor-intensive. A weighting based on the planned cost of each work package is more comprehensive, although, as mentioned earlier, the plan for some projects does not include costs at the level of individual work packages.

Types of Reports

Three somewhat different types of information flow to managers.

1. *Reports of Trouble.* These report both on trouble that has already happened (such as an unforeseen delay resulting from any of a number of possible causes) and also anticipated future trouble. Critical problems are flagged. It is essential that these reports get to the appropriate manager quickly so that corrective action can be initiated. In fact, they often are transmitted by face-to-face conversation or by telephone. If significant, the oral report is later confirmed by a written document so that a record is maintained. Precision is sacrificed in the interest of speed; rough numbers are often used—man hours rather than labor costs, or numbers of bricks rather than material cost.

2. *Reports of Progress.* Progress reports compare actual schedule and costs with planned schedule and costs for the work done, and contain similar comparisons for overhead activities not directly related to the work. Variances associated with price, schedule delays, and similar factors may be identified and measured quantitatively, using techniques for variance analysis that are similar to those used in the analysis of ongoing operations.

3. *Financial Reports.* Accurate reports of project costs must be prepared if there is a cost-reimbursement contract, and usually even if there is a fixed-price contract. These reports are relatively unimportant for management control purposes, however. Since they must be accurate, they are carefully checked, and this process takes

time. Less precise information prepared quickly is more important to project management.

Use of Reports

Reports of Trouble

Managers spend much time dealing with reports of trouble. The typical project has many such reports, so many that one of the manager's tasks is to decide which ones have the highest priority. In the limited number of hours in a day, the project manager cannot possibly deal with all the situations that cause, or may cause, the project to proceed less than smoothly. The manager therefore must decide which problems will get personal attention, which will be delegated to someone else, and which will be disregarded on the premise that operating personnel will take the necessary corrective action. Note, incidentally, that resolving troubles is essentially a process of problem solving; since problem solving is planning, this is another indication of the close linkage between the planning process and the control process in the management control of projects.

Reports of Progress

Not only do managers limit the number of trouble spots to which they give personal attention, they also are careful not to spend so much time fighting fires that no time remains for careful analysis of the progress reports. Such an analysis may reveal incipient problems that are not apparent in the reports of trouble, and the manager needs to identify these problems and plan how they are to be solved.

The temptation is to spend too much time on current problems and not enough in anticipating problems that are not yet apparent. Some managers deliberately set aside a block of time to reflect on what lies ahead, matters that might be overlooked in the pressure to resolve current problems.

The approach to analyzing progress reports is the familiar one of "management by exception." If progress in a particular area is satisfactory, no attention need be paid to that area (except to congratulate the persons responsible). Attention is focused on those areas in which progress is, or may become, unsatisfactory.[9]

The analyses of reports on actual cost compared to budget and actual time compared to the schedule are relatively straightforward. In interpreting the time reports, the usual presumption is that if a work package is completed in less than the estimated time, the responsible supervisor is to be congratulated, but if more than the estimated time has been spent, questions are raised. The interpretation of the cost reports is somewhat different, for the possibility exists that if actual costs are less than budget, quality may have suffered. For this reason, unless there is some independent way of estimating what costs should have been, good cost performance is often interpreted as meaning being on budget, neither higher nor lower.

Cost-to-Complete

Some companies compare actual costs to date with budgeted costs for the work accomplished to date. Others report the current estimate of total costs for the entire project compared with the budgeted cost for the entire project. The current estimate is obtained by taking the actual costs to date and adding an estimate of the costs required to complete the project. The latter type of report is a useful way of showing how the project is expected to come out, provided that the estimated costs-to-complete are properly calculated.

In most circumstances, the estimates of cost-to-complete should at least equal the original estimates made for the remaining work. If managers are permitted to use lower amounts, they can hide past overruns by making overly optimistic future estimates. In fact, if overruns to date are caused by factors that are likely to persist in the future, such as unanticipated inflation, the current estimates of future costs probably should be higher than the amounts estimated originally.

Informal Sources of Information

Because written reports are visible, the description of a management control system tends to focus on them. In practice, the documents are usually less important than information that the manager gathers from talking with others, from regularly scheduled or ad hoc meetings, from informal memoranda, and from personal inspection of how the work is going. From these sources, the manager learns of incipient problems and of circumstances that may cause actual progress to deviate from the plan. This information is also necessary in understanding the significance of the formal reports because it often describes circumstances not apparent in them. In many cases a problem may be uncovered and corrective action taken before a formal report is prepared, and the formal report does no more than confirm facts that the manager has already obtained from informal sources. This is an illustration of the principle that the formal reports should contain no surprises, a point emphasized in Chapter 4. Nevertheless, formal reports are necessary. They document the information that the manager has learned informally, and this documentation is important if questions about the project are raised subsequently. Also, subordinate managers who read the formal reports may discover that they are not an accurate statement of what has happened, and they take steps to correct the misunderstanding.

Revisions

If a project is complex, or if it is lengthy, there is a good chance that the plan will not be adhered to in one or more of its three aspects: scope, time, or cost. A common occurrence is the discovery that there is likely to be a budget overrun, that is, that actual costs will exceed budgeted costs. If this happens, the sponsor might decide to accept the overrun and proceed with the project as originally planned; to cut back on the scope of the project with the aim of producing an end product that is within the original cost limitations; or to replace the project manager if the sponsor concludes that the budget overrun was unwarranted. Changes in scope or schedule may also be decided. Whatever the decision, it usually leads to a revised plan.

The question then arises: Is it better to track future progress against the revised plan or against the original plan? The revised plan is presumably a better indication of the performance that is now expected, but the danger exists that a persuasive project manager can negotiate unwarranted increases in budgeted costs or that the revised plan will incorporate, and thus hide, inefficiencies that have accumulated to date. In either case, the revised plan may be a *rubber baseline;* that is, instead of providing a firm benchmark for measuring progress, it may be stretched to cover up inefficiencies. (A similar problem exists in revising the budgets of responsibility centers in ongoing operations.)

This possibility can be minimized by taking a hardheaded attitude toward proposed revisions; but even so, there is a tendency to overlook the fact that a revised plan, by definition, does not show what was expected when the project was initiated. On the other hand, if performance continues to be monitored by comparing it with the original plan, the comparison may not be taken seriously because the original plan is known to be obsolete.

A possible solution to this problem is to compare actual cost performance with *both* the original plan and the revised plan. Such a summary report starts with the original budget, and in the first section sets forth the revisions that have been authorized to date and the reasons for making them. Another section shows the current cost estimate and the factors that caused the variance between the revised budget and the current estimate of costs.

PROJECT EVALUATION

In ongoing operations, the evaluation of current performance suggests ways of improving future performance and affects decisions about the reward, assignment, promotion, or other actions for the manager whose performance is evaluated. The evaluations of projects and of project management have similar objectives. Each evaluation is made in terms of the three aspects of a project: the quality of the product, the time required to complete it, and its cost. These elements are judged both separately and in relation to one another.

Once the project has been completed, evaluation obviously cannot improve performance on that project. Nevertheless, it may lead to better ways of doing similar projects. Judgments made about managers influence their reward and their assignment to future projects.

Because work on a project tends to be less standardized and less susceptible to measurement than work in a factory, evaluation of a project is more subjective than evaluation of production activities. It resembles the evaluation of marketing activities in that appraisal of performance requires that the effect of external factors on performance be taken into account. A judgment as to whether actual accomplishment was satisfactory under the circumstances is highly subjective.[10]

Hindsight

In looking back at how well the work on the project was managed, the natural temptation is to rely on information that was not available at the time. With hindsight one can usually discover instances in which the "right" decision was not made. If, however, the manager did not have all the information at that time; if the manager did not address a particular problem because other problems had a higher priority; or if the manager based the decision on personality considerations, trade-offs, or other factors that were not recorded in written reports, the decision may have been entirely reasonable.

If the project is completed with satisfactory quality, on schedule, and at budgeted cost, management is usually credited with doing a good job even though these results may actually reflect either a relatively loose plan or simply good luck. Conversely, if the project did not meet these standards, the tendency is to fault the management even though an unrealistically tight plan or unforeseen circumstances may have accounted for this. Although his armies lost the Civil War, Robert E. Lee is usually judged to have been a superb general.

Some positive indications of poor management may be identified. Diversion of funds or other assets to the personal use of the project manager is one obvious example. Another example is failure to tighten a control system that permits others to steal, but this is more difficult to judge because overly tight controls may impede progress on the project. Evidence that the manager regards cost control as much less important than an excellent finished product completed on schedule is another indication of poor management, but it is not conclusive. The sponsor may overlook budget overruns if the product is outstanding, as often happens in the case of motion picture projects.

SUMMARY

The most important difference between the management control of ongoing operations and the management control of projects is that the ongoing operations continue indefinitely, whereas a project ends. Exhibit 5-1 illustrates this point. The

Exhibit 5–1
Phases of Management Control

A. In an Operating Organization

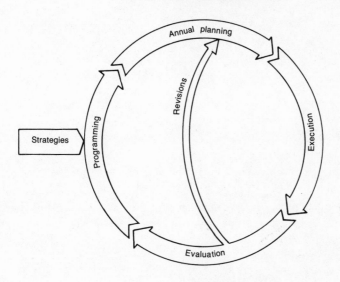

B. In a Project

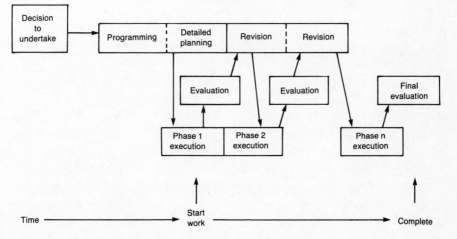

elements in the management control of operations recur; one leads to the next in a prescribed way and at a prescribed time. Although some operating activities change from one month to the next, many of them continue relatively unchanged, month after month, or even year after year.

By contrast, a project starts, moves forward from one step to the next, and then stops. During its life, plans are made, they are executed, and the results are evaluated. The evaluations are made at regular intervals, and these may lead to revisions of the plan.

6

INFORMATION SYSTEMS
FOR MANAGEMENT CONTROL

THIS chapter discusses the design and installation of information systems that are used in the management control process. It is divided into two parts: technical aspects and behavioral aspects. Because significant, but unpredictable, changes related to computers are certain to occur, some aspects of the technical discussion probably will become obsolete in the near future. Human nature is unlikely to change drastically, however, so the behavioral points are less subject to obsolescence.

INFORMATION PROCESSING IN GENERAL

The relationship between information processing and the management control function roughly resembles the relationship between a telephone network and the users of that network. The designers and operators of a telephone network try to assure that messages flow quickly, accurately and clearly; in order to accomplish these objectives, they do not need to know the content of the messages themselves. Similarly, designers of information systems in an organization need an expertise in the construction of databases, in the design of hardware, in computer programming, in forms design, in methods of transmitting data, in data display, and the like, but this expertise is separate from the expertise involved in *using* information for planning and control. (The analogy is not exact, because designers of information systems do need to know considerable about how the information will be used.)

Conversely, just as users of the telephone don't need to know much about how the telephone system works, so users of management control information don't need to know much about the computers that produce this information.

The relationship between information processing and the management control function is indicated in Exhibit 6-1. The information system collects detailed data about each transaction occurring in the organization, about other internal events, and about relevant external events. Many of these data are used directly in performing tasks. Data on an employee's hours worked, wage rate per hour, and

121

Exhibit 6–1
Flow of Information

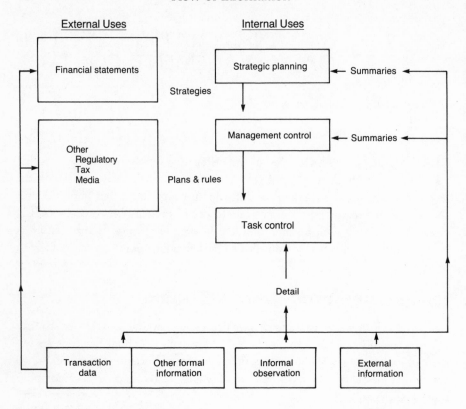

payroll deductions are used to prepare the payroll check. For most other purposes, the information is summarized.

Exhibit 6-1 also indicates the basic relationships of the three planning and control processes. Strategic planning sets the goals and strategies that govern management control. Management control sets the rules and procedures that govern task control.

Source Data

The systems designer decides on the nature of the source data to be collected. With the development of bar codes and devices for reading them automatically, there are now many practical options. For example, not too many years ago, a grocer could feasibly record only the total dollar amount of revenue in an individual sales transaction. With the electrical cash register, sales could be recorded by a dozen or so product lines. With electronic cash registers and bar code readers, sales, and even gross margins, can be recorded for individual items.

The trend is not always in the direction of more detail, however. In some factories, the product costing system that collected the direct labor cost for each operation has been superseded by a system that summarizes the labor costs for an entire production line; the labor content of the product has become so insignificant that its details are no longer worthwhile.

Decisions about what data to collect are also influenced by the necessity of building in safeguards in order to ensure the integrity of the data, and also to minimize defalcation. Absolute protection is not feasible. Some people are careless, and others want to steal; a system that included sufficient checks to find all careless errors and that provided complete protection against a clever thief would cost too much and would unduly delay the production of useful information.

Thus, the basic problem is to decide whether the benefits of more detail or more safeguards are worth the cost. Because the source data are used for many different purposes, the ultimate benefit of a given amount of detail cannot be measured.[1] The decision is therefore a judgmental matter.

> CAUTION: *There is a large theoretical literature on measuring the value of information. It is of little use to practitioners, however.*

The Ideal: An Integrated System

The ultimate aim of some systems designers is to develop a completely integrated information system, that is, a system in which each item of source data is entered only once, and thereafter is combined in various ways to provide the summaries needed for all purposes. Except in organizations with simple activities (which are not necessarily small organizations), this ideal is not now achievable. The problem of making the pieces fit together, and especially being able to revise the system as the need changes, is beyond the capability of humans.[2]

Nevertheless, steps toward this goal are feasible. Many companies have separate systems for payroll, inventory control, production scheduling and control, and product costing. Some are finding it feasible to combine two or more of these separate systems, thus reducing the quantity of data and eliminating the inconsistencies that are almost inevitable when similar information is collected in separate systems.[3]

Moreover, many companies are developing what are called "executive information systems," which are integrated systems for the use of managers. These systems consist of a central database, which is available to managers via their personal computers. Each manager has a program that accesses the central database for information that the manager finds useful. The gain in the consistency of data furnished to all managers is a big advantage of such a system. There are also programs for communication among managers. Development of such systems is expensive, however.[4]

Financial Accounting

In addition to information needed for internal purposes, a company must also collect information for investors, creditors, and other outside parties. This is financial accounting information. Financial accounting information must conform to standards that, for the private sector, are set by the Financial Accounting Standards Board. Some regulatory agencies also prescribe accounting systems. Although there are no official rules governing the content of management accounting information, there are two strong reasons for making this information reasonably consistent with financial reporting requirements.

First, in many companies the "name of the game" is net income as reported on the bottom line of the income statement, and there is a strong tendency for managers to act in a way that increases the reported bottom line, which sometimes is not in the long-run best interest of the organization. (Much more often than not, decisions that increase net income *are* in the company's long-run best interest.) To the extent that senior management approves this attitude, management accounting information should be consistent with financial accounting information.

Second, the cost of having two information systems is obviously more than the cost of a single system. In fact, the cost is more than double because of the confusion that arises when the same facts are reported in two different ways.

Although there is a predisposition to use information for management control purposes that is consistent with FASB standards, there are cases in which departure from these standards is warranted. For example, in financial accounting, the cost of using capital—interest—is counted as a cost only when it relates to the construction of capital assets and certain types of projects. However, capital tied up in inventory and receivables does have an interest cost, and if this cost is overlooked, managers may make unwise decisions about the level of these current assets. Interest is therefore recorded as a cost in many management accounting systems. The problem of adjusting the information to meet the requirements of financial accounting usually is not serious.

Decision Support Systems

In the last decade much effort has been devoted to developing *expert systems*, which are computer programs that model the decision process that an expert would use and thus, unless countermanded, can actually make the decision.[5] Currently, development of an expert system requires tens of person years and a million dollars or more. This effort is worthwhile only if this cost can be spread among many users. Not many management decisions (as distinguished from problems that nonmanagerial professionals deal with) meet this criterion.

Computer models for certain tasks have been in use since the 1950s. Examples are inventory replenishment, linear programming, and production scheduling. Beginning in the 1970s, expert systems have been developed for certain professional tasks: for example, certain types of securities transactions, newspaper layout, auditing, cash management, geological exploration, and credit decisions.[6]

As the name suggests, decision support systems do not make decisions; they help the decision maker. Models for analyzing proposed capital investments have been around for a long time. They do not decide whether a proposal should be accepted; rather, they narrow the area within which judgment is required. Some recent and prospective development of decision support systems for management control will be discussed in the next section.

MANAGEMENT CONTROL INFORMATION

General Considerations

The nature of information that is useful in the management control function has been described in Chapter 4. The focus is on responsibility centers. Consistent with the organization's goals and strategies, and using information from other sources, plans and objectives for the responsibility center are formulated. These are intended to guide its operations. The responsibility center is also influenced by rules, guidelines, job descriptions, manuals, standing instructions, and informal understandings of various types. It receives information relevant to current conditions from a number of sources. Its performance is measured, and reports of performance are prepared; these reports compare actual performance with what performance should have been under the circumstances. If performance was satisfactory, the manager is rewarded; this is positive feedback. If performance was unsatisfactory, either corrective action is taken via feedback to the responsibility center, or the plans are revised.

Points that are relevant in designing such an information system are discussed in this section.

A Unified, Total System

Task control systems are designed to assist in the performance of specific tasks. By contrast, management control systems are designed for the organization as a whole. Although an information system may be developed initially for a division or other part of the organization, eventually a single system should encompass the whole organization.

Since the resources used in responsibility centers are heterogeneous (hours of labor, pounds of material), they must be converted to some common denominator. That common denominator is money.[7]

> CAUTION: *This does not mean that all the numbers in a management control system are monetary; rather it means that the system is built around a monetary core. Nonmonetary items, such as quantities of product produced or ordered, are also included.*

The system is a total system in that all significant resources in the organization are controlled. We sometimes hear that a certain manager has carte-blanche spending authority, implying that he or she is exempt from control. Such cases are rare. And even a manager who is told that he or she has a free hand knows that the organization's resources are limited and that there is a corresponding limit on anyone's use of these resources.

An Internally Consistent System

Since the budget states planned amounts and the accounting system reports actual amounts, it seems obvious that useful comparisons between planned and actual spending cannot be made unless the budget numbers have the same meaning as the actual numbers. Unfortunately, this is not always the case. The worst offender is the federal government. By law,[8] government agencies are supposed to control spending on the basis of the costs they incur, but the budget, which shows the funds appropriated by Congress, is on an "obligation" basis that is fundamentally different. For operating activities, obligations occur when contracts are entered into, whereas costs are incurred when resources are actually consumed. Although consumption cost provides a much better basis for the control of operating activities than does the obligation basis, most agencies control on an obligation basis. This is not surprising; the power of the purse is stronger than the concepts of sound management control.

Consistency also means that the numbers should have the same meaning throughout the organization. In a large organization, especially one that has grown by acquiring established companies, the meanings may differ. For example, there are many ways of defining such apparently clear-cut terms as "direct labor." Some divisions may define direct labor as the compensation earned by direct employees, while other divisions may include some or all of the fringe benefits and taxes associated with the work done. Differences in the definitions that are used in various parts of the organization can cause significant misunderstandings by those who use the numbers and a lack of comparability of amounts that should be comparable.

Even if the accountants read and follow a manual that defines terms carefully, users of the information may not be aware of the accounting definition. Because of prior experience in another organization, or because they mistakenly believe that "everyone knows" that a number means such-and-such, users may have an incorrect perception. Such misconceptions may persist for years. This suggests that systems designers should spend much time making certain that the meanings of the labels for the numbers are clearly stated, and they should develop ways to educate users as to the specified definitions.

Adaptation to Individual Wishes

Although the system should be consistent throughout the organization, the content and format of information furnished to individual managers should be what those managers want. Until the advent of computers, especially personal computers, the possibilities of tailor-making information were sharply limited. Senior management could get whatever it wished in whatever form it wanted, but others had to take whatever the computer spewed out. It is now possible to take from the management control system the information that a given manager finds useful and to present it graphically, in tables, or in whatever format the individual wishes.

If the formal system does not provide information in the form desired, managers usually create "private" records in the form that they find useful. Maintaining such bootleg records is an inefficient use of the manager's time (or the time of an assistant). When the manager uses this unofficial information in conversations with others who are unfamiliar with it, misunderstandings can result.

Writing individual software for all the managers in an organization is time-consuming, and relatively little has been done so far, but the effort should grow rapidly. Indeed, after a few tailor-made reports are developed, it is likely that a manager will see one that appeals to him or her and will say, "I want that." When this happens, the movement will be rapid.

Information Overload

Human beings can process only a relatively few items of information at a time.[9] The computer can spew out in a few minutes more than the user can assimilate in a month. There are, therefore, concerns in the literature about "information overload," providing more information than the manager can use.[10] In many cases, these concerns are unwarranted. Although managers may receive more information than they want, they learn to focus on the items that are important to them and to disregard the remainder. (A newspaper reader similarly gets more information than possibly can be assimilated, but learns to focus on sports, the comics, certain sections of the classified ads, or whatever else is of interest.)

Nevertheless, reporting unneeded data can be distracting and can reduce the respect that managers have for the system. For example, no one can use more than three (or at the most, four) significant digits of information about a given item, yet many systems report all seven digits for items with magnitudes in the millions of dollars.

Benefit/Cost Analysis

The information provided by a system should be worth more than the cost of collecting and disseminating it. Because much management control information is a summary of data that must be collected in any event for task control purposes, the additional cost of massaging it for management control reports is relatively small.

> CAUTION: *However, the information is not costless. The systems builders cannot know what managers actually want, and they tend to provide more than the optimum amount of information so that managers can have whatever they want. In total, the cost of collecting and disseminating information that no one uses can be substantial.*

As mentioned earlier, there are theoretical ways of measuring the cost of one item of information, but they are not practical. In a management control system, a single item of information is used by a number of people, and there is no way of knowing how much any one user thinks it is worth, let alone its aggregate benefit to all users.

Unfortunately, most systems do process information that no one uses. Originally, this information was collected to satisfy someone's need, or at least someone's request. As time passed, the need no longer existed or the user was transferred, but the report continued to be disseminated. A reporting system therefore needs to be weeded out on a regular basis.

Decision Support Systems

Almost all decision support systems developed to date are related to task control, not management control. Indeed, development of automated production lines has transformed what once was a management control activity into a task control activity, and this is characteristic of many such systems.

Relatively little has been done so far to help managers make better decisions, however. A few developments are described in the following sections. In the annual task of budget preparation, models may help the manager decide what the appropriate amount for an expense item should be, in view of probable relationships between inputs and outputs, probable inflation, and the like. For certain problems, such as make-or-buy or buy-or-lease, excellent software is available. But for the recurring job of analyzing actual performance, not much has yet been done.

It seems likely that programs will be developed that compare actual performance with budgeted performance, adjust the variance for the effect of noncontrollable circumstances, and flag those adjusted variances that seem to be significant. Conceptually, this seems doable. As a practical matter, it may not come for a fairly long time. Physicians have a roughly comparable problem in deciding what, if anything, a patient should be treated for; but although software programs for patient diagnosis were developed in the 1970s, very few doctors use them.

Some proprietary programs whose purpose is to process information for all steps in the management control function do exist. The better ones provide an excellent starting point in the development of a computer-based information processing system. They are only a starting point, because they require considerable work in adapting them to the needs of managers in the specific organization.

Environmental Factors

Developments in information processing are likely to have significant implications for an entity's organization structure, and for the nature of communications between managers at various levels, topics discussed in Chapter 3.

Organization Structure

Many operating decisions are made by managers at low levels, because the information required to make these decisions is available on a timely basis only at these low levels. With the development of rapid, inexpensive information flows, certain of these decisions now can be made in a central office. Moreover, they can be sounder decisions than those made by an individual low-level manager, because the central office has information from throughout the organization, whereas the first-line manager knows primarily what is going on in his or her own responsibility center.[11]

It follows that the number of managers required for an activity of a given nature and size will decrease. In addition to the point made above, there are two other reasons for this. First, as computers take over task activities formerly done by humans, the number of people decreases, and the number of managers required is in part a function of the number of people involved in the activity. Second, as managers receive more decision support from computers, less time is required to make a given decision, so more decisions can be made by each manager. At the extreme, some decisions once made by managers will now be made by computers (subject, of course, to a management veto or override). These reductions in the number of managers are not proportional to the time saved by using decision support systems. Some of the management time that is freed up by computers will undoubtedly be used in improving the quality of decisions.

Although the number of managers is likely to decrease, the number of locations at which an organization does business is likely to increase. A bank customer can now do business at any of thousands of locations that have automated teller machines. Employees of many businesses work at home, with a computer connection to the office. Thus, there is centralization at the top and dispersion at the bottom of an organization.

Rules and Guidelines

Faster and better interchange of information between lower levels and the central office means that instructions for certain matters can be disseminated in more detail by the central office to operating managers and to nonmanagement employees. In the absence of timely, detailed information about what is happening, the central office could issue guidance only in general terms. For example, the head office of an insurance company can now analyze the type of insurance that customers are buying, how various types are affected by legislation, and other factors, and issue fairly specific guidelines to branch offices as to how customers should be approached.[12]

Programming and Budgeting

Nearly all organizations prepare an annual budget, and many prepare a program, or long-range plan. Few companies integrate these two types of planning into a single system, however. Most go through the programming process annually and use program decisions as the basis for building the budget, but then they put the long-range plan aside. The following year they develop a new long-range plan, in some cases referring back to the previous plan, but in other cases developing a new one from scratch. The basic reason for this approach is that managers do not have much confidence in the validity of the numbers for the out years of the long-range plan.

Actually a long-range plan is, or should be, the best available estimate of what the numbers in the next few years are going to look like. It has the following meaning: "If the decisions that we have made to date are implemented, and if circumstances are as were assumed in formulating the long-range plan, then this is what the numbers in the out years should look like." Although the assumed circumstances are likely to change, information about the future effect of decisions already made is useful.

The long-range plan is also useful as a means of keeping track of the effect of decisions whose impact will not be felt in the near future. For example, if a decision to introduce a new product was based on certain beliefs as to its future sales and costs, it is important to know whether these beliefs were borne out. If a decision to acquire labor-saving equipment was based on someone's estimate of the savings that will be made for several future years, future budgets should assume that these savings will be made, in the absence of compelling reasons to do otherwise. Unless the long-range plan is carefully maintained, the promised savings may disappear through the crack.

Another important use of the long-range plan is to provide a model that can be used in analyzing proposed changes in strategies. These proposals do not necessarily arise during the programming process; they can be made at any time. The best way to analyze them is to study their probable impact on how the organization would look, as set forth in the long-range plan.

Thus, a good case can be made, not merely for paying attention to the annual long-range plan after it has been accepted in a given year, but also for a process that updates the long-range plan whenever an important decision is made. A continuously updated long-range plan does involve additional paperwork; there must be a document spelling out the estimated effect of a decision in each future year and on each element of the program. The document should be easy to prepare, however, because the analysis made in arriving at the decision presumably included the same estimates. A continuously updated long-range plan has been technically feasible for years; the low cost of modern computers makes it even more attractive.

Decision Support Systems

Most sizable organizations and many small ones use computer analyses in formulating the budget. These range from simple "what if?" spreadsheet programs used by individual managers to companywide models that incorporate all the estimates entering into the budget and check them for reasonableness and consistency. Many commercial programs are available for this purpose. An example is the Interactive Financial Planning System, which was introduced in 1975 and which has been made increasingly sophisticated with annual updates.

Computers should also mitigate the horrendous problem of coordinating the various pieces of the budget. Spreadsheets prepared in individual responsibility centers can be transmitted to the central office instantaneously and fitted into an overall corporate budget. If the pieces do not fit together, the program can quickly identify the discrepancy.

Overemphasis on Quantitative Information

With the increased sophistication of computer programs for assisting in budget and other decisions, there is a tendency to regard the computer output with some awe and to overlook the fact that the estimates provided by the numbers cannot be an accurate picture of what is actually going to happen. The impressive appearance of the numbers may divert users from adequate recognition of the softness of some of the estimates. No software can take all the relevant variables into account, and no one knows how some of these variables are going to behave.

A striking example is the collapse of the roof of the Hartford Civic Center in 1978 under the accumulated weight of snow and ice, only a short time after several thousand people had left it. The computer program used to verify the safety of the roof construction neglected to take into account one variable, and although people noticed that the roof was sagging immediately after its completion, management trusted the computer rather than its own eyesight.[13]

Execution

In the program execution phase of the management control function, there are essentially two types of useful information: (1) information about what is happening, and (2) information useful in making decisions.

Much of a manager's judgment about what is happening is obtained from conversations and personal observation, rather than from formal reports. The reports can be helpful, but unless they are carefully structured, they provide a torrent of data that may hide vital information. An important guide in designing these reports is that the focus should be on *key variables*; that is, those relatively few variables that have important consequences to the organization and that change quickly and unexpectedly. The volume of incoming orders is a key variable in many organizations, for example. In addition, there must obviously be a way of bringing catastrophic occurrences to management's attention quickly. Deciding what information is relevant requires close cooperation between managers and systems designers. They may include both financial and nonmonetary information, and both internal information and information about what is happening in the external environment.

A market research axiom, applicable to management "howgozit" reports, is "We can provide cheap data, fast data, or good data, but not all three." This suggests that providing reports quickly often requires that accuracy be sacrificed. The need for a compromise among these criteria is reduced with the development of inexpensive, fast computing power.

Decision Support Systems

Many decision support systems are available to aid managers in resolving day-to-day operating issues: making price quotations, inventory replenishment, equipment replacement, make-or-buy, and others. As has been emphasized, these programs *support* the decision-making process; they do not make decisions. The rules and computational procedures built into a decision support program should be those with which the manager is comfortable, which are not necessarily those that the systems designer prefers. And the word "support" implies that the program helps managers; it does not replace a manager. So long as organizations consist of human beings (and by definition all organizations do), human managers are necessary. A computer cannot possibly take all the variables into account, nor can it deal with interpersonal relations.

Evaluation

Conceptually, the information required to evaluate performance is easy to state: A report should compare actual performance with planned performance and identify the reasons for significant differences. The differences, or variances, can be classified as efficiency, volume, price (or cost), mix, and other. (The "other" category is for unusual causes that do not occur in most organizations.) Distinguishing between variances that have short-run versus long-run implications is also important.

Although textbooks have described the calculations of these variances for years, few formal reporting systems identify any but the most obvious ones, and many systems do not identify any. With the computation power of computers, calculations for most variances can be made routinely and quickly.

> CAUTION: *I do not understand why managers do not require the identification of many textbook variances that seem to me to be important. Whatever the reason, the current nonuse of these variances indicates that acceptance of more sophisticated calculations may not come quickly.*

Similar calculations can greatly improve the method of calculating management incentive compensation. Because not all the significant factors can be identified— especially the long-run impact of current actions—the incentive compensation formula never can be made completely objective. To the extent that the degree of subjectivity is reduced, however, the results will be fairer, and the manager should be motivated to act in a more goal-congruent manner.

In repetitive production operations, statistical techniques can be used to identify the significant variances. Although some of the academic literature recommends that these techniques be used for management reports, this recommendation is unrealistic. There is rarely the succession of comparable observations that is an essential requirement for the application of statistics. The decision as to which variances are significant is a matter of judgment. The amount of variance that is judged to be significant depends on the specific item. For some items, any unfavorable variance is significant. For others, a percentage, such as 5 percent or 10 percent, is the "red flag." For some items a variance is not significant unless it persists for several periods.

Computers can provide reports quickly. Along with the increased speed is the desirability of providing managers with only what is needed. The solution is to arrive at the optimum balance between collecting the same information for everyone, which simplifies the data collection operation, and tailoring the information provided each manager to what he or she needs, which is expensive. This is easier said than done. In part, the problem of arriving at the optimum balance is mitigated by the fact that managers can, within limits, skip over information that is not of interest to them. Thus, although management reports are basically similar throughout the organization, the specifics of the report provided to individual managers should reflect their personal wishes.

Decision Support Systems

From the above it follows that systems designers should work closely with individual managers to develop reports that draw from the central system the information needed and to present it in the form that the manager finds most useful. Reports prepared for other managers, or commercially available software, can be used to illustrate the possibilities.

So far as I know, software that does an adequate job of identifying the various types of variances is currently not available. Probably, such software will be developed in the near future.

SYSTEM INSTALLATION

Introduction of a new system is a traumatic experience for managers.[14] A new system changes the way in which plans are made; it alters the way in which performance is measured and judged; and it establishes new patterns of communication and discussion between managers. The new information provided by the system is presumably better information, but it is certainly different information, and it takes some getting used to.

The problems of installing a management control system are much more severe that those of installing task control systems. A new system for processing payroll, for billing, or for keeping track of inventory may initially contain technical bugs, but it is unlikely to cause serious organizational problems. If the system works, managers are unlikely to resist its introduction. Indeed, they will support it as soon as they recognize that the system helps them do their job better.

This section discusses two aspects of systems installation separately: (1) revisions of overall systems and (2) development of decision support systems for individual managers.

Revision of Overall System

Top Down

Opinions differ as to the relative roles of senior management and operating managers in the revision of a system. Some people maintain that the impetus must come from operating managers and that a new system cannot be installed successfully unless operating managers request, welcome, or at least support the effort. Others maintain that the impetus must come from senior management.

I support the latter view. I think that the driving force must come from senior management, and that it is unlikely that operating managers will voluntarily embrace a new management control system in advance of its installation, let alone be enthusiastic advocates of it. If systems designers wait until operating managers are sold on the idea of revising the management control system, they will have a long wait indeed. Some reasons why operating managers are suspicious of new management control systems are discussed in a later section of this chapter.

Senior Management Support

Ideally, support for the systems development effort should come from the chief executive officer. However, in some organizations the chief executive is primarily involved in policymaking and relations with the investment community, important customers, or other outside parties. If so, the necessary support can come from the Number 2 person; this person in fact has the principal management authority. Without the support of one of these two top people, the effort is likely to be unsuccessful.

Support means more than acquiescence. Although the time of senior management is precious, they must be willing to allocate a significant amount to a systems development effort. Senior management must understand the objectives and general concepts of the proposed system well enough to see its benefits, and they must explain to principal subordinates how the system will help them as individuals and help the organization as a whole. If roadblocks arise during the development and installation effort, senior management must be prepared to listen to the conflicting points of view and then make a decision which removes the roadblocks. Most important, operating managers must be convinced that the CEO will in fact rely on the new system once it has become operational. If the CEO's management style is principally one of personal observation and discussion, rather than analyzing numbers, operating managers may not be convinced that the proposed system is important.

Senior management commitment to a systems development effort may originate from any of several reasons. Two are common. (1) A new CEO takes over and is dissatisfied with the existing system; it does not fit his or her personal style. (2) The organization faces a crisis, and the CEO is convinced that the existing system either did not properly anticipate the crisis or is inadequate to resolve it. A third reason is less common, but is becoming more important in this era of explosive information technology: the CEO becomes convinced—by the executive responsible for information processing, by an outside consultant, or by his or her own awareness—that the existing system has become outdated.

Systems Design Team

The team responsible for designing and installing the system should have a strong charter from the CEO. Systems designers, of course, should have the competence and the expertise that is necessary for the job. They need ready access to senior management, because the system must reflect the style of management that senior management wants, and the only way of assuring that the system does this is to discuss the proposed design personally with senior management.

Systems designers also must consult with operating managers, who are busy people. Senior management must convince operating managers that the systems design effort is important enough for them to take time away from their always pressing operating problems to discuss their needs for information. Few, if any, of the other staff specialists require a corresponding amount of an operating manager's time.

Typically, outside consultants participate in the effort. They have a general expertise in systems design and, in many cases, experience in designing systems in similar organizations. Furthermore, outside consultants are usually perceived by operating managers as being unbiased; they are not involved in internal politics. On the other hand, outsiders *are* outsiders. They may not understand "how things really work in our organization."

Consultants should never have complete responsibility for developing and installing a system; in-house personnel should have an important role. All good consulting firms insist on such involvement. When the development effort is completed, the consultants leave; and after they leave, there must be in-house personnel who will regard the system as *their* system and who will continue to work to ensure its success. This attitude can be generated only if in-house personnel have been involved in the development in a substantial way.

Relationship with Operating Managers

Although life would be more pleasant if this were not the case, it is quite probable that operating managers will resist efforts to introduce a new system, or at least they will be unenthusiastic about it. The reason is not that people resist change. A salary increase is a change, and no one resists a salary increase. Rather, people tend to resist change when the effect on them is uncertain.[15]

Even if operating managers perceive that the existing system is inadequate, it is nevertheless something that they have worked with and are comfortable with. They have learned to interpret the information it provides, they know its virtues, and they also know its limitations and how to make allowances for them. They now must learn how to interpret new information, and how to recognize and allow for *its* limitations. They also are uncertain as to exactly how the new system will affect what they do. There is no way of removing this uncertainty completely, because there is no way of communicating accurately to them what will happen when the new system becomes operational. Its impact must be experienced to be understood.

A new system can change the style of management and the desired qualifications of managers. It may shift power from lower-level managers to higher-level managers, or (less frequently) vice versa. It often requires professionally educated managers rather than those qualified principally by experience. The new system may help the manager obtain better control over subordinates, which is good; but, by the same token, it helps the superior obtain better control over the manager, which may be uncomfortable, or a threat to the manager's autonomy. Further, systems are designed and run by staff people, and operating managers tend to mistrust staff people. Perceptions of these factors can easily lead to resistance. This is especially the case in a mature organization whose managers are interested primarily in job security.

There are several ways of lessening hostility and resistance to a new system. First, to the extent that operating managers are convinced that the new system will on balance benefit them, they will support it. Educational efforts should therefore stress the benefits, some of which are that (1) the system will help them to do a better job, which will be perceived as such by their superiors; (2) the system will facilitate smoother coordination with other units; (3) managers can exercise better control over their subordinates; (4) by providing an orderly, rapid flow of reliable information, the system will make life less hectic; (5) the system will permit them to make better decisions about the allocation of resources (this is especially important in periods when budgets are tight); and (6) the system will provide a more equitable measurement of performance.

Finally, those who design, and those who will eventually operate the system, must never forget that people, not systems, get things done. Managers manage; the system helps them manage.

Steps in Systems Design and Installation

Details of the systems design and installation process are set forth in several texts on this subject. The main steps are described in the following paragraphs.

Diagnosis

Analyze the goals and objectives of the organization, the general nature of the existing system, and the organization structure. This analysis may reveal possible weaknesses in the existing system and organization structure. Discussion with management may lead to changes in the organization structure. If so, these changes should be taken into account in designing the new system. If management prefers not to change organizational relationships, for whatever reason, this decision must, of course, be accepted. The system should fit the organization that senior management wants; the organization structure should not be changed simply to facilitate the structure that the designer prefers.

Planning

Develop a plan, including a timetable (preferably in the form of a PERT diagram or similar scheduling device), an estimate of personnel and other resources required, the estimated costs of these requirements, a statement of the units or individuals that are to be responsible for each step of the development process, and a description of the cooperation that is expected from each part of the organization. Obtain approval of this plan.

In estimating the time requirements, the principle should be to allow not quite enough time. There is no upper limit to the time that might be spent in fine-tuning a system, and the designers should accept less than perfection in the interest of getting a useful system on-line as soon as feasible.

CAUTION: *The time required to develop and install a workable system should not be underestimated. It is rarely less than one year, and five years, or more, are frequently needed in sizable organizations.*

Inventory of Current Information

Examine the existing sources of information in considerable detail. Most of this information must be collected routinely for operating purposes, and its use for management control involves little incremental cost. This information should therefore be used in the new system if feasible. Moreover, managers probably understand the definitions governing this information, and will be more comfortable with it than with alternatives that the systems designer might prefer.

Development of the Information Structure

This involves decisions on revenue, expense, assets, liabilities, equities, and nonmonetary items that are to be incorporated in the system, their sources, and how they are to flow through the system to managers. The data elements should not be specified in detail. Only key elements—those that will be used in high-level summaries—need be defined centrally. More detailed information can be developed to fit the specific needs of individual responsibility centers.

The systems designer must work with operating managers. At one time the recommended approach was that the systems designer should ask managers what information they needed. In recent years, this approach has generally been abandoned, because it has been found that many operating managers do not know what information they need. In particular, they cannot visualize the nature of the new information that might be made available and therefore cannot comment on its usefulness.

The approach currently favored, therefore, is for the systems designer to find out by indirect methods the information that the operating manager needs. The designer does, if for no other reason than courtesy, ask managers what information they need; but the interviews are focused primarily on the job itself, the relationship of one responsibility center to another, the environmental influences that affect the work in the responsibility center, and so on. Based on this information, a system is designed that provides the information that the manager *should* need. The systems designer must resist the inclination to recommend information that he or she personally wants, and instead try to think of what the operating manager *should* want.

Systems designers should not bite off more than they can comfortably chew, or more than the organization can reasonably be expected to digest at one time. One of the principal causes of failure of a new system is that it is too complicated. A complete system, using the most up-to-date techniques, requires an unduly long development time, probably includes design errors, and involves a difficult education task. The preferable approach is piecemeal, with only moderate sophistication, and particularly with no attempt to tie all subsystems into a grandiose integrated system. If the elements of a sound system are installed and accepted by the operating organization, refinements can be added after users become familiar with the essentials. Both systems designers and managers have an opportunity to learn and grow with the system, and the cost of initial development is not excessive.

The system should be completely documented, and the instructions should include a mechanism for keeping the documentation up-to-date. All systems experts emphasize this, but documentation is a dull task that sometimes is neglected. There may come a day when the organization discovers that there is no adequate record, which makes removing bugs or initiating improvements a difficult task indeed.

Test

Test the proposed system in one part of the organization. Not only is this desirable for debugging, but also the pilot installation provides a concrete example that helps educate managers throughout the organization in what is coming. The test may require that a "fence" be built around the pilot installation, and that the new information collected in the pilot system be converted to that needed for the existing system in order to arrive at overall reports for the whole organization. This extra work is preferable to the alternative of installing the whole system at one time, risking a crash that will result in the permanent loss of data.

Education

Develop a comprehensive education program. Systems designers are intellectually aware of the importance of a thorough educational program as a part of the educational process. As a practical matter, however, they sometimes do not devote enough time to this effort. There are so many technical problems that must be solved by prescribed deadlines that not enough time may be left for an adequate educational campaign. In retrospect, many wish that they had devoted more time to education.

The preparation of manuals, explanations, sample reports, and other written material is a necessary part of the education process, but it is not the important part. The important part is to explain to managers how the new system can help them do a better job. Systems experts, who are the only ones with detailed familiarity with the new system, necessarily play a large role in these educational programs, but management should also be involved.

Above all else, operating managers must become convinced that the new system is in fact going to be used. Systems designers can say this, but they are, after all, only staff people. The only message that carries conviction comes from the words and deeds of line managers. Thus, within the limits of their knowledge about the new system, managers should teach other managers; that is, senior managers should discuss the new system with their subordinates, who then convey the message to *their* subordinates, and so on. Moreover, once the system becomes operational, even on a test basis, management use of the new information is the best educational device there is.

Implementation

If feasible, run the new system in parallel with the existing system. If this is done, eliminate the obsolete parts of the old system fairly quickly. As long as the old system continues to exist, some managers may not embrace the new one, hoping it may fade away.

Decision Support Systems

Most managers have, or soon will have, a personal computer. In large companies, this computer is tied into a corporate database, and it will permit managers to communicate with other managers. Currently, many managers are not making optimum use of their computers. Reasons for this, and suggestions for alleviating the problem, are given in this section.

Reasons for Nonuse

Almost all stock market traders make extensive use of computers. The reasons why managers do not use computers to the same extent can be understood by contrasting the job of the stock market trader with the job of the manager.

First, and perhaps most important, since practically every trader relies on a computer, those few who don't use one feel that they are behind the times. By contrast, relatively few managers touch a computer keyboard. Some feel that having a computer in the office is beneath their dignity: computers are for secretaries or assistants. Few managers are convinced that they need a computer to keep up-to-date with other managers.

Second, traders use computers all day long, and for essentially one task: making decisions about buying or selling securities. A single computer program suffices. Managers don't have a single task; they deal with a variety of problems in the course of a day. Each type of problem would require a different computer program. As a related point, traders deal mostly with numbers, whereas managers deal mostly with people; computers are of little use in interpersonal relations.

Thus, the trader's investment of time in learning to use the computer pays off quickly, whereas for managers the ratio of learning time to the time that elapses before worthwhile results are obtained is much greater. Until recently, managers were correct in judging that the required investment in learning to use a computer was greater than was warranted by the personal benefits.

Third, the software that has been developed for traders is sophisticated but easy to use; its value is obvious. By contrast, managers can't readily identify the software that will help them. When they do locate a useful program, it may be difficult to master. Unless they use it frequently, they can easily forget how to make it work. Moreover, they need data. Although the data probably exist somewhere in the organization's databanks, managers don't know how to retrieve them, and the data they do retrieve is unlikely to be in a form that fits their needs.

CAUTION: *Managers don't need to know how a computer functions; only how to use it.*

Gaining Acceptance

Someday managers will learn to use computers, just as a few years ago their predecessors learned to use telephones. Following are some steps that may help speed up the process.

- Encourage them to learn touch-typing (now called "keyboarding"). An adult may be unwilling to invest the forty hours or so that this requires. The skill actually should have been learned in grammar school. The typical person will make much more use of it than of cursive writing.
- Get them interested. Provide personal computers, and do not criticize if the first uses are for stock market quotations, personal budgets, a calendar, an address list, or even playing games. Provide introductory lessons on request (but don't require them). Some companies frown on using the computer for such personal activities; I believe that anything that entices the manager to get interested is worthwhile.
- Provide personal assistance. Recognize that searching through the thousands of available software programs for the few that meet their needs, studying the detailed instructions that come with a program, and figuring out how to call up the data needed for the program, are not good uses of management time. Make available the services of a knowledgeable person to give advice, to suggest new programs, and to install and explain them. Many companies have

a large staff of experts who work on the overall computer system. Not many have people who will help individual managers on request.

- Start with programs that automate the arithmetic involved in problems with which the manager is already familiar. The manager is much more likely to trust these programs than programs that require a different way of thinking. Although most computers come equipped with a programming language (for example, BASIC), never expose the manager to it. If BASIC is required, the resource person should write the program.

- Make certain that the assumptions and algorithms in the program are those that the manager is comfortable with (and do not expect the manager to know what "algorithm" means). Resource persons should not substitute their opinion for that of the manager.

- Find programs that help with "what-if" calculations. Managers probably want to test out alternative courses of action and alternative assumptions, and to have a quick way of reacting to proposals made by others.

- Eventually, start to think about expert systems. As noted earlier, development of an expert system is an expensive, time-consuming job. Even if the product is useful, managers are unlikely to trust it unless they are already comfortable with commercially available decision-support programs. When that day does come, the manager's life will be made much easier. The computer will take on much of the day-to-day drudgery, and the manager will have more time to work with other people and to think about the future.

CONCLUSION

In the ideal world, an organization would have a single information database, and stored information would be retrieved for use in all activities. In the real world, this ideal is not attainable. Except in the simplest organizations, the task of designing a single system that will meet all the diverse needs for information is beyond the capabilities of humans. The perceived need for information varies with individuals, for a given individual it varies with different tasks, and it changes over time. Humans cannot identify the one best system that accommodates all these variables.

The closest that an organization can come to a single system is its management control system. This system should be total and integrated, in contrast with task control systems that are designed for specific tasks. Summaries from task control systems feed into the management control system. Strategic planning requires information from the management control system, but its precise information needs depend on the particular strategy that is being studied, and no system can anticipate all these needs.

The accounting model, constructed within the constraint that debits must equal credits, is an important unifying device for the management control system, but the information needed for management control is broader and less detailed than that flowing through the accounts.

Thus, although currently computer-based systems are primarily task control systems, ultimately their most important use is likely to be in the management control function.

7
VARIATIONS IN
MANAGEMENT CONTROL PRACTICES

IN the preceding description of the management control process, I have implicitly assumed a sort of "typical" situation. (I cannot prove that it is, in fact, typical because there are no good data on the prevalence of various practices.) In this chapter I shall describe briefly the nature of factors that lead to modifications of these "typical" practices and suggest the nature of these modifications.

Currently, some management consulting firms and academic researchers analyze variables that are relevant to a phenomenon by setting up a 2 x 2 matrix in which the vertical dimension is divided into a "high" half and a "low" half according to some criterion, and the horizontal dimension is similarly divided, thus giving four cells or quadrants.

HIGH LOW	HIGH HIGH
LOW LOW	LOW HIGH

Some matrices have nine cells, with the permutations of High-Medium-Low. I have tried to devise such a matrix as a way of organizing this chapter, but I have been unable to do so. There are more than two or three important dimensions.[1] I have grouped what I think are the important variables under three headings:

The first is a set that relates to the external environment. I think it constitutes a continuum, with highly uncertain factors at one end and relatively predictable factors at the other end. I describe the extremes of this continuum and their implications for management control.

The second is a set of variables relating to the internal environment. I list several such variables and their implications.

145

The third is a list of specific industries that have atypical management control problems, with the causes of these problems and their impact on the management control function.

Many of these factors are inherent in the situation; management salary must accept their existence and adjust to them. For other factors, differences in management strategies and style can, within limits, mitigate their influence.

EXTERNAL ENVIRONMENTAL INFLUENCES

The factors in the external environment that influence the management control function can be arranged along a single continuum having to do with uncertainty. Factors that are associated with a highly uncertain environment are at one end, and factors associated with a relatively predictable environment are at the other end.

Exhibit 7–1
External Environmental Influences

Uncertain	*Predictable*
Characteristics	
New product	Mature product
Differentiated product	Commodity product
Aggressive competition	Price competition
Uncertain sources	Few sourcing problems
Uncertain political situation	Few political uncertainties
Implications for Management Control	
Much attention to programming	Little or no programming
Broad budget estimates	Detailed budgets
Budget revisions	No budget revisions
Discretionary cost ceilings	Cost controls, variance analysis
Much management latitude	Little management discretion
Rapid information flow	Early warning signals only
Evaluation results oriented	Evaluation based on compliance
Evaluation subjective	Evaluation objective
Compensation: high % bonus	Compensation: high % salary
Entrepreneurial management (sometimes)	Professional management

Uncertainty results both from inadequate knowledge about what is happening or what is going to happen and from the difficulty of predicting what will actually happen as a consequence of a given course of action.

These factors are listed in Exhibit 7-1 and described below. They affect both the organization structure and the management control function, but analysis of organization structure is outside the scope of my analysis. The list is illustrative, rather than definitive; others would select different factors.

Environmental Characteristics

Product Life Cycle

Typically, products go through a cycle whose main stages are initiation, growth, maturity, and decline. For a new product, estimates of success are highly uncertain. Similarly, if a company's strategy involves the frequent introduction of new products, the overall success of this strategy is uncertain. As a product reaches the maturity stage, its sales volume, the nature of its customers, the best way of reaching potential customers, and similar marketing characteristics are much better understood, and plans can be made with greater confidence.

Nature of Products

Products can be grouped into two general classes: differentiated products and commodities. Differentiated products succeed because customers perceive that they have some advantage over competing products. Commodities succeed primarily because they have lower costs than competing products. Since customer perception is difficult to understand and since customer loyalty is subject to change because of actions of competitors or other reasons, the demand for differentiated products is typically much more difficult to predict than the demand for commodities. This is, of course, only a generalization; Ivory soap and Bayer aspirin are differentiated products the demands for which in most years have been relatively easy to predict. (However, the introduction of branded detergents had a significant effect on sales of Ivory soap, and the development of other analgesics affected Bayer.)

Nature of Competition

If a company's competitors are numerous and if some of them are especially skillful and aggressive, the moves of competitors may be difficult to anticipate or counter. This makes for uncertainty. If the nature of competition is well understood, and if new competitive moves do not occur frequently, predictions of the effect of competition are easier to make. The nature of competition in an industry may change unexpectedly, as happened when the Japanese introduced automobiles and steel products into the United States, and such developments can move the industry from the predictable end of the spectrum to the highly uncertain end.

Sourcing

Some companies deal with an environment in which the sources, quality, or price of their materials, components, energy, labor, or other resources are highly uncertain. In most cases this uncertainty is temporary, as was the case of crude oil in the early 1970s. In a few cases it is chronic. In many companies, sources are dependable, and sourcing is not a major uncertainty.

Politics

Uncertainty about political developments can be an important environmental factor. This uncertainty can exist at the global, national, state, or local level. The factor relates to uncertainty, not to whether the situation is favorable or unfavorable. In making its plans, a company can adjust to an unfavorable political development if it is reasonably sure that this situation will continue.

Technology

Rapid changes in technology are of course a major source of uncertainty. Management control activities in computer, biotech, ceramics, and similar high-tech companies must take into account uncertainties that affect their marketing tactics and their production methods. Many companies are relatively little affected by changing technology.

Implications for Management Control

In Uncertain Environments

When the environment is uncertain, the company's *programming* process is especially important. Management needs to give much thought to how to cope with the uncertainties, and this usually requires a longer-range view of planning than is possible in the annual budget. A few companies develop alternative programs with scenarios for different developments in the uncertain environment, but most believe that the effort to do this is not worthwhile.

In developing the long-range plan, all available information regarding the probable future environment is of course gathered and carefully analyzed. However, the available data are by definition inadequate, and much reliance is therefore placed on the personal opinions of knowledgeable people. As contrasted with programming in a stable environment, in an uncertain environment more weight is given to the opinions of knowledgeable line managers than to analyses made by staff (although the staff may analyze these opinions, judging their validity according to their logic, their internal consistency, and their consistency with known facts).

The *budget* prepared in an uncertain environment is not regarded as an accurate statement of what is going to happen. If the uncertainties affect revenues, the bottom line of the budget cannot be taken too seriously as a valid estimate of what net income will actually be. If they affect costs, the affected items are likewise regarded as being tentative. The plan for the year may contemplate specific tactics for dealing with uncertainty, such as increased spending for research/development or advertising. If so, the corresponding budget items are viewed as being definitive guidelines. Thus, part of the budget is tentative, but another part is prescriptive. The cash budget provides an adequate margin of safety in estimating cash requirements and the sources of cash.

The budget may be revised in the course of the year as the situation becomes clearer. However, this practice runs the risk of losing the original benchmark. Thus, some companies prefer to leave the original budget untouched and prepare a current "best estimate" of results as a separate report.

In the *execution* phase, operating managers are given considerable latitude in deciding how to cope with the situation as it develops. For new products, the ideal manager is the entrepreneur. The entrepreneur gets things done without being much constrained by rules and guidelines, and without being concerned about cost control. The manager's skill in dealing with uncertainties and his or her knowledge of the environment are important qualifications. Managers who operate in uncertain environments tend to be highly paid.

Information about the environment needs to be conveyed to managers at all levels accurately and quickly. Much of it is "soft" information—tips, gossip, rumors obtained from telephone calls, and informal conversations, as contrasted with formal reports. Managers who are not directly affected by developments in the external environment, such as production managers when the volatility relates to sales, also need quick, reliable information. Those on the firing line need to convey what they learn to others.

Evaluation in an uncertain environment is results oriented, and the manager has considerable latitude in deciding the best way of seeking the organization's objectives. Evaluation of performance is highly subjective; that is, relatively little attention is given to quantitative comparisons of actual amounts with the budget or to other quantitative measures of performance. More attention is given to effectiveness (that is, how well the job was done) than to efficiency (that is, how well costs were controlled). In judging performance, the superior tries to recognize the long-run consequences of current decisions. For example, spending more than the budgeted amount for research/development is not criticized—indeed may be praised, if the results appear to be promising. Considerable reliance is placed on comparing performance with that of other organizations in the same industry. A large fraction of the compensation package may consist of a bonus, even though the amount of the bonus is arrived at subjectively.

In Predictable Environments

If the environment is stable, there may be no *programming* process at all, or only a long-range plan that is developed on a broad-brush basis. Senior management may decide that the process described in Chapter 4 is not worth the effort. If there is a long-range plan, it often extends for a longer future period than is feasible in an uncertain environment, simply because reasonable estimates of the longer period can be made.

Although there may not be a programming process for the whole entity, there may be a "zero-base review" of selected activities on a rotating schedule. Conducting such a review is much easier in a stable environment, because data on past performance are not influenced so much by fluctuating conditions and therefore provide a more valid basis for comparison. The review is also more useful for subsequent planning because the assumptions used in recommending spending levels are not likely to change.

Proposed *budgets* are analyzed in depth. There is a tendency for costs to creep up with the passage of time, and careful scrutiny of the budget can reduce (although probably not entirely eliminate) this tendency. Managers are expected to attain budgeted profits within close limits. Shortfalls are the subject of criticism, but even profits in excess of budget may not be cause for rejoicing; they may indicate only that the budget preparation process was defective. Budgeting in a stable environment is much easier than budgeting in an uncertain one, and much more importance is paid to the budget.

In a stable environment, the entrepreneur is not so likely to be as effective as the professional manager (and indeed the entrepreneur is unlikely to be interested in working in such an environment).

With one exception, the flow of information need not be rapid or detailed. The exception is that the system should provide early warning signals. A stable environment may not remain stable indefinitely. Managers tend to become complacent, and they need to be made aware of shocks from the environment as far in advance as possible.

Evaluation of performance can be relatively objective. Compensation can be set largely by formula. The focus can be both on process measures (the quantity, quality, and cost of individual activities) and on results measures (the end product of what the manager accomplished).

INTERNAL FACTORS

Internal factors are those that exist within an organization, and therefore can be affected by the actions of its managers. My list is as follows: strategies, input/output relationships, internal consistency, interdependence, flexibility, key variables, and management style. Probably it is not conclusive, but I believe it contains the principal factors.[2] For each, the nature of the factor and its implications for management control will be described.

Strategies

Nature of the Variable

The process of formulating strategies is outside the scope of this book.[3] In recent years, consultants and authors have classified strategies in various ways that they find useful in analyzing an entity's situation and recommending courses of action.[4] These classification systems have implications for management control. Two of them are discussed briefly below.

Competitive Strategies

Michael Porter proposes three types of competitive strategies: (1) cost leadership, (2) differentiation, and (3) focus. Each has implications for management control. In the *cost leadership* strategy, management attempts to be the low-cost producer, and the control system therefore emphasizes cost control. This strategy is most relevant to commodity products, as discussed in the preceding section. In the *differentiation* strategy, the emphasis is on developing a product, a method of distribution, or some other feature that is perceived as being unique to the industry. Such a strategy emphasizes product and market research. In the *focus* strategy, the aim is to differentiate but to do so by finding a unique niche in a market segment. The management control process is similar to that of differentiation.

Position in Product Life Cycle

Most products go through a typical life cycle, and some observers, particularly consulting firms, maintain that management controls should be different at different phases in this cycle. One model, for example, classifies the phases as "build," which is the initial stage of development and obtaining market share; "maintain," which is the stage of optimum profitability after market share has been developed;

and "harvest," which is when the product no longer has a competitive edge. Although models such as this tend to be overdone, they are worth thinking about occasionally.

Implications for Management Control

The following implications of this classification are adapted from works of Gupta and Govindarajan.[5] For *harvest* products (that is, mature products), capital investment and other spending decisions are carefully controlled. Performance measurement is focused on short-term performance. A *build* product, (that is, a newly introduced product) needs an organization led by a manager who is willing to take risks, and one who is tolerant of ambiguity and of imprecise, soft information. Performance measurement is focused on long-term performance. Nonfinancial measures (for example, market share) are important. Decisions are more decentralized. Also, a new-product organization should have fewer and less restrictive rules, and evaluation of its performance is more subjective. These organizations ordinarily make more contingency plans than other organizations. For *hold* products, management control is that of the typical situation discussed in Chapter 4.

Input/Output Relationships

Nature of the Factor

This factor is similar to the degree of uncertainty in the external environment that was discussed in the preceding section. If an electricity generating plant uses a certain amount of fuel as input to a turbine, the amount of electricity that will be generated is known within close limits. (This is a general rule, applicable only when the turbine is working properly.) Many production operations have a similar characteristic: there is a known relationship between inputs and outputs. For example, the leather used for two pairs of shoes should cost twice as much as the leather used for one pair, and the optimum amount of costs for a given level of output can be estimated within close limits. These costs are called *engineered costs*. I shall refer to responsibility centers whose activities are predominantly of this nature as *predictable* responsibility centers.

In other activities, however, one does know the optimum relationship between outputs and inputs: spending twice as much on research will not necessarily produce twice the research output; "throwing dollars at the problem" may, in fact, result in less output if the researchers get in each other's way. Earlier, the costs in these activities were referred to as *discretionary costs*. I shall refer to such responsibility centers as *less predictable*, with the implication that the optimum relationship between effort and accomplishment cannot be known.

In certain types of production activities, the optimum relationship between inputs and outputs also is uncertain. The optimum cost for a production process that requires close tolerances with consequent high spoilage rates, such as microchips, is less certain than the optimum cost of a production operation that makes shoes. In a job shop working on nonstandard products, the optimum costs are more difficult to predict than in certain closely controlled process operations. In the corn wet milling process, for example, a difference of one percentage point in the product yield is cause for concern; in the production of certain computer chips, yield fluctuations of ten percentage points are common. The optimum cost for a construction project that involves uncertain soil conditions, weather, and other factors is less certain than the optimum cost of building a conventional house.

Uncertainty as to the relationship between effort and accomplishment also characterizes the nonroutine activities of many professionals: lawyers, ministers, engineers, professors, accountants, actors, musicians, social service workers, legislators, consultants, and so on. Since the causal relationship is unknown, one also does not know whether spending an incremental amount will add a corresponding amount to attainment of the organization's objectives. (Is attending a professional convention worth the cost?) Moreover, the output itself may not be measurable. (How much do students actually learn in a college?)

In short, the greater the relative uncertainty of the relationship between inputs and outputs, the more important judgment becomes in the management control process. In this context, "uncertainty" refers to the difficulty of predicting the outputs that will occur as a consequence of a given set of inputs, that is, the difficulty of knowing the causal relationship between efforts and accomplishments.[6]

Implications for Management Control

In all phases of the management control process, the greater the uncertainty of the causal connection between effort and accomplishment, more reliance must be placed on management judgment than on quantitative methods of making plans or evaluating results.

In programming for less predictable units, the central question may be: How much can we afford to spend? rather than: How much is it necessary to spend in order to attain a specified output? In annual planning, the emphasis also is on affordability, with the current level of spending taken as a starting point. The agreed level of discretionary costs often indicates an amount that is to be neither exceeded nor underspent.

The evaluation of performance in less predictable units is necessarily subjective. It therefore is based on personal observation more than on any numerical measures. Conformance to a budget is one aspect, but a relatively minor one. At most, conformance measures how well the manager followed instructions; it says nothing about how well the job was done.

In predictable organization units, the criterion of efficiency is dominant. This is so by definition because efficiency measures the relationship between inputs and outputs. In less predictable units, performance is measured primarily in terms of effectiveness: how much did the unit's output contribute to the entity's objectives?

In less predictable units, the only objective measures of output may be *process measures:* how many hours were spent on a research project, but not what was accomplished in these hours; how many contacts the public relations person made; how many patients the physician saw. In predictable units, the focus can be on both process measures and *results measures:* how much profit was generated; the cost per unit of output.

In predictable units, performance can be evaluated frequently—hourly or daily for production units, clerical units, and the like; monthly for entire responsibility centers. In less predictable units, valid estimates of performance necessarily require longer time intervals. The success of an advertising campaign, or indeed any marketing innovation, usually cannot be judged until months after the effort was undertaken (although interim measures, such as Nielsen ratings or coupons returned from a media advertisement, may be more prompt). One of the most serious management control problems with less predictable units is that information about performance necessarily relates to the current period, whereas an objective basis for action is available only in the long run. This is a basic reason why the performance evaluations of such units is largely subjective.[7]

> CAUTION: *Even though causal relationships may not be known for an entire responsibility center, they may be sufficiently well known for certain parts of it so that standards can be set and efficiency measured. The efficiency or effectiveness of the controller's organization cannot be measured, but valid standards can be set for certain clerical operations within it.*

Internal Consistency

Nature of the Factor

If the organization has several responsibility centers with similar functions that are physically separated from one another, the management control system should ensure that these responsibility centers act consistently and in accordance with the wishes of senior management. One type is an organization with several branch offices. Senior management of the Internal Revenue Service attempts to assure that all taxpayers are treated alike, no matter what office they deal with. Local branches of a life insurance company, a public accounting firm, a bank, an auto rental agency, or a fast-food chain are expected to conform to organizationwide policies. Staff units of individual profit centers such as personnel, quality control, controller, and finance provide another example; each should follow procedures developed at headquarters.

Implications for Management Control

In order to assure the desired consistency of operations, headquarters develops detailed rules for the operation of such responsibility centers, and it usually has training programs to promote the understanding and use of these rules. The formal organization structure, job descriptions, and divisions of responsibilities are written out in considerable detail.[8]

Programming and annual planning are done within the constraints of these rules. For example, standards may be developed that permit so many square feet of office space per employee, number of clerical workers for a given volume of transactions, pay scales and number of employees in each pay grade, and the amount of contributions to local charities. These govern the numbers included in the budget, and they reduce the opportunities for negotiation about the budget amounts.

Some organizations with branches of this type tend to require detailed, frequent reports from the branches, although there may be no real need for them. These reports seem to proliferate with time; often, a new management can prune them substantially.

Entities with detailed rules are referred to as "bureaucracies," a word that usually has a pejorative implication. Actually, given the need for consistency throughout the organization, such details are necessary. Especially in bureaucracies whose output cannot be satisfactorily measured, a focus on adherence to rules, including spending only as authorized in the budget, is an important criterion in judging performance. This criterion may be given more importance than is warranted; the real criterion is how well the work was done.

Interdependence

Nature of the Factor

The structure of an organization is determined partly by its strategy and partly by the interdependence among its units. The relationship between strategy and structure has already been mentioned.

Interdependence has two related aspects. First, there is the interdependence that results when several responsibility centers are part of a single production process, such as the departments in a factory, or even a single marketing-production process. The output of one unit is the input of the next unit. A marketing unit may be a member of a set of interdependent units; production activities are in direct response to sales orders taken. Second, there is the interdependence between units that provide internal services and the responsibility centers that receive these services.

Implications for Management Control

In interdependent organizations, responsibility centers make their annual plans in accordance with detailed guidelines. The first cut of the budget may uncover inconsistencies relating to the interdependency among units. For example, users may collectively budget for more data processing work than the data processing department's capacity. These discrepancies are reconciled before the final budget is approved.

There is an obvious need for a rapid flow of accurate, detailed information among interdependent units.

In evaluation, the fact that the responsibility centers must act as a team causes complications. If too much emphasis is given to the reported profitability of individual units, managers may be unwilling to sacrifice a little of their own profitability for the overall good of the organization. For example, a production manager may be unwilling to authorize overtime costs that are necessary to fill a rush order that the marketing department regards as being essential in maintaining good relations with that customer. For this reason, great care must be exercised in developing a bonus plan that encourages individual sacrifices for the overall good. Also, one manager may blame other managers for poor performance (for example, blame the purchasing department for a shortage of parts that caused down time), and actual responsibility may be difficult to pinpoint. In short, an interdependent organization requires teamwork, but the management control system tends to focus on individual managers without adequate recognition of the importance of teamwork.

Flexibility

Nature of the Variable

Organizations differ as to the ability of management to change the conduct of their operations. At one extreme are *capital-intensive* organizations such as electrical generating plants; having built a plant, the organization is committed to operating it for a long period of time. Similarly, an organization may commit itself with a long-term supply contract, or it may sign a construction contract that implies a long-term commitment. At the other extreme are *labor-intensive* organizations whose size can be varied by hiring and layoffs (although management may be loath to see the size of the organization contract).

Implications for Management Control

Capital-intensive organizations need to give much attention to the programming process. They need a mechanism for controlling the actual construction of plant. In annual planning, they need to consider carefully the consequences of having idle plant if sales volume is lower than plant capacity. In evaluation, they need to take into account, to the extent feasible, the long-run consequences of those current decisions that reduce flexibility. This is, of course, difficult because the actual consequences may not be known for some years. An important control device is a mechanism for comparing actual experience with the assumptions on which the decision to go ahead with the project were based. (However, such a comparison is not of much use if the persons involved subsequently move to other positions.)

Key Variables

Nature of the Variable

In every organization, something can go seriously wrong. It can be as unlikely as a fire or a flood. It can be an out-of-control situation that has serious consequences unless corrected promptly, such as a breakdown in a chemical process or in an automated production line. The loss, or even the possible loss, of an important customer is another example. Obviously, managers need information about the existence of such situations quickly. Hopefully, instructions as to the remedial steps to be taken are already in place.

Implications for Management Control

By their nature, the events in this category are difficult to predict. Nevertheless, the control system should identify those variables that can change quickly and when changed have a major effect on the organization. Key variables vary in different organizations, and I don't try to list them. The point is that they need to be taken into account in designing a management control system.

Management Style

Nature of the Variable

Overlapping the other variables, the management control function in an organization is influenced by the style of its senior management. The style of the chief executive officer affects the behavior of the organization as a whole, and the style of subordinate managers affects those parts of the organization that they manage. Some management styles and their implications for management control are described in this section.[9]

The style preferred by a particular manager may not be a good fit with the management control requirements of the organization. If the manager recognizes this incongruity and adapts his or her style accordingly, the problem disappears. If, however, the manager is unwilling or unable to change his or her style, the organization will be in serious trouble. The solution in this case is to change the management.

"Tight" versus "Loose" Controls

Managers exercise tight control when they define subordinates' roles in detail, when they participate frequently in decision making by subordinate managers, and when they monitor actual results closely. Managers exercise loose control when they permit subordinates to decide what should be done, within broad limits, and when they focus on overall results (the *bottom line*), rather than on the details of how the results were obtained.

As suggested in earlier sections, in some situations management control is necessarily somewhat tight and in other situations somewhat loose. A manager's style affects the *degree* of tight versus loose control in any situation. Thus, the manager of a routine production responsibility center can be controlled either relatively tightly or relatively loosely, and the actual control reflects the style of the manager's superior.

The degree of looseness tends to increase at successively higher levels in the organization hierarchy. Higher-level managers tend to pay less attention to details and more to overall results than lower-level managers. However, this generalization does not apply if a given manager has a different style.

> CAUTION: *The degree of tightness or looseness is often not revealed by the content or the forms or aspects of the formal control documents, rules, or procedures. It depends on how these formal devices are used.*

Personal versus Impersonal Controls

Managers differ as to the relative importance they attach to formal budgets and reports, contrasted with informal conversations and other personal contacts.[10] Some managers are "numbers-oriented"; they want a large flow of quantitative information, and they spend much time analyzing this information and deriving tentative conclusions from it. Other managers are "people-oriented"; they look at a few numbers, but they usually arrive at their conclusions by talking with people; they judge the relevance and importance of what they learn partly on their appraisal of the other person. They spend much time visiting various locations and talking with both management people and hourly employees to obtain a feel for how well things are going. These differences in style are matters of degree; all managers need both formal reports and informal sources of information.

Management's attitude toward formal reports affects the amount of detail they desire, the frequency of these reports, and even such matters as their preference for graphs rather than tables of numbers, or for supplementing numerical reports with written comments. Designers of management control systems obviously need to identify these preferences and accommodate them.

Entrepreneur

As mentioned in earlier sections, the manager responsible for starting a business or for introducing a new product is often an entrepreneur. An entrepreneur is a special type of manager; in fact, some people regard "entrepreneurial manager" as a contradiction in terms. However, even a small new venture involves several people, and the entrepreneur who leads these people is by definition a manager.

Many entrepreneurs will not tolerate good management controls, even though they recognize that theoretically such controls are desirable. They do not spend much time in developing long-range plans, or even annual budgets. Working with the formal planning and control system distracts them from the more exciting work of making the new idea come to fruition; it is boring.[11] If the entrepreneur is willing to delegate the management control function to a Number 2 person in the organization, this inattention causes no great problem. Even if the function is not delegated, the entrepreneur's contribution to the initial success of the enterprise may far outweigh the lack of optimum control.

In any event, it is unlikely that an organization can be managed indefinitely by an entrepreneur who is not adequate at management control. A new venture may succeed spectacularly with the leadership of an entrepreneur, but it is unlikely to continue to prosper unless the entrepreneur is, or learns to be, a person who is able to exercise good management control.

Other Characteristics

Managers differ in other dimensions. Some think in concrete terms; others think abstractly. Some are analytical; others are heuristic. Some are "Theory X" (they dominate decision making); others are "Theory Y" (they encourage organization participation in decision making). Some are influenced primarily by monetary rewards; others have broader goals. To the extent feasible, the management control system should be an extension of the CEO's individual personality.

Change in Management

Managers inevitably succeed other managers. If the successor's management style is considerably different from that of the predecessor, the organization may have difficulty in adjusting to this change. Subordinates will attempt to judge what the new superior really wants, and this is discerned from how the superior acts (for example, how much attention he actually gives to performance reports), rather than from speeches or directives.

INDUSTRY-SPECIFIC FACTORS

Some of the practices described in earlier chapters need to be modified as applied to certain industries. (As used here, "industry" refers to a group of entities that are engaged in similar activities. Some of those listed here are not ordinarily described as separate industries.) The modifications are not major; they are matters of emphasis rather than basic changes in the management control function. Characteristics that lead to these changes and their implications for management control are described in this section.

Service Industries

Although not explicit, the description in the earlier chapters usually referred to companies that produce and sell tangible goods. Services are intangible, and this is the central reason why certain management control practices in service industries differ from those described earlier.

Services cannot be stored. The airplane seat, hotel room, or consultant's hour that is not sold today is gone forever. There is no inventory to act as a buffer between production and delivery. (In some service industries, such as consulting, there may be a backlog of orders, which acts as a buffer.) Furthermore, many service organizations cannot adjust costs to meet variations in demand, because most of their costs are fixed in the short run; today's differential cost of an empty hotel room is not much lower than the cost of a room that produced revenue today.

Consequently, service organizations work hard to minimize the amount of unsold capacity. They seek ways to level out seasonal fluctuations (for example, low weekend rates at commercial hotels, low midweek rates at resort hotels, special fares on airlines). To the extent feasible, they reduce the cost of idle capacity by personnel planning. They devote much attention to analyzing what can be done to sell all available services and to adjust costs to changes in demand. The percentage of available resources that produced revenue is a key results variable ("sold time" in a professional organization, "load factor" in an airline, "occupancy rate" in a hotel).

The quality of tangible goods can be inspected before the goods are released to the customer, but the quality of many services can be inspected only as the services are delivered. (An exception is the draft report of an engineering, law, or consulting organization.) Information about the quality level, although of crucial importance to the success of the organization, is obtained from customer complaints and from personal observations; these are much more subjective than the instruments used to measure the quality of goods. In some service organizations, such as hospitals and public accounting firms, there is a formal mechanism for reviewing the quality of service, but this is not typical of other service industries.

Because in many situations neither the quality nor the quantity of output can be measured satisfactorily, judgments about performance are necessarily subjective. Incentive compensation is therefore based primarily on the opinion of the manager's superior, rather than on performance measured against quantitative standards.

Problems specific to several types of service organizations are discussed in the following sections: financial institutions, professional organizations, nonprofit organizations, and governments.

Financial Institutions

Banks, insurance companies, stockbrokers, and other financial organizations are service organizations, with the characteristics mentioned above. In addition, they have certain problems of their own that complicate the management control function. Among these are (1) the need to match borrowed funds with loaned funds, (2) the long time horizon of certain transactions, and (3) the transfer price of money.

Matching

Many financial institutions are in the business of obtaining money from depositors and lending these funds to borrowers. They must match the interest cost and maturities of loans with the interest revenues and maturities of deposits. As many savings and loan associations found out in the 1980s, they can get into great difficulty if current revenues are not sufficient to pay current interest costs plus operating expenses. Thus, lending officers need guidelines as to their authority to lend at prescribed rates and maturities, and these guidelines require knowledge of the current pattern of deposits. The system for reporting the information needed to decide on the guidelines, to communicate them, and to ensure that they are adhered to, needs to be prompt and accurate. In some organizations the guidelines are changed daily.

Long Time Horizon

Life insurance companies and banks that make long-term loans do not know the actual profit on an individual transaction until many years after the contract was signed. Nevertheless, they must have a means of estimating profitability in order to judge the performance of branch managers, insurance agents, and lending officers, as a basis for deciding on premiums or interest rates, and for deciding what products to promote. Until fairly recently, these estimates were crude. Since the 1960s, estimating techniques have improved greatly, although they can never overcome the inherent difficulty of judging what is going to happen in the future.

Although the actual profitability of these transactions cannot be known until many years after the sale or loan was made, the performance of the person involved needs to be judged currently and, if feasible, compensation should be based on this performance. In particular, methods of identifying likely problem loans or canceled policies are essential. By definition, they cannot be known with certainty, but criteria can be developed, and the management control system can measure and report conformance with these criteria.

Transfer Price of Money

Loans, investments, and other transactions that generate revenues for a financial institution are made by different departments from those that obtain funds from deposits, fees, and other sources. In order to measure the expenses of the former and the revenues of the latter, transfer prices for money must be established. There can be more than one transfer price, depending on the characteristics of the particular funds. This is a particularly difficult transfer pricing problem, and in recent years excellent techniques have been developed.

Professional Organizations

Organizations that provide services in law, medicine, management consulting, architecture, engineering, research/development, and other professions have a special problem. The professionals in these organizations tend not to appreciate the importance of the management control function, and to resent the guidelines, budgets, and reports that managers in industrial companies take for granted. In recent years, especially with the availability of computer software that eases the paperwork burden, this attitude has lessened considerably in many types of professional organizations (with the notable exception, unfortunately, of higher education).

Similar attitudes tend to exist in professional staff departments in industrial companies, but they are less strong because the overall culture typically found in these companies recognizes the importance of good management control.

The evaluation of performance, and indeed even the measurement of what performance was, may be primarily judgmental. Conformance to the spending expressed in the budget is one aspect, but mere conformance does not indicate how well the job was done. Routine aspects of certain professional activities (for example, the preparation of routine documents by a lawyer) can be measured and evaluated in a manner similar to that of production operations, but nonroutine aspects require judgment. One can tell which 15 percent or so of the professionals did an excellent job and which 15 percent were at the bottom, but the 70 percent in the middle often cannot be arrayed with confidence along a scale. (These percentages are similar to those involved in grading students.)

Nonprofit Organizations

Although profit is rarely the sole goal of a for-profit organization, it is an important goal, and it provides a unifying focus for management control. Proposed programs can be judged in terms of their profitability, and performance of many responsibility centers can be judged on the basis of their contribution to corporate profits.

By definition, such a focus does not exist in nonprofit organizations. The financial objectives of these organizations is on average to break even or do a little better. If the organization generates a large profit, the indication is that it is not providing as many services with available resources as it should. If it consistently operates at a loss, it will go bankrupt, just like a business.

The profit focus provides a unifying theme to the management control function in a for-profit organization that is not present in a nonprofit organization. In a profit-oriented organization, a manager who spends more than the budgeted amount but produces a correspondingly greater profit is often congratulated. In a nonprofit organization, adherence to the budget is more important.

The basic objective of a nonprofit organization is to deliver the maximum amount of services with available resources. In the planning activity, the relationship between the amount of resources devoted to an activity and the resulting benefits is tenuous. (Will an additional professor add enough more to the education delivered to warrant the additional cost?) In the evaluation activity, the quantity and quality of services delivered rarely can be measured satisfactorily.

The budget is especially important in nonprofit organizations. In a for-profit organization, managers can, within certain limits, use their own judgment in deciding whether a proposed additional expenditure will generate substantially more additional revenue, and they can depart from the budget accordingly. In a nonprofit organization, additional revenues are unlikely to be generated by additional expenditures, so the manager's discretion is more limited. The budget is therefore a tight constraint on spending.

Chief executive officers of many nonprofit organizations were appointed because of their expertise in the organization's activities, rather than because of their management skills (although this tendency has been greatly reduced in recent years). Members of governing boards tend to be unpaid people who are interested in the activities of the organization but who are not well acquainted with management practices; they therefore do not exercise as much oversight over the organization as is the case with corporate boards of directors. In such organizations, top-level support for sound management control practices is likely to be less than in for-profit organizations.

> CAUTION: *Differences between for-profit and nonprofit organizations are not as significant as many people make them out to be. In both types of organizations, managers are responsible for the wise use of resources. There is no significant difference between a for-profit hospital and a nonprofit hospital, for example.*

Government Organizations

Federal, state, and local government organizations are nonprofit organizations, so the comments in the preceding section apply to them. They have other characteristics that inhibit sound management control.

One is that their senior managers are elected, or they are appointed by elected officials. Consequently, decisions are partly influenced by the desire for reelection. This means that their decisions are not necessarily consistent with the presumed goals of the organization. The planning, execution, and evaluation aspects of management control must take this fact into account.

In government organizations, authority and responsibility are diffused. In federal and state governments, there is a division of authority among the legislative, executive, and judicial branches. At the local level, responsibility for delivering certain services may be divided among local, state, and federal organizations. These organizational arrangements increase the difficulty of planning and of assigning responsibility for performance.

Government organizations are subject to stronger outside influences than those that affect for-profit organizations. Various pressure groups influence decisions. Citizens, especially the media, assume that they have a right to know the details of government activities, and this assumption is reinforced by "freedom of information" acts. Reports, both for planning and for evaluation, therefore tend to be written with the possibility of publication in mind, and some sensitive information is never reduced to writing.

Regulated Industries

Regulators of public utilities, banks, railroads, pipelines, insurance companies, and other regulated industries usually prescribe accounting principles for the companies within their jurisdiction. These principles often are different from generally accepted financial accounting principles, and they may differ from the principles that the companies would prefer for their management control systems. In many cases, the prescribed systems are poor. The railroad industry, for example, must use an archaic system (although in 1987 the Railroad Accounting Principles Board completed the development of modern principles).

In these circumstances, the regulated company must decide whether to build its management control system around the system prescribed by the regulatory body or to develop a separate system. The latter alternative is expensive and can cause confusion when numbers describing the same events are presented differently in the two systems. Nevertheless, some companies have decided that a separate system is worthwhile. They provide "crosswalks" for recasting the numbers they find useful into the form required by the regulatory agency. Other companies live with the prescribed system, trying to overcome its inadequacies by various informal devices. In their view, the "name of the game" is the bottom line as prescribed by the regulators, even though this may not make much sense as a matter of sound business.

Public utilities, pipelines, and certain other regulated industries are capital-intensive. This influences their programming process. They may plan their capital requirements for as much as 20 years in the future, and such plans may be reasonable because the demand for their product is predictable. Even so, these plans need to be reviewed periodically so as to assure that the assumptions on which they were based continue to be valid. For example, the growth curves for electrical generating plants were upset in the 1970s by the conservation movement touched off by the skyrocketing cost of petroleum, and the feasibility of building nuclear plants has become doubtful because of the success of certain groups in challenging their safety.

Multinational Companies

Multinational companies have the obvious problems associated with foreign exchange fluctuations. (Many people do not realize that this is a fairly recent problem; until the demise of the Bretton Woods agreement, most exchange rates were fixed.) They need rapid, accurate procedures for making decisions on these matters and for evaluating the soundness of these decisions. They also need systems for translating the financial status and performance of foreign subsidiaries, especially in countries with high rates of inflation.

Multinational companies also have a special transfer pricing problem. Section 482 of the Internal Revenue Code spells out detailed rules governing the pricing of international transactions between an American corporation and its foreign subsidiaries. These rules are not necessarily the same as the rules that the company would prefer to use for the management control purpose of promoting goal congruence. This suggests the possible need for a transfer price for management control that is different from the price used for income tax purposes. However, this would involve the cost of operating two systems and create the confusion that exists when two systems give conflicting signals. Also, the very existence of a separate system for management control may cause the Internal Revenue Service to question the system that is used for income tax purposes.

Corporations that operate in several countries should take account of cultural differences that affect control. On the basis of 116,000 responses to a questionnaire administered to employees of one organization that had offices in 40 countries (whose results were consistent with 38 other studies that he analyzed), Geert Hofstede grouped these cultural differences into four dimensions.[12]

1. *Power Distance.* The perception of the amount of inequality between superiors and subordinates. For example, the more that superiors exclude subordinates from the budget preparation process, the greater the power distance.

2. *Uncertainty Avoidance.* The tendency to use rules and rituals to reduce uncertainty, the importance of stability of employment, the level of anxiety or stress that is tolerated.

3. *Individualism.* The importance the employee attaches to personal and family life, compared with his or her regard for the organization.

4. *Masculinity.* The relative importance of qualities associated with men (who are said to be assertive and whose goals are said to be high earnings and promotions) and with women (who are said to be nurturing and whose goals are said to be to render service).

Hofstede classified the principal countries of the world into four groups, based on the above categories. He says that control systems originating in the United States reflect below-average Power Distance and low Uncertainty Avoidance, and therefore need to be modified when they are used in countries in which these dimensions are high. Others may use somewhat different classification schemes, but the existence of cultural differences cannot be denied. Not too many years ago, American managers tended to minimize the importance of these factors. Currently, the need to take them into account in exporting management control systems is generally recognized.

APPENDIX
GENERALIZATIONS AND EVIDENCE FOR THEM

THE book describes what I believe to be currently useful generalizations about the management control function. In this appendix I explain the intended meaning of "currently useful generalizations" as they apply to management control and the nature of the evidence on which these generalizations are based.

CURRENTLY USEFUL GENERALIZATIONS

A generalization is a statement that is believed to be valid much more often than not; that is, the person who accepts a generalization will do well to act in accordance with it, even though in certain circumstances it will turn out to have been invalid. Some generalizations in this book are definitions; others are descriptions of good management control practices.

A generalization also is a principle. The usual definition of "principle" is "a settled guide to action," a phrase implying that the principle must be of practical use.

Useful Generalizations

Generalizations are useful only if action taken in accordance with them produces beneficial results. As one author puts it, valid generalizations are "rules to which it is best to conform in the absence of very strong countervailing considerations."[1] It is always difficult to determine whether a given result really was caused by the application of a generalization, or was brought about for other, unrelated reasons. The best evidence that a generalization is useful is a series of observations showing that application of the generalization was useful, and another series of observations showing that failure to apply the generalization produced some undesired result, or no result.

To be useful, a generalization must be specific enough to indicate a preferred course of action. If after learning a particular generalization, a potential user asks "So what?" the generalization will not be useful to that person. Such a question suggests that the generalization is so broad or so vague that no practical use can be made of it.

Currently Useful

The word "current" is always implicit in the notion of generalizations. In even the oldest and best developed sciences, accepted principles change. Until the twentieth century, the conservation of matter was accepted as a principle of physics; and as recently as 1957, so was the principle of parity. The principle of the conservation of matter was superseded by the principle of the conservation of energy, and the principle of parity was found to be inapplicable to elementary particles. These facts illustrate two of the ways in which principles are modified over time: they can be superseded entirely, or the range of their applicability can be narrowed. A third way is that the range of their applicability can be broadened; for example, when a drug originally developed for one use is found to have other uses.

Generalizations

The words "generalization" and "guide" both have the implication that the statement is usually true, but not always. It must be true much more often than not; otherwise, it is not useful. However, exceptions can occur, in every field except mathematics, without destroying the principle.

In order to be a generalization, a statement must be useful in a variety of situations; otherwise it is nothing more than a report. The assertion that "such-and-such a practice works well in my company" is a report of a single experience, and therefore is not a generalization. Anyone who attempts to apply such a statement to other situations runs the risk of being misled.

There can be no doubt that generalizations about the management of organizations do exist. To deny this is to claim that each problem must be approached de novo, that an experienced person has no advantage over an inexperienced person, and that attempting to learn about management in school, or in reading articles, or in listening to speeches, is pointless. Experienced persons have built up generalizations that are useful to them. Although they may not have verbalized these generalizations, they nevertheless exist, and they can be communicated to others once these persons have learned how to articulate them.

"Motherhood" Statements

Some general statements are such that nearly everyone will agree with them. We tend to accept these "motherhood" statements as being valid and do not need evidence to support them. This is often quite proper. An example is "Control should be related to personal responsibility." Such a statement is a cliché, but clichés are not to be disparaged. Occasionally, however, evidence turns up that casts doubt on a time-honored motherhood statement, in which case the presumption of validity must be carefully examined.

Generality of Generalizations

Statements can be made that have a very broad application, but the broader the applicability, the less useful the statement is likely to be. As Kenneth Boulding says, "We always pay for generality by sacrificing content."[2] The statement "The benefit of a control practice should exceed its cost" is a valid generalization, but it is so broad as to be of little practical use. Statements describing the circumstances in which a practice is likely to be worth more than its cost are more useful, but less general. They are also more difficult to find; one of the most difficult tasks in formulating useful generalizations is to specify the conditions under which they are valid.

The opposite side of this coin is, of course, that to be useful, a generalization must be general. A statement that is valid only in a particular company at a particular time is not a useful generalization except in that company at that time; it cannot be extrapolated safely to other situations. Reporting such a statement serves no useful purpose, except to stimulate thinking.

Thus, good generalizations must be valid under certain specified conditions, but at the same time they must not have so many qualifications attached to them that they have no broad applicability. They should be somewhere between the extremes "All companies should use variable costing" (which is not true) and "Company A should use variable costing" (which may be true but not useful as a generalization). The useful generalization answers the question "Under what circumstances should variable costing be used?"

Organization Characteristics Related to Generality

Following are some comments about the relevance of certain organizational characteristics that influence the development of generalizations about the management control function. They are generalizations about generalizations. They were discussed in more depth in Chapter 7.

1. By and large, generalizations should not be conditioned by differences in the personalities of managers. The personality of the chief executive is, of course, an important factor in determining the optimum management control system, since the system should be, in an important sense, an extension of the CEO's per-

sonality. Differences in the personalities of subordinate managers should not be governing, however. The use of the system will vary from person to person, but the system itself should be affected by human nature in general rather than by specific idiosyncrasies. Separating the influence of individuals from an analysis of the system itself is a difficult task.

2. Organization size is often, but incorrectly, thought to be an important consideration. Although there is a fundamental difference between organizations with only one manager and other organizations, I doubt that fundamental differences exist between, say, medium-size and large organizations with respect to sound management control concepts and practices.

3. Organization complexity, as distinguished from size, is an important consideration. The problem of management control in a single-product cement company is quite different from that in a job shop or in a company with a wide product line or complex manufacturing operations.

4. The philosophy of the organization has an important bearing on the validity of generalizations. Decentralized organizations—that is, organizations in which subordinates have considerable independence of action—have different problems from centralized organizations, in which individual authority is sharply circumscribed.

5. The strength of competition is probably an influential factor as a practical matter, although theoretically management should try to manage as well as possible regardless of the spur of competitive forces.

6. The relative proportions of discretionary costs and engineered costs undoubtedly affect the nature of management control.

7. The rate of change and the degree of change in what the organization does over time also are important considerations.

8. Companies that produce and market commodities have different management control practices from those that deal with differentiated products.

9. Multinational companies have additional management control problems beyond those of domestic companies.

In this book I have tried to handle the problem of variations in practice by describing in Chapters 3 to 6 what I believe to be a "typical" situation, and discussing departures from this typical situation in Chapter 7. Admittedly, my judgment as to what is typical is based largely on personal experience rather than on formal evidence, so the reader may disagree with my analysis. I hope he or she will be charitable. In any event, this arrangement greatly simplifies the problem of describing management control; the alternative would be to deal with these variations in connection with each topic that I discuss in the earlier chapters. This would be cumbersome.

MY GUIDELINES

I tend to use the following guidelines as bases for judging the validity of proposed generalizations about management control systems. My reasons are suggested by the nature of the available evidence, as discussed in the next section.

1. If a generalization is consistent with the theories of scientists and with practice in organizations I believe to be well managed, there is a strong presumption that it is valid.

(a) If the environments of these organizations are similar, then the presumption of validity applies only where these similarities exist. If these organizations have different environments, then the presumed validity is broadened.

(b) If well-managed companies of one type use management control practices that are different from those used by well-managed companies of another type, a generalization should be limited to the applicable type.

2. No matter how many theorists have advocated a procedure, if the procedure has been given a thorough trial and then abandoned, most likely it is unsound. However, this presumption can be rebutted by showing that those making the trial were not competent, that the procedure was not properly applied, or that unusual circumstances were involved.

3. If a proposed procedure has been widely known for a long time, especially if it has been frequently written about, but still has been adopted by only a few organizations, there is a presumption that it is not a good procedure.

(a) However, the force of inertia is strong, and there are notable exceptions to this guideline. The merits of variable costing were described in 1936 (under the name "direct costing"), but variable costing was not widely adopted until the 1950s.

(b) Evidence of nonuse also can be challenged by showing that each of the alleged objections is invalid.

4. As between competent practitioners, who must live with their decisions, and theorists, who have no such responsibility, what the former *do* is likely to be a more valid guide than what the latter *say* should be done. However, practitioners tend to perpetuate the status quo, and practice is therefore not conclusive evidence.

EVIDENCE FOR GENERALIZATIONS

As is the case with any applied discipline, generalizations about the management control function are based on inputs from two quite different sources: theoretical science and practice. The best generalizations are those that are consistent with both sound theoretical principles and valid evidence from practice. The next best generalizations are those that have strong support from practice, even though there may be no known scientific explanation of the relationship between cause and effect. The generalizations that curare assists heart action, that certain drugs help mental patients, that aspirin relieves headaches, and that cigarette smoking causes lung cancer were useful, even before we knew the scientific explanation for them.

Of course, a theory that is not consistent with good practice is not a sound theory. There are many such theories.[3]

Theoretical Underpinnings

Hypotheses are scientific theories that are not supported by adequate evidence from practice. As such, they can be valuable in pointing the way to improved practice, but a judgment as to their validity is difficult to make. One must examine carefully the assumptions and the reasoning that lie behind a particular hypothesis. Often, an unrealistic assumption is made about conditions in the real world. For example, game theory appears to be a sound approach to solving problems that involve interactions between two competitors, but in order to apply game theory to most practical situations, the user must estimate the payoffs from each of the strategies being considered. If such estimates are not feasible in a certain class of situations, we should not generalize that game theory is useful in such situations.

Although unsupported hypotheses must be examined carefully, they should not be rejected outright. Inertia is a powerful force that must be overcome before new ideas are put to practical use. The problem is to isolate from the great mass of untested proposals those few that will turn out to have merit.

Relevant Disciplines

The disciplines relevant for a study of management control systems are general systems theory, the behavioral sciences (especially social psychology), and microeconomics.

General Systems Theory

Although general systems theory is not a science in itself, it brings together ideas about systems that have been developed in other sciences, both physical and behavioral. The analogies that it draws provide useful ways of thinking about management control systems, and I have referred to them in several places.[4]

Behavioral Sciences

In the behavioral sciences, theories typically are not based on adequate evidence; often there is no evidence at all, and few accepted theories are relevant to management control problems. This is simply a fact, and not to be taken as criticism of the behavioral scientists. Their task is vastly more difficult than that of the physical scientists; yet the research resources available to them, especially money, are vastly less. Furthermore, much of the evidence developed in the behavioral sciences is derived from research in which the subjects are nonmanagerial employees: college students or others not currently employed in an organization, or even nonhumans such as white rats and pigeons. The application to management problems of findings based on this evidence is suspect.[5]

Behavioral scientists, including some who do research in organizational behavior, also tend to use new names for concepts that have been around for a long time. As a minimum, this requires the user of the research to study an article or book in enough depth to find out that there is nothing really new, which is a waste of time. Worse, it can lead to confusion and misunderstanding.

In some cases the new terms are developed by consulting firms or others who want to sell an old product in a new package. (The use of "experience curve" to replace "learning curve" is an example.) In other cases, the new terms are used because the author does not know that the old term exists. In still other cases, the author genuinely believes that there is something new when this is in fact not the case.

Currently, the terms that give me the most trouble are in the area that is called "agency theory." Agency theory is used in several subject areas. As used in research on organizational behavior, the terms "principal" and "agent" seem to me to be nothing more than new labels for "superior" and "subordinate." (Of course, if a new term is more descriptive, there is a good reason to use it. I changed "operational control" to "task control" for this reason.)

Until recently, behavioral researchers stayed away from mathematical models. They believed that there is no way of making a realistic model of the dynamics of interpersonal behavior; the subject is too complicated. Research based on agency theory frequently uses models, however. Researchers develop equations that purport to represent the interactions between superiors and subordinates. Because the assumptions in these models are overly simplistic and not based on evidence about actual behavior, conclusions drawn from these models are worthless.[6]

Microeconomics

The essential first step in appraising the usefulness of economic theories is to examine the assumptions that economists make—either explicitly or implicitly—to see whether these assumptions are realistic. If we conclude that the assumptions do describe, at least approximately, the real world, then we can pay attention to the conclusions derived from the mathematical manipulations and logical deductions of the economists.

Many models that simplify the real world are nevertheless useful. Physicists develop models that assume perfect vacuums, the existence of gravity as the sole basic force, or the absence of friction. Such models are useful, provided that their limitations are understood. For many purposes, practical conclusions are not affected by the simplification.

A microeconomic model necessarily simplifies the real world. Although *simplification* is always necessary, *oversimplification* makes the model worthless. By definition, oversimplification means that there is too much simplification for the purpose for which the analysis is being made. Many microeconomic models are oversimplifications. When an economist reasons about a world that does not exist, the conclusions are useless to people in the world that does exist.

For example, some economists assume that selling prices are normally based on variable costs rather than full costs. Although there may be situations in which this assumption is valid, most studies of real world situations reach the opposite conclusion: more often than not, selling prices *are* based on full costs. When confronted with these facts, the variable coster may say that prices *should* be based on variable costs. This is an arrogant statement, implying that the economist knows more than the managers who make their living by deciding on the appropriate selling prices. My generalizations about transfer pricing in Chapter 4 are based on the premise that in the absence of market prices, transfer prices should be based on full costs, rather than variable costs, and I believe this to be a realistic premise.[7]

EVIDENCE FROM PRACTICE

Evidence for generalizations about the management control function comes from any of the following, listed in descending order of their probable validity: (1) experiments, (2) observations, (3) statistical analyses, (4) surveys, (5) case studies, and (6) models. A seventh item, personal experience, is listed last but is by no means least. I shall discuss each of these, contrasting the available evidence relevant to my topic with the evidence used as a basis for generalizations in medicine.

Medicine is a practical discipline that deals with the functioning of individuals, while management control deals with the functioning of organizations, which are groups of individuals. Management control is therefore a much more complicated discipline than medicine. For this reason, evidence about what management control practices keep an organization healthy is, and always will be, less satisfactory than evidence about what practices keep individuals healthy. Nevertheless, the contrast highlights the weakness of evidence about management control, and helps to show why that evidence is necessarily weak.

Experiments

Medicine

The best evidence is that obtained from a controlled experiment. If the experimental design has adequate controls for factors that otherwise would confound the relationship between the variables being studied, and if the sample is representative, the results of such an experiment can be conclusive. This is the way new drugs are tested (but only after there have been experiments with animals), and no drug can be offered to the public until its efficacy has been demonstrated by such experiments. (Even so, the results are not always conclusive. The Dalkon shield showed excellent results in clinical trials, and the possibility that it was sometimes harmful was not known until years after it had been approved.)

Management Control

Virtually no controlled experiments relating to management control have been undertaken, and those few that do exist are of limited usefulness. One of the first was the work by Roethlisberger and Dickson in the Western Electric Company in 1939.[8] They studied the effect of various environmental and behavioral influences on the productivity of workers in one department. Although their report has been used as a model ever since, its conclusions are by no means universally accepted. Indeed, as recently as 1983 a spate of articles debated the validity of the findings.

So far as I know, controlled experiments with managers as the subjects have not been made, nor is it likely that they ever will be made. Such an experiment would require that one group of managers act in a certain way, that another group act in a different way, that all the important variables other than management action be identified and allowed for, and that a valid method of measuring which result was better be developed. Even if senior management were willing to risk the undesirable consequences of the course of action that was hypothesized to be the less desirable, which is highly unlikely, the situation is too complicated to permit a valid experimental design.

A number of experiments of management actions have been conducted, but the subjects were not managers; frequently they were students in a college classroom. The first such experiment that I know of involved having students fill as many glasses of water as they could in a given time period, with differences in their behavior being influenced by monetary rewards and by their participation in the preparation of a budget for their activities.[9] The experiment was interesting (and earned a Ph.D. for the researcher), but it didn't tell anything about the behavior of real live managers in a real organization setting. Its value is in teaching about the problems of experimental design, not in generalizing about desirable management control practices.

Some experiments have involved managers, but not in the environment in which they actually work. This is frequently done with participants in an executive development program. Valid generalizations cannot be drawn from the behavior of a manager who is confronted with a classroom problem rather than one in the environment with which he or she is familiar. A classroom experiment isn't worth much if the subject doesn't draw on knowledge built up from experience with the actual people involved and doesn't have the incentives provided by the actual reward structure in an organization.

Observation

Medicine

Ethical experiments on human beings can be conducted only if the researcher believes that the participants will not be harmed. Moreover, the long-run effects of new drugs take time to discover, and it is difficult and expensive to hold experimental subjects over a long period. For example, studying the effects of cigarette smoking by requiring an experimental group to smoke heavily and a control group to refrain from smoking is neither feasible nor socially desirable. An alternative is to *observe* the effect of certain practices on a group of individuals over time, without asking some of them to act in a way that is believed to be harmful. A properly designed observation study has the same problem of controlling for extraneous variables that exist for a controlled experiment. In addition, it has the problem of assuring that results are reported accurately.

Such a study may provide conclusive evidence. Alternatively, it may demonstrate that an *association* exists, even though it may not prove that there is a *causal* relationship. For example, there is no doubt that an association between cigarette smoking and lung cancer exists. The experimental evidence does not unequivocally explain what causes this relationship. Nevertheless, the evidence from observations involving tens of thousands of subjects over a period of 30 years is so overwhelming that no rational person would reject the generalization that cigarette smoking does cause lung cancer. (This is a generalization: "If you want to avoid lung cancer, you shouldn't smoke cigarettes." However, not all cigarette smokers get lung cancer, nor is cigarette smoking the only cause of lung cancer.)

Management Control

The analogous evidence for management control would involve a large, representative sample of subjects, observed over a long enough time so that statistically valid generalizations could be made (as distinguished from the small sample from case studies, discussed below). Few attempts to collect such samples have been made. The largest is probably the PIMS study, which contains some relevant information even though it is not directly aimed at management control problems.[10]

Statistical Analyses

Medicine

Much information about the functioning of the human body is based on an analysis of data collected by such organizations as the National Center for Health Statistics and by the life insurance industry. As of this writing, the most important information about the AIDS epidemic comes from such sources. These analyses do not show directly what causes AIDS nor how it is transmitted, but they do provide extremely important inferences that are helpful both to public health officials in dealing with AIDS and to laboratory researchers in suggesting useful directions for experiments.

Management Control

There is no remotely comparable body of statistics about the prevalence of various management control practices. In connection with the price-control programs in World War II, in the Korean War, and in the early seventies, extensive information on cost accounting practices was collected. The Cost Accounting Standards Board collected similar information until its demise in 1980, and it provided some useful summaries of this information. The Federal Trade Commission started a program in the late 1970s, but gave it up. All these efforts involved cost accounting, which has some relevance to management control.

Statistically valid information about what companies do would be useful; for example, the prevalence of alternative ways in which companies define direct labor costs (include taxes? fringe benefits? overtime? and so on). The prevalence of a practice would give some indication as to its desirability (with many qualifications, of course). As a minimum, such information could be a useful counter to the assertion, "everybody knows" that such-and-such a practice is generally adopted.

Surveys

Medicine

Creating and following up on an observation longitudinal study is expensive and time-consuming. In particular, it is difficult to keep many subjects involved for the time period required to obtain valid results. A less expensive alternative is a survey. In this approach, people are asked questions about the topic being studied, either in writing, by telephone, or by personal interviews. A large body of literature describes the proper way of conducting such surveys. It deals with such matters as the sample size, making the sample representative, framing unambiguous questions, the optimum length of the questionnaire, avoiding biased responses, treatment of nonrespondents, and statistically sound methods of adjusting for characteristics of the respondents and deciding whether the results are significant. There is general agreement that this approach has to be limited to specific topics for which clear-cut questions can be framed. Questions such as the prevalence of the use of harmful substances have been studied in this manner.

Management Control

Surveys about management control practices are common. The *Fortune* 1000 companies receive several requests a month. Most of them are amateurish; that is, they are made by people who have not learned survey techniques. For example, recipients may be asked, "Does your company use net present value?" with either a yes/no answer or a ranking from "not at all" to "very much" on a five- or seven-interval scale. Some recipients may not know what net present value is and are nonrespondents for this reason. The questionnaire is rarely constructed to give results that show the weight given to net present value in making a decision, the types of problems for which net present value is used, or a number of other considerations that are necessary to understand the responses. Most respondents are unwilling to spend much time on a survey, so unless the survey instrument is short, the response rate will be so low that the results are unreliable. At best, surveys find out what current practice *is,* whereas we are more interested in what practice *should be.* The majority opinion may not reflect important recent developments that have yet to gain general acceptance, for example.

Despite their limitations, well-designed surveys are far superior to anecdotal evidence obtained from conversations or articles about the practice in one company.[11] In particular, surveys are a good way of finding out about trends. If a succession of surveys shows that an increasing number of organizations have adopted a new practice, this is a strong indication that the idea has merit. If, on the other hand, successive surveys report first an increasing adoption of an idea, and later a decline, the idea probably was a fad.

Case Studies

Medicine

Case studies deal with one or a few situations that are studied in some depth. They do not purport to provide results that are statistically valid. Clinical studies in medicine are nevertheless useful. The first heart transplant was a single observation, but it showed that the procedure did work. Later cases led to even more useful conclusions about how best to do the procedure and the circumstances in which it was likely to be successful.

Management Control

Case studies are probably the most important source of evidence about management control practices. They are of several types: a study prepared by an outside researcher either for teaching purposes or as a research project, a study prepared by employees of the organization, a study growing out of a consulting assignment.

Thousands of cases have been written for classroom use. Since their purpose is to provide the basis for classroom discussion, they are not necessarily valid as a description of actual practice; that is, if the company is disguised, some facts may have been altered so as to bring out certain points for teaching purposes. The situation described in some cases is fictitious. Nevertheless, particularly if the case names the actual company, study of a number of such cases can give one a feel for which practices seem to be better than others under various circumstances.

No single individual or team can make a thorough firsthand investigation of enough situations to provide an adequate basis for generalizing about organizations as a whole. Nevertheless, the cumulative evidence of a series of well-conducted investigations of individual companies or a few companies is perhaps the best source of generalizations. The most useful investigations are those that analyze contrasting situations, such as current practice compared with prior practice in the same organization, a proposed practice compared with present practice, two substantially similar divisions that have different management control systems, divisions in one organization that have different environments but use similar management control systems, different companies in the same industry, or organizational units performing the same function in different industries.

The best-selling book on management ever is *In Search of Excellence*.[12] It is based on case research in 38 presumably well-managed companies. It contains many generalizations, but there is little indication of the number of companies that practice what the authors recommend (and the number is certainly smaller than

38), or why other companies follow different practices. A sample of 38 is too small to warrant valid generalizations, in any event. The book's popularity results from the authors' writing style, not from the validity of the evidence.

Books and articles by practitioners must be used with caution, both because they are likely to be biased, even self-serving, and because the reader usually cannot determine the crucial variables in the situation being described. A rash of articles in the 1970s described a new management control system in ITT. Did this system represent a new development of wide applicability? Did the articles describe a system that produces results primarily because of the vigorous personality of its chief sponsor? Or did the articles describe a gimmick that was publicized in order to please Harold Geneen? The reader is in no position to judge.[13]

Some practitioners, such as Chester Barnard and Alfred Sloan, have provided extremely valuable insights based on their cumulative experience.[14] The value of their conclusions, however, derives more from their wisdom than from verifiable evidence.

Valuable insights are not necessarily reduced to writing. Many students, including me, have been greatly influenced by the observations about management control we learned from Professor Ross Graham Walker, a practitioner turned academic.

On the basis of their own work with clients, consulting firms probably have the best information about current practice and the advantages and pitfalls of new practices. For example, a few firms dominate the field of executive compensation plans; they have tried out various schemes and have some feel for what works and what doesn't work. This is proprietary information, however; it helps give the firm a competitive advantage. Members of a firm do write articles and give speeches about new techniques they have developed, but the purpose of most of these is to sell a service, rather than to inform. The information therefore is sufficiently unspecific so that the reader or listener can't apply the idea without hiring the firm.

Models

Medicine

Biochemists, neurologists, and other researchers who study what goes on inside the human body develop mathematical models (or, in some cases, mechanical models) as an aid to understanding. The validity of the relationships assumed in these models can be verified by actual observation, and the results obtained from manipulating the model are therefore highly useful.

Management Control

The models referred to here are those purporting to describe the management control function, not models of the economics of a firm, of a production operation, or of some other activity. The diagrams given in earlier chapters are models; they are intended to help the reader visualize relationships, but they do not predict relationships. Unfortunately, the most important aspects of management control are behavioral, and we do not know enough about cause/effect relationships of behavior in organizations to construct models that help predict the consequences of a proposed management control practice.

Nevertheless, models do exist.[15] A popular model currently is called "agency theory." The name comes from the basic assumption that senior managers (or directors, or shareholders) are principals and the people who work for them are agents. Principals hire agents to perform services, and the theory asserts that this is a contractual relationship similar to that set forth in agency law. (Advocates say that they do not claim that the relationship is identical with the contractual relationship between principal and agent, but they do not point out the differences.) The model also assumes that both the principal and the agent are motivated solely by self-interest (principally monetary), that they act rationally, that the more they are rewarded, the harder they work (which implies that people are inherently lazy), that they dislike taking risks, that the principal knows the cost of obtaining information about the agent's activities, that the principal knows the effect of various types of incentives on the agent's behavior, and that the principal and the agent arrive at an equilibrium in some sense (it is not clear to me what this sense is). Based on these assumptions, a model is constructed and manipulated to find the optimum compensation plan, the optimum amount of information, and so on.

These models are worthless. The relevant relationship is not the legal relationship between a principal and an agent, but rather it is the relationship between employer and employee, between superiors and subordinates, or between leaders and followers, which are quite different. In fact, the phenomena depicted in the model are the same as those reported in studies of organization behavior for years, but the organization behaviorists are not so presumptuous as to assume that they can be reduced to mathematical equations. As Charles Horngren has written, the assumptions of agency theory are "enormous and distasteful."[16]

Agency theory is primarily a way of getting doctoral students to collect and manipulate data. I have a manuscript by one of them (who shall remain anonymous) reporting on a study of franchise companies. He collected data on 10,240 units, of which 80 percent were franchised and 20 percent were owned by the parent company. One data item was the distance of each of these 10,240 units from headquarters (imagine the work of assembling this information!). Running these data through an agency model led the researcher to conclude that (a) owned units were more closely controlled than franchise units, and (b) owned units were closer to headquarters than franchised units. These do not seem to be unexpected or significant findings. Does the latter imply that McDonald's would be wrong to own a restaurant in China?

Personal Experience

Medicine

Notwithstanding the almost overwhelming quantity of evidence from the sources described above, the physician rarely relies completely on evidence from others. In addition to generalizations derived from this evidence, a physician has developed generalizations based on personal experience. These can temper the evidence, and even, in some cases cause the physician to have a "gut feeling" that a generalization from the evidence is not to be trusted, or that it does not apply in the specific case being diagnosed.

Management Control

Since the evidence for sound management control practices is vastly inferior to that for sound medical practices, the manager necessarily relies much more on personal experience than does the physician. Indeed, it is safe to say that many successful managers have never read a book or article on management control. Authors like me hope that our material will be helpful, but we are not so naïve as to believe that what we say is anywhere near as useful in a particular situation as the personal generalizations that excellent managers have developed. In many cases, they cannot even articulate these generalizations, but they nevertheless exist.

The Literature

Medicine

Evidence developed from the sources described above is reported in the literature. In medicine, thousands of additions to the literature are made monthly. Medicine is divided into specialties, and physicians subscribe to journals covering their specialty. Related sciences, such as biochemistry, are also divided into specialties, each with its own journals. Articles are abstracted, and the abstracts are carefully indexed and made available both in hard copy and in computer databases. Some of these databases have millions of items. Authors of reports are careful to refer to earlier research on the same topic, so that the reader can determine whether the new report is an advance, a confirmation of earlier work, or a review of the state of the art.

The medical literature also contains books and articles intended for a lay audience, such as how to lose weight or how to relax. In general, the physician can distinguish between these books and those that are based on scientifically sound evidence.

Management Control

Reports of management control practices number in the dozens per month, rather than in the thousands. There are only rudimentary mechanisms for abstracting, indexing, and reporting these studies. We know little about the prevalence of various practices or about favorable and unfavorable experiences with innovative practices. A beginning in organizing reports on management practice is being made in the form of abstract services, but these are sketchy at present. Much of the literature, including some best-selling books, describes practices that turn out to be fads, comparable to the diet fads in medicine.[17]

An especially annoying practice of authors who write scholarly articles on management is to refer to earlier sources without specifying whether the conclusions in those sources were valid, or even whether there were any conclusions at all. For example, a 1953 article that described budgeting practice in five companies is cited as if it were relevant as a basis for generalizations about the current prevalence of certain budgeting practices.[18] Articles on agency theory refer to numerous other articles, without pointing out that none of these articles contains useful information. Textbook authors tend to perpetuate unsubstantiated statements made by previous authors. Someone who takes the trouble to read the footnote references usually finds that they are the same unsubstantiated assertions used in support of the author's point. This situation is especially true of the textbooks in the "Introduction to Management" category.

Another annoying characteristic of the literature, which I have already mentioned, is the use of new names for old ideas. An author can, of course, choose new terms (I have done so in this book), but there should be a good reason for doing so. For example, there is a whole branch of accounting called "positive accounting," which I thought was something new until I discovered that it is nothing more than a study of what accounting practices actually are. New terms that are more descriptive, and definitions that are more precise, than the ones they replace are of course helpful. Merely thinking up new names for old ideas is not helpful.

Many books and articles—certainly a high proportion of the total management control literature—are based on the author's opinion, unsupported by research other than that developed from personal experience. Their acceptance depends largely on how convincingly the author writes, rather than on evidence.

Judging the Literature

Management is a "soft" discipline, which means that generalizations cannot be based on "hard" evidence. Individuals working in the field therefore must make personal judgments about the material they find in the literature. Statistically sound evidence is available only for relatively unimportant topics.

Everyone has a way of making such judgments. My own judgments are based partly on what I know about the author, and partly on my feeling about the internal soundness of the views expressed. Others, of course, have different bases for their judgment. For example, in the automobile industry, I have a high regard for Alfred Sloan's book, even though I have never met him. I have a high regard for Bob McNamara, even though much of his wisdom about management control has not been written down. I have a less high regard for Lee Iacocca, even though his public reputation is high and his book was a bestseller. The author's reputation, a cumulative impression, is important to me, but not conclusive.

In general, I mistrust bestsellers, and especially ten-minute, or fifteen-minute, solutions to management problems. They are superficial. *In Search of Excellence* is my current illustration; I found it cute, rather than insightful, even though I have a high regard for Bob Waterman, one of its authors.

I don't find much useful material in news journals, such as *The Wall Street Journal, Business Week, Forbes,* and the *New York Times.* Their fact checking is superb, but the conclusions that reporters draw from the facts tend to be superficial. After all, most stories are based on a few interviews, usually by telephone, by a reporter who has no deep knowledge of the topic. Accordingly, I am skeptical of quotations from these publications cited by authors, with the implication that they provide a reliable basis for generalizations. (*Fortune* articles tend to contain a more thorough analysis.)

An Example: Zero-Base Budgeting

Zero-base budgeting (ZBB) is an excellent example of how a new practice can get adopted despite very little evidence as to its soundness, and how it fades away when companies generally find that it is not worthwhile.

As the name implies, zero-base budgeting requires that a company build its budget starting from a base of zero, as contrasted with incremental budgeting, which takes a certain level of expenses as a starting point. It involves breaking the annual budget into "decision packages," estimating the costs and benefits of the topic of each package, ranking these packages in order of priority, selecting the relatively high ranking packages at lower organization levels for consideration at higher levels, and finally arriving at a budget that consists of the highest ranking packages for the whole organization.

The first article, by Peter Phyrr in the November–December 1970 *Harvard Business Review*, described this practice as used in Texas Instruments Corporation. The asserted benefits were glowing. However, a careful reader would note that the technique was used in only certain staff units at Texas Instruments, and that the conclusion that the results were favorable was entirely the author's and was based on a single year's experience.

In 1971, Governor Jimmy Carter hired Phyrr to help install ZBB in the State of Georgia. Again, there were articles of highly favorable results. Not many people knew that shortly after the installation started in Georgia, "zero" became 80 percent of last year's expenditures; that the packages were in fact "increments" above the 80 percent, despite the criticism of incremental budgeting; that theoretically the governor should review 11,000 packages in order to arrive at a budget, and that there was very little agreement on how to arrive at priorities. Not until 1975 was a thorough analysis of the Georgia experience published.[19]

In 1973, when Governor Carter became President Carter, he ordered all government agencies to adopt ZBB. The idea was picked up by several companies and many government agencies. Many articles and several books were written about it. Most of them were descriptions of the process, rather than reports of concrete results, and several were written by consultants as marketing devices. Before too long, it became apparent that the amount of paperwork required by ZBB was far more than could be handled in the time available during the budget preparation process. (One federal official estimated that the cost of the paper alone exceeded any conceivable savings that could be identified with ZBB.) ZBB as such thereupon faded away in practice (although some textbooks devoted several pages to it for several years thereafter). The name persists in some quarters, in order to take advantage of the favorable publicity, but the technique to which the name is now applied is the technique of program budgeting.

Ironically, the history of another practice called Planning-Programming-Budgeting System (PPBS) is quite different. PPBS was the federal name for program budgeting, which, as indicated in Chapter 4, is a useful practice. In 1967, President Johnson ordered that it be introduced throughout the federal government. Unfortunately, his timetable was too short to permit sound development efforts, and the system got a bad name. President Nixon abandoned it. Nevertheless, although the PPBS label is gone, the technique continues to be used in most government agencies, with slightly different acronyms.

NOTES

Chapter 1

1. The term "administered organizations" is a good label for the organizations of interest here. As defined by Thompson et al., organizations consist of groups that have four characteristics: (1) they exhibit sustained collective action; (2) they are integral parts of a larger system; (3) they have specialized, delimited goals; (4) they are dependent upon interchange with the larger system. (James D. Thompson et al., eds., *Comparative Studies in Administration* [Pittsburgh: University of Pittsburgh Press, 1959], pp. 5–6).

2. Some people state that there are two strategic planning processes, one for the development of goals and the other for the development of strategies for the attainment of the goals. Although in theory this is the case, the nature of the planning, the types of people involved, the temporal characteristics, and other elements are so similar that I see no point in separating the two. In military doctrine, a distinction is made between "strategy," which relates to a particular battle, and "grand strategy," which relates to the whole war, but there seems to be no valid reason to set up analogous categories for purposes of the framework suggested here.

3. William J. Sullivan, *Public Affairs* (Fall 1966).

4. Peter Lorange and Michael S. Scott Morton, "A Framework for Management Control Systems," *Sloan Management Review* (Fall 1974), pp. 41–56.

5. Kenneth A. Merchant, *Control in Business Organizations* (Marshfield, Mass.: Pitman, 1985).

6. In a 10-minute skimming of the July 1982 issue of *The Academy of Management Review*, I noted the following strange terms: "phenomenology," "attribution leadership," "noesis," "nosma," "eidic reduction," "intentional analysis," "Leibnitzian IS," "moxie," "reciprocal determinism," "social learning," "internal validity," "competitive symmetry," "relational communication," "instrumental motivation," "calculative commitment."

7. Geert Hofstede, *Cultural Consequences: International Differences in Work-Related Values* (Beverly Hills, Cal.: Sage, 1980).

8. *Management Services* (March–April 1966), p. 26.

Chapter 2

1. In a sample count of one widely used management text, Nugent and Wollman found that "system" was used, on the average, as every thirty-third word. (Christopher E. Nugent and Thomas E. Wollman, "A Framework for the System Design Process," *Decision Sciences* [January 1972], p. 85.

Ida Hoos has a whole chapter describing various meanings of "system," including a mathematical definition that is 37 lines long. (Ida R. Hoos, *Systems Analysis in Public Policy* [Berkeley: University of California Press, 1972], chapter 2.)

2. The first exposition of general systems theory was a 1947 article by Ludwig von Bertalanffy. His ideas were developed in his "General Systems Research" (1956). For an excellent article, see James G. Miller, "Living Systems: Basic Concepts," *Behavior*, vol. 10, no. 4 (1965), pp. 192–236. See also Norbert Wiener, *Cybernetics: Or Control and Communication in the Animal and Machine* (New York: Wiley, 1948); and W. Ross Ashby, *Design for a Brain*, 2d ed. (New York: Wiley, 1960).

3. Some authors distinguish between "management" and "administration." I see no point in doing so. Originally "adminstration" meant policy formulation and "management" meant the execution of these policies. In current usage, however, these meanings are often reversed. For example, several

cabinet departments in the federal government have an Assistant Secretary for Administration, whose responsibilities mainly have to do with "housekeeping" functions. For a thorough discussion of this point, see Henrietta M. Larson, *Guide to Business History* (Boston: Canner, 1964); and Alfred D. Chandler, Jr., *The Visible Hand* (Cambridge, Mass.: Harvard University Press, 1977).

4. For example, Hofstede defines control as follows: "Control within an organizational system is the process by which one element (person, group, machine, institution, or norm) intentionally affects the actions of another element." G. H. Hofstede, *The Game of Budget Control* (London: Tavistock Publications, 1967), p. 11. Every planning decision fits this definition.

Nevertheless, it is possible to make useful statements about the control process without reference to planning. Kenneth A. Merchant, *Control in Business Organizations* (Boston: Pitman, 1985), has many perceptive ideas on control.

5. In *Planning and Control Systems*, I used essentially the same idea, but spelled it out in more detail:

> *Strategic planning* is the process of deciding on objectives of the organization, on changes in these objectives, on the resources used to attain these objectives, and on the policies that are to govern the acquisition, use, and disposition of these resources.

This definition used "objectives" instead of "goals." I now believe that "goals" is a more precise term, for reasons given in the text. I now prefer "strategies" to "policies" because "strategy" has a broader connotation. The term "policies" has the same meaning as "strategies" if it is restricted to broad policies (as distinguished, for example, from a policy that states who can travel first class on an airplane). The word "strategy" is intended to encompass all the types of decisions listed in the earlier definition.

6. Some authors use these two terms as synonyms, and others reverse the meanings given above. For example, Vancil describes "objectives" as being stated in broad and general terms without reference to a time horizon, with a focus on the external environment, and in relative terms (for example, performance in the top 10 percent of comparable companies); and he describes "goals" as being time-phased, stated in terms of a particular result, internally focused, and measured in absolute terms. (Richard F. Vancil, "Strategy Formulation in Complex Organizations," *Sloan Management Review* [Winter 1976], pp. 2, 3.)

My use is consistent with the etymology of these terms (although abridged dictionaries typically do not distinguish clearly between them). My use is also consistent with the meaning in "management by objectives", which is a phrase used frequently in the management control process. Goals are developed in the strategic planning process, and objectives are developed in the management control process.

7. I think that "satisfactory return on investment" describes the economic goal of business organizations much more accurately than the terms "profit maximization" or "wealth maximization." For my analysis, see "The Trouble with Profit Maximization," *Harvard Business Review* (November–December 1960), pp. 126–134. See also Herbert A. Simon, *The New Science of Management Decision* (New York: Harper, 1960).

8. For a more thorough description of the goals of nonprofit organizations, see R. N. Anthony and D. W. Young, *Management Control in Nonprofit Organizations* (Homewood, Ill.: Irwin, 1988), chapter 2.

9. For an excellent summary of types of strategies, based on an analysis of about 100 books and articles, see Charles W. Hofer, "Research on Strategic Planning: A Summary of Past Studies and Suggestions for Future Efforts," *Journal of Economics and Business* (Spring 1976), pp. 261–286. Results of the principal research projects are summarized in an organized manner. E. Ralph Biggadike, in *Corporate Diversification* (Boston: Division of Research, Harvard Business School, 1979), has an excellent bibliography on strategy as well as useful insights into the strategic planning process.

10. For descriptions of the strategic planning process, see Kenneth R. Andrews, *The Concept of*

Corporate Strategy (Homewood, Ill.: Dow-Jones Irwin, 1980); C. Roland Christensen et al., *Business Policy: Text and Cases* (Homewood, Ill.: Irwin, 1982); Gordon Donaldson and Jay W. Lorsch, *Decision Making at the Top* (New York: Basic Books, 1984); Michael E. Porter, *Competitive Strategy* (New York: Free Press, 1980); Bruce Henderson, *The Logic of Business Strategy* (Boston: Ballinger, 1985); D. E. Schendel and C. W. Hofer, eds., *Strategic Management* (Boston: Little, Brown, 1979).

11. Thornton Bradshaw (in an interview in *Across the Board*, February 1985, p. 41) gives a candid statement of how a set of strategies was formulated:

> When Robert Anderson became the chairman and I became the president of Atlantic Richfield in 1964, we didn't even know each other very well. We [Atlantic Richfield] had bought his company [Honda Oil & Gas Company], he had come on the board and then there was a board revolt against the old management. And the board, at that time, selected Anderson and me. Shortly after this happened, he and I went on a trip to Europe. We talked a lot on the way over. We used the back of the airline's menu to write down what we thought the company could do, what it should do. We wrote down six points [including finding more crude oil to feed the refineries, using alternate-energy sources, diversification against the gradual depletion of oil and gas supplies].

These points were never changed during the tenure of Anderson and Bradshaw.

12. The authors of several recent articles and books do not agree with this statement. Some of them cite the following quotation (*Business Week*, July 8, 1972, p. 52) attributed to Reginald Jones, at that time chief executive officer of General Electric Company:

> Strategic planning has become GE's route to faster corporate growth. It is basically a technique that treats the company's vast array of ventures as an investment portfolio, sorting out the winners and losers through systematic analysis.

I do not accept this quotation as evidence that strategic planning at GE is "systematic." At most, it refers to a systematic review of *existing* strategies; it does not imply anything about the development of *new* strategies. Moreover, his successor, John F. Welch, Jr., "slashed the corporate planning group from 58 to 33, and scores of planners have been purged from GE's operating sectors, groups and division" (Reported in *Business Week*, September 17, 1984, p. 62).

A more realistic statement is: "in geopolitics and in military strategy as well as in business strategy the pattern of competition contains long periods of natural competition punctuated by relatively sudden and major shifts in relationships as a result of strategy" (Bruce D. Henderson, *Strategic and Natural Competition* [Boston: Boston Consulting Group] p. 2).

13. For example, Frank Aguilar, *Scanning the Business Environment* (New York: Macmillan, 1967).

14. In 1984 *Business Week* reexamined a sample of 33 companies whose corporate strategies had been reported in that magazine in 1979 and 1980. It found that 19 of these strategies had failed, run into trouble, or been abandoned; therefore, only 14 could be deemed successful (*Business Week*, September 17, 1984, p. 63).

15. The best-known research is the "Profit Impact of Market Strategy" (PIMS) project originated at General Electric Company, and expanded by the Marketing Science Institute, a nonprofit corporation formed for this purpose by Professor Robert Buzzell and Dr. Sidney Schoeffler. PIMS developed important insights about the relationship of various factors to profitability. As the name suggests, however, this system is a way of analyzing the *impact* of proposed strategies (in particular, marketing strategies), which is not the same as originating the idea that eventually becomes a strategy.

For a description, see Robert D. Buzzell and Bradley T. Gale, *The PIMS Principles: Linking Strategy to Performance* (New York: Free Press, 1987). For a summary of PIMS research, see Vasudevan Ramanujam and N. Venkatraman, "An Inventory and Critique of Strategy Research Using the PIMS Database," *Academy of Management Review*, vol. 9, no. 1 (1984), pp. 138–151.

16. "Goal programming" is a technique which conceptually solves problems in which there are multiple goals, but this technique can be used only if each goal can be quantified and if the relative importance of the goals can be determined. This is unlikely to be possible in the real world.

17. For a perceptive description of these developments, see Bruce Henderson, *The Logic of Business Strategy*.

18. In *Planning and Control Systems*, I used essentially the same idea, but with an emphasis on the acquisition and use of resources:

> *Management control* is the process by which managers assure that resources are obtained and used effectively and efficiently in the accomplishment of the organization's objectives (p. 17).

The newer definition also links management control to the implementation of strategies, which is its direct purpose, rather than to the attainment of objectives, which is a more indirect purpose.

19. In *Planning and Control Systems* I used "operational control" rather than "task control," but with the same definition. This term led to the misconception that the process applied to all operating activities, rather than to specified tasks. Management control also has to do with operating activities, of course.

Also, in describing the process I did not mention the informal interactions discussed in the next paragraph; this was an error. Human beings are involved in many tasks; however, the interactions involve two individuals, or at most a small group. These interactions are usually informal: that is, they are not associated with reports or other formal devices. Since I focus on formal systems, discussion of them is omitted.

Many, but not all, tasks, as used here, correspond approximately to what Simon has called "programmed" activities: "Decisions are programmed to the extent that they are repetitive and routine, to the extent that a definite procedure has been worked out for handling them, so that they don't have to be treated *de novo* each time they occur" (Simon, *The New Science of Management Decision*, pp. 5–6).

Task control corresponds to what Head calls "transaction control" (in Robert V. Head, *Manager's Guide to Management Information Systems* [Englewood Cliffs, N.J.: Prentice-Hall, 1972]). This is a descriptive term, except that to an accountant it suggests bookkeeping transactions, which is too narrow, and to a sociologist it suggests all human interactions, which is too broad.

References on various types of task control activities are R. B. Chase and N. J. Aquilano, *Production and Operations Management*, 3rd ed. (Homewood, Ill: Irwin, 1981; John F. Magee, *et al.*, *Modern Logistics Management* (New York: Wiley, 1985); Sharon M. McKinnon and William J. Bruns, Jr., "Evaluating Tasks for Operational Control," *Management Accounting* (October 1984), pp. 60–63.

20. Human beings may also be used for other reasons. For example, McDonald's probably could serve its fast-food customers more efficiently by using machines rather than human beings at the counter, but it evidently has decided that customers want to place their orders with a person. However, drive-through customers place their orders via a microphone, and they hear, but do not see, a human order taker.

21. See R. K. Mautz and James Winjum, *Criteria for Management Control Systems* (New York: Financial Executives Research Foundation, 1981). Despite its title, this book focuses mainly on criteria for control *of* the management control system, rather than on the management control system itself. See also Institute of Internal Auditors, *Control: Its Meaning and Implications for the Professional Practice of Internal Auditing* (Altamonte Springs, Fla.: Institute of Internal Auditors, 1985).

22. Stephen Kahne, Irving Lefkowitz, and Charles Rose, "Automatic Control by Distributed Intelligence," *Scientific American* (June 1979), pp. 78–90.

23. These informal sources are often referred to as the "grapevine," and the grapevine is sometimes referred to as an "informal system." The grapevine meets the broad definition of "system," even though it is unsystematic.

24. For a description of these activities, see Graham Allison, *Essence of Decision: Explaining the*

Cuban Missile Crisis (Boston: Little, Brown, 1971); Joseph L. Bower, *Managing the Resource Allocation Process* (Boston: Harvard Business School Press, 1986); and Gordon Donaldson and Jay W. Lorsch, *Decision Making at the Top* (New York: Basic Books, 1983).

25. The discussion in this section assumes that strategic planning is done at the top of the organization. In some organizations the divisions are almost autonomous, and division management may make most of the strategic decisions, subject to ratification by top management. The discussion here applies at the divisional level in such organizations.

26. The term "sales orders booked" is an example. In one division, sales orders may be counted as bookings only if they are validated by a written confirmation that the goods are, or will be, available and also that the customer has a satisfactory credit rating. In another division, bookings may be defined as amounts submitted by salesmen on order forms that carry the customer's signature, without checking availability or credit ratings. In still another division, any report received by a salesman may be counted as bookings, even if it contains no customer signature, and even though some of these "orders" may be merely the salesman's way of reserving inventory in the hope that the customer will take it. These different meanings of "sales orders booked" require significantly different interpretations of the sales order picture in the three divisions.

27. George A. Miller, *The Psychology of Communication: Seven Essays* (Baltimore: Penguin Books, 1969), pp. 45–55.

28. For an elaboration of this point, see Geert Hofstede," The Poverty of Management Control Philosophy," *Academy of Management Review* (July 1978), pp. 450–461.

Chapter 3

1. So far as I know, the first description of the idea of "responsibility center" and of the relationship of responsibility centers to accounting was by John Higgins in "Responsibility Accounting" (*The Arthur Andersen Chronicle* [April 1952], pp. 93–111). Until that time the focus of internal accounting was on "cost centers," which were devices for collecting items of cost as a way of arriving at overhead rates, but which were not necessarily related to the responsibility of a single manager.

For example, "occupancy" is often the name of a cost center that consists of costs related to the occupancy of premises. Building maintenance costs may be the responsibility of the factory superintendent, insurance may be the responsibility of the insurance department, and depreciation on the building may not be the responsibility of anyone.

2. Previously, I have used a fourth category, revenue centers, with branch sales offices as an example. As a practical matter, these organization units are responsible for expenses as well as revenues, so they fit the definition of expense center. They differ from profit centers in that revenues and expenses are controlled separately; that is, expenses are not subtracted from revenues to give a measure of the profitability of the unit.

3. For a discussion of profit center criteria, see Richard F. Vancil, "What Kind of Management Control Do You Need?" *Harvard Business Review* (March–April 1973), pp. 75–86; and Raymond Villers, "Control and Freedom in a Decentralized Company," *Harvard Business Review* (March–April 1954), pp. 89–96.

4. For a thorough discussion of the implications of these restrictions on autonomy, see Richard F. Vancil, *Decentralization* (New York: Financial Executives Research Foundation, 1978 and 1979). Vancil reports the results of a survey of 291 large manufacturing companies. Excluding profit centers that were essentially self-contained businesses, the median profit center manager believed that the profit center relied on other units for about one quarter to one third of the resources used in its activities and that the manager had authority to make autonomous decisions affecting about three quarters of the profit center's costs. The book contains much detailed information on profit center practices.

5. For a discussion of some possible solutions to this problem, see the following *Harvard Business Review* articles by John Dearden: "Measuring Profit Center Managers" (September–October 1987),

pp. 84–88; "Case Against ROI Controls" (May–June 1969), pp. 124–130; and "Problems in Decentralized Financial Controls" (May–June 1961), pp. 72–80.

6. For an article advocating "opportunity cost" (which is variable cost plus the foregone contribution margin) see Ralph L. Benke, Jr., James Don Edwards, and Alton R. Wheelock, "Applying an Opportunity Cost General Rule for Transfer Pricing," *Management Accounting* (June 1982), pp. 43–51. They provide no evidence whatsoever that companies follow this practice. The research on which this article was based was sponsored by the National Association of Accountants (NAA). The NAA also sponsored research by Thomas H. Bruegelmann et al., reported in *The Use of Variable Costing in Pricing Decisions* (Montvale, N.J.: National Association of Accountants, 1986). That study concluded: "most companies set target or list prices on the basis of full costs." See also the study by V. Govindarajan and Robert Anthony, "How Firms Use Cost Data in Pricing Decisions," *Management Accounting* (July 1983), pp. 30–34, which arrived at the same conclusion.

7. Texts on industrial psychology expand on these points at length. See especially B. F. Skinner, *Beyond Freedom and Dignity* (New York: Appleton-Century-Crofts, 1971).

8. Some authors assert that there is a relationship between the strength of the achievement need of the leaders of an organization and success of that organization. See David C. McClelland and David G. Winter, *Motivating Economic Achievement* (New York: Free Press), 1971.

9. See Edward E. Jones, "Interpreting Interpersonal Behavior: The Effects of Expectancies," *Science* (3 October, 1986), pp. 41–46.

10. Douglas McGregor, *The Human Side of Enterprise* (New York: McGraw-Hill, 1960).

11. Although the traditional view of evolution focused on the theme of competition (that is, "survival of the fittest"), more recent research indicates that cooperation among its members is also an essential characteristic of the behavior of a successful species. See Robert Axelrood and William D. Hamilton, "The Evolution of Cooperation," *Science* (27 March, 1981), pp. 1390–1396.

12. For a thorough treatment of this topic, see Kenneth A. Merchant, *Control in Business Organizations* (Marshfield, Mass.: Pitman, 1985).

13. Material in this section is condensed from George David Smith and John E. Wright, "Alcoa Goes Back to the Future," *Across the Board* (September 1986), pp. 23ff.

14. For material on organization cultures, see: J. P. Campbell et al., *Management Behavior, Performance, and Effectiveness* (New York: McGraw-Hill, 1970); F. A. Heller, *Managerial Decision Making: A Study of Leadership Styles and Power-Sharing Among Senior Managers* (London: Tavistock, 1971); Paul R. Lawrence and Jay W. Lorsch, *Organization and Environment* (Homewood, Ill.: Irwin, 1969); Jay W. Lorsch and Stephen A. Allen III, *Managing Diversity and Independence* (Boston: Harvard Business School Division of Research, 1973).

15. Kenneth R. Andrews, *The Concept of Corporate Strategy* (Homewood, Ill.: Dow Jones–Irwin, 1980).

16. For criticisms of *In Search of Excellence*, see the Appendix, Note 12.

17. In the 1980s, a young, rapidly growing microcomputer manufacturing company attempted to prepare a statement of its "corporate culture." One sentence in the statement read, "Management by personal communication is part of our way of life. We encourage open, direct, person-to-person communication as part of our daily routine." Notwithstanding the "open communication" buzzword, the statement itself was developed by senior management in strict secrecy, without consultation with middle management, and it was not communicated to the organization until after it had been adopted. Management's deeds were the exact opposite of its words. (Reported by Peter C. Reynolds in "Corporate Culture on the Rocks," *Across the Board* [October 1986], p. 53.)

18. Perhaps stimulated by the contrast between Japanese and American workers and managers with respect to their willingness to accept change, there has been much research on this topic. See Richard E. Walton, "Planned Changes to Improve Organization Effectiveness," *Technology in Society*, vol. 2, no. 4 (1980), pp. 391–412.

19. Ralph Waldo Emerson, *Self Reliance* (1841).

20. An interesting contrast in management styles is that between two chief executive officers of General Electric Company. As described by Lamb:

When he [Reginald Jones] was tapped to run GE, it was a large, multi-industry company that performed fairly well in a number of mature markets. The company, however, was experiencing a bit of a mid-life crisis: a price-fixing scandal that sent several executives to jail, coupled with GE's sound defeat in, and subsequent retreat from, the mainframe computer business. Jones provided the salve for those wounds. He instituted formal strategic planning and built up one of the first strategic-planning units of a major corporation. Jones was psychologically suited for such an operation: dignified, refined, very bright, able to delegate enormous amounts of authority. GE moved into new areas, but carefully, after much thought, and efficiently. Business was good....

[When he retired,] Jones and the GE board had the wisdom to select not a man just like him, but one as different as night from day: Jack Welch....Welch nearly eliminated the planning group, shifting planning to line managers. He cut the work force by 20 percent, closed dozens of plants....Not surprisingly, Welch became as well known for his extroverted personality as the introverted Jones had been for his. "He demands action immediately," said one top GE executive. (Robert B. Lamb, "CEOs for This Season," *Across the Board* [April 1987], p. 38.)

21. In the modern corporation, the person responsible for the operation of the management control system is often called the chief financial officer. The chief financial officer is responsible for functions that prior to the 1950s were performed by two separate people, the treasurer and the controller. Both these officers now report to the chief financial officer in many organizations. The Controllers Institute, which is the principal association of controllers, changed its name to Financial Executives Institute. In my opinion, the reason for this change was that the treasurer function required a highly competent person, but he made important decisions infrequently. Combining this function with the controller function provided a full-time job for a highly competent person.

22. See Vijay Sathe, *Controller Involvement in Management* (Englewood Cliffs, N.J.: Prentice-Hall, 1982).

Chapter 4

1. For more detailed descriptions of the management control process, see Robert N. Anthony, John Dearden, and Norton M. Bedford, *Management Control Systems* (Homewood, Ill.: Irwin, 1988); Robert N. Anthony and David W. Young, *Management Control in Nonprofit Organizations* (Homewood, Ill.: Irwin, 1988); Charles T. Horngren, *Introduction to Management Accounting* (Englewood Cliffs, N.J.: Prentice-Hall, 1987); Kavasseri V. Ramanathan, *Management Control in Nonprofit Organizations* (New York: Wiley, 1982).

For a survey of the literature and a summary of practices in 86 profit centers, see Richard L. Daft and Norman B. Macintosh, "The Nature and Use of Formal Control Systems for Management Control and Strategy Implementation," *Journal of Management*, vol. 10, no. 1 (1984), pp. 3–66.

2. Authors can, of course, use whatever terms they wish. Several books and articles that have "strategic planning" in the title are actually discussions of programming as the term is used here. For example: George A. Steiner, *Strategic Planning* (New York: Free Press, 1979).

3. The programming process is more highly developed in government than in business. For a good description, see Robert J. Mowitz, *The Design of Public Decision Systems* (Baltimore: University Park Press, 1980). See also Richard G. Hamermesh, *Making Strategy Work: How Senior Managers Produce Results* (New York: Wiley 1986).

S. S. Thune and R. J. House studied the performance of 36 firms, consisting of 18 pairs matched by size and industry group, with one firm in each pair a firm that did long-range planning and the other a firm that did not. They concluded that the planning firms outperformed the nonplanning firms in terms of return on investment, return on equity, and earnings per share ("Where Long-Range Planning Pays Off", *Business Horizons* [August 1970], pp. 81–87).

D. M. Herold, in a follow-up study, concluded that the planning firms continued to outperform the nonplanning firms ("Long-Range Planning and Organization Performance," *Academy of Management Journal* [March 1972], pp. 91–94).

These studies, plus seven other studies of the same topic are discussed in Charles W. Hofer, "Research on Strategic Planning: A Survey of Past Studies and Suggestions for Future Efforts" *Journal of Economics and Business* (Spring 1976), pp. 261–286. Not all these studies support the hypothesis that companies that program outperform those that do not, and the methodology of some of these studies has been criticized.

Incidentally, some authors state that programming in business was an adaptation of a process originally developed in government. In fact, the origin was the other way around. The original government system (called Planning-Programming-Budgeting System, or PPBS) was developed in the Department of Defense in the early 1960s. Secretary Robert S. McNamara brought the general outlines of this system with him, based on the system he developed for Ford Motor Company (he was its controller and later its president). This system had some resemblance to the system General Motors Corporation had used for years.

4. See Suk H. Kim, Trevor Crick, and Seung H. Kim, "Do Executives Practice what Academics Preach?" *Management Accounting* (November 1986), pp. 49–52. This reports the results of a survey, with responses from 367 of the *Fortune* 1000 companies, on the prevalence of various capital budgeting practices, and summarizes previous surveys on this topic. See also Thomas P. Klammer and Michael C. Walker, "The Continuing Increase in the Use of Sophisticated Capital Budgeting Techniques," *California Management Review* (Fall 1984), pp. 137–147. For a description of capital budgeting techniques, see Harold Bierman, Jr., and Seymour Smidt, *The Capital Budgeting Decision* (New York: Macmillan, 1980).

5. This process is called a "zero-base review" because ideally it assumes that all activities and expenses in excess of zero must be justified. It is to be contrasted with "zero-base budgeting," which was a gimmick advocated during the 1970s, but now largely discredited. The rise and fall of zero-base budgeting is described in the Appendix.

Consulting firms have well-developed techniques for making zero-base reviews. See, for example, Charles W. Roush, *A New Perspective on Controlling Overhead Costs* (Cambridge, Mass.: The MAC Group, 1987).

6. The British government has a formal review procedure, for which it claims considerable success. However, the reviews are conducted by employees of the agency being reviewed, with only advice from a central organization. Although this procedure may be necessary in order to overcome the opposition of civil servants, I doubt that employees of the agency will be as tough-minded as an outside review team would be.

7. In the late 1960s, Norton Company's formal programming system was often cited as an example of an innovative system; it was the subject of a series of Harvard Business School cases. Shortly after a new management took control, however, the formal system was abandoned. The new chief executive officer, Robert Cushman, explained the reasons in "Is This Group Necessary?" *MBA* (May 1973), pp. 8ff. Basically, Cushman didn't think the effort was worth the management time involved.

8. There seems to be no agreement on the circumstances in which a "management by objectives" (MBO) system is worthwhile. There is agreement that an MBO system is time-consuming and therefore should not be undertaken unless management believes that the results are worth more than the effort involved. For a description of MBO, see Stephen J. Carroll, Jr., and Henry L. Tosi, Jr., *Management by Objectives* (New York: Macmillan, 1973); Charles R. MacDonald, *MBO Can Work: How to Manage by Contract* (New York: McGraw-Hill, 1982); Edward S. Greenberg, *Workplace Democracy: The Political Effect of Participation* (Ithaca, N.Y.: Cornell University Press, 1986); Wilson Learning Corporation Staff, Ruth Cavin, ed., *The Positive Managers* (New York: Wiley, 1985).

9. Michael F. van Breda, in an unpublished MIT paper, uses the term "financial control system," rather than "budget." He defines the structure of this system as "a set of related variables that constitute a model of the enterprise." The literature on budgeting goes back to about 1900. For a

review, see Atsuo Tsuji, "Some Notes on the Early Development of the Budgetary Control Concept in the United States," *Business Review* (Osaka: Osaka City University, 1972), pp. 1–18.

10. See Edmund J. Hall and Richard J. Kolkmann, "A Vote for the Probabilistic Pro Forma Income Statement," *Management Accounting* (January 1976), pp. 45–48; Robert J. Lord, "Budgeting," *Cost and Management* (May–June 1973). Most companies that have experimented with probabilistic budgets have found that attention focused on the "best estimate," and the other estimates were symmetrically distributed around it. Consequently, the expected value of the frequency distribution was the same as the best estimate. Companies that attempted to use probabilistic PERT for production planning and control had the same experience, and almost all PERT systems today are deterministic (that is, expressed as single amounts, rather than frequency distributions).

11. For an excellent description of how managers operate, see John P. Kotter, *The General Managers* (New York: Free Press, 1982). Although the book focuses on the general manager, much of it applies to the work of functional managers.

12. For further discussion of critical success factors, see Anthony, Dearden, and Bedford, *Management Control Systems*, pp. 109–114.

13. For examples of dysfunctional measures of performance, see Note 5 to Chapter 3.

See also Ida R. Hoos, *Systems Analysis in Public Policy* (Berkeley: University of California Press, 1972); and her *Retraining the Workforce: Analysis of Current Experience* (Berkeley: University of California Press, 1967).

For the results of a questionnaire survey on supervisors' attitudes toward budget evaluations, see Paul J. Carruth, Thurrell O. McClendon, and Milton R. Ballard, "What Supervisors Don't Like about Budget Evaluations," *Management Accounting* (February 1983), pp. 38–45.

14. So far as I know, the concept of strategic funds was first stated by Norman Berg in *The Allocation of Strategic Funds in a Large, Diversified Industrial Company* (D.C.S. Dissertation, Harvard Business School, 1964). See also his "Strategic Planning in Conglomerate Companies," *Harvard Business Review* (May–June 1965) pp. 79–92. For the experience in one company, see the Texas Instruments, Inc. cases (Harvard Business School, 184–109 and 184–111, 1984) prepared under the direction of Richard F. Vancil.

15. For material on compensation plans, see Anthony, Dearden, and Bedford (1984), chapter 13.

16. The best work on program evaluation is probably that done by the Program Evaluation and Methodology Division of the U.S. General Accounting Office. It publishes a series of "transfer papers" on the topic. One is "Designing Evaluations" (Washington D.C.: U.S. GAO, 1986). Other references: T. D. Cook and D. T. Campbell, *Quasi-Experimentation: Design and Analysis Issues for Field Settings* (Chicago: Rand McNally, 1979); C. M. Judd and D. A. Kenny, *Estimating the Effects of Social Interventions* (Cambridge, Mass.: Harvard University Press, 1981).

Chapter 5

1. See Paul R. Lawrence and Jay W. Lorsch, *Organization and Environment* (Homewood, Ill.: Irwin, 1969).

2. Frank P. Moolin, Jr., manager of the Trans-Alaskan Pipeline Project, one of the largest and most complex privately financed construction projects ever undertaken, sums up the characteristics of these giant projects as follows:

> A giant project is compressed change. Change is what project management is all about. Starting with nothing, other than a concept in someone's mind, a giant project eventually becomes something that affects the lives, economics and the entire fabric of our society. Because of the velocity of projects, because of the tremendous physical impact these projects have, because of the fact that we start with nothing and end up with something very significant, it is necessary to frequently change the strategy of the organization and management approach to a project. Frequent organizational changes, including different styles of management, are required. Giant projects experience as many organization and management changes in a period of three to five years as corporations see in ten to fifteen years.

(Frank P. Moolin, Jr., "Giant Projects Require New Management Approaches...What We Learned from the Trans-Alaskan Pipeline," speech at the School of Architecture and Urban Planning, University of Wisconsin at Milwaukee, April 23, 1979.)

3. For further discussion of many of the points made in the remainder of this chapter, see: Joseph A. Maciariello, *Program-Management-Control Systems* (New York: Ronald Press, 1978); Linn C. Stuckenbruck, *The Implementation of Project Management: The Professional's Handbook* (Reading, Mass.: Addison-Wesley, 1980); L. R. Sayles and M. K. Chandler, *Managing Large Systems: Organizations For the Future* (New York: Harper & Row, 1971).

4. The price for a fixed-price contract is bid by, or at least proposed by, the contractor. In arriving at this price, a competent contractor includes an allowance for contingencies, and the size of this allowance varies with the degree of uncertainty. Thus, for a project with considerable uncertainty and a correspondingly large contingency allowance, the sponsor may end up paying more under a fixed-price contract than under a cost-reimbursement contract, in which there is no such contingency allowance. This extra payment is the contractor's reward for the assumption of risk.

Fixed-price contracts work best when the scope of the project can be closely specified in advance and when environmental uncertainties are low. In these circumstances, the contractor cannot increase the price by negotiating change orders and is motivated to control costs. If the contractor signs a contract that does not include adequate provisions for adjustments caused by changes in scope or by environmental uncertainties, it will resist the sponsor's requests to make desirable changes and in the extreme case may be unwilling to complete the job. If the contractor "walks away from the job," no one gains: the sponsor doesn't get the product, and the contractor doesn't get paid.

5. In a cost-reimbursement contract the profit component, or fee, usually should be a fixed dollar amount; if it is a percentage of costs, the contractor is motivated to make the costs high and thereby increase its profit. (However, the fixed fee is normally adjusted if the scope of schedule or the project is significantly changed.)

6. There are many variations within these two general types of contracts. In an *incentive contract*, schedule and/or cost targets are defined in advance, and the contractor is rewarded for beating the targeted schedule or for incurring less than the targeted costs. This reward is in the form of a schedule bonus set at an amount per unit of time saved, and/or a cost bonus set as a fraction of the costs saved. Such a contract would appear to overcome the inherent weakness of a cost-reimbursement contract, which has no such incentives. However, if there is no reliable way of arriving at the targets, the ultimate effect may be no different from a cost-reimbursement contract. Thus, an incentive contract is a middle ground; it is useful when moderately reliable estimates can be made.

Analysis of the work to be done may indicate the desirability of using different contract types for different activities on the project. For example, direct costs may be reimbursed under a cost-reimbursement contract because of the high degree of uncertainty, while the contractor's overhead costs may be covered by a fixed-price contract, either for the total project or for each month. A fixed-price contract for overhead motivates the contractor to control these costs; avoids the necessity of checking on the reasonableness of individual salary rates, fringe benefits, bonuses, and other amenities; lessens the contractor's tendency to load the overhead payroll with less qualified personnel, and encourages the contractor to complete the work as soon as possible so that supervisory personnel are freed for other jobs. However, such a contract may also motivate the contractor to skimp on supervisory personnel, a good control system, and other resources that help get the project completed in the most efficient manner.

If unit costs can be reasonably well estimated, but the quantity of work is uncertain, the contract may be for a fixed price per unit applied to the actual number of units. An example is a catering contract with payment made at a specified cost per meal.

7. James G. March and Herbert Simon, in *Organizations* (New York: Wiley, 1958), make a useful distinction between two types of work packages: (1) those that can be *programmed*, that is, the nature of the work required and the time and cost required to do it can be reliably estimated, and (2) those that are *unprogrammed*. Both in planning and in the conduct of operations, these two types of work packages should be treated quite differently.

8. Techniques for analyzing proposed projects are outside the scope of this study. See Robert N. Anthony and James S. Reece, *Accounting Principles* (Homewood, Ill.: Irwin, 1988); Harold Bierman and Seymour Smidt, *The Capital Budgeting Decision*, 5th ed. (New York: Macmillan, 1980); Eugene L. Grant et al., *Principles of Engineering Economy* (New York: Wiley, 1982); O. Maurice Joy, *Introduction to Financial Management and Policy* (Englewood Cliffs, N.J.: Prentice-Hall, 1980); and J. Fred Weston and Eugene F. Brigham, *Managerial Finance* (Hinsdale, Ill.: Dryden Press, 1981). For a review of the literature and an excellent bibliography, see Arnoldo C. Hax and Karl M. Wig, "The Use of Decision Analysis in Capital Investment Problems," *Sloan Management Review* (Winter 1976), pp. 19–48.

9. Moolin emphasizes this point in describing his approach to the management of the Trans-Alaskan Pipeline Project:

> Collecting manhour and progress data and comparing it to a pre-construction estimate and past performance is the most basic and universally accepted type of cost reporting used on any construction project. Of course, such a report doesn't do management's job for it. Rather, the report is a *tool* used by project management to identify the existence of problems (if, in fact, the problem has not already surfaced through other sources of information).
>
> Let's take a hypothetical example. If the Field Labor Daily Report for Section 2 [one of five sections of the pipeline] showed a dramatic increase in the manhour unit rate for ditching, you can be sure that Dave Haugen concentrated his attention on the ditching operation and, unless he already knew the cause of the problem and was confident that it was being attacked properly, worked closely with his Below-Ground Supervisor, the Perini Project Manager and the Perini Below-Ground Superintendent to isolate the cause and take appropriate action. And I can assure you that if the increase in ditching manhours for Section 2 was particularly dramatic, or extended over several weeks, Kay Eliason and I would be in direct contact with Dave to find out what was going on and what was being done about it, if we did not already know. And, of course, the Weekly Critical Items Reports gave us all an ability to compare productivity among the five sections, so that the best and worst performers stood out dramatically—we investigated and spread among the other sections the techniques which allowed the best performers to achieve high levels of productivity and insisted that the worst performers more closely bring themselves in line with their competition.

(Source: Prepared Direct Testimony of Frank P. Moolin, Jr., Federal Energy Regulatory Commission, Docket No. P-81-1, pp. 230–232.)

10. Professor J. Ronald Fox, in an unpublished memorandum, lists the following questions as important in evaluating the manager of a large construction project:

> 1. Did the project manager select contractor organizations and personnel with records of effective and efficient performance? Were the selected contractors and personnel assigned specific objectives and assisted where necessary with timely approvals and the removal of barriers to their performance?
>
> 2. Were reasonable efforts made to plan the project tasks, to allocate resources commensurate with the task requirements, and to anticipate and confront foreseeable problem areas (known unknowns) within the time and resources available?
>
> 3. Were reasonable steps taken to prepare for problems that were not identified in advance (unknown unknowns)?
>
> 4. Did the project manager have a reasonable way of comparing actual performance with planned performance throughout the life of the project and for timely identification of deviations from planned schedule, cost, and technical performance?
>
> 5. Once problems arose, were reasonable steps taken to deal with them expeditiously and to prevent or minimize the likelihood of their recurrence?

Chapter 6

1. The classic is Claude E. Shannon and Warren Weaver, *The Mathematical Theory of Communication* (Urbana: University of Illinois Press, 1949). Shannon was a researcher at Bell Telephone Laboratories, and the mathematical model he developed was of practical use in the design of telephone networks and other communication equipment. It has not, however, had practical applications in the design of information systems in organizations. The model requires data on the probability that a message conveys information, the value of that information, and other quantitative variables that are not obtainable for systems in organizations. The following Studies in Accounting Research (Sarasota, Fla.: American Accounting Association) have some practical information, but not much: #2, Baruch Lev, *Accounting and Information Theory* (1969); #13, Theodore Jay Mock, *Measurement and Accounting Information Criteria* (1976); #17, Robert H. Ashton, *Human Information Processing in Accounting* (1982). See also Joel S. Demski, *Information Analysis* (Reading, Mass.: Addison-Wesley, 1980); and Henri Theil, *Economics and Information Theory* (Chicago: Rand McNally, 1967).

2. As this is written, the Department of Defense is attempting to develop a strategic defense ("Star Wars") system. Its success depends on an integrated system in which information about incoming missiles automatically directs weapons that will destroy these missiles. Many experts believe that such a system is beyond the capabilities of systems designers. Systems in individual companies are far simpler, but the failure to develop integrated systems for companies, despite the obvious advantages, indicates the difficulty.

For an argument that a company can develop an "ideal" single system, see William E. McCarthry, "The REA Accounting Model—a Generalized Framework for Accounting Systems in a Shared Data Environment," *The Accounting Review* (July 1982), pp. 554-558.

3. Integration can occur among entities as well as within a single organization. For example, automobile manufacturers and their suppliers are working collectively to develop systems for handling data required to order and receive parts. It is said that the paperwork previously (1985) required for these activities added $200 to the cost of an automobile, a total of $2 billion a year. The aim is to exchange information electronically. Some grocery and pharmaceutical manufacturers already have developed such systems for handling transactions with retailers. *(Business Week, August 26, 1985, p. 94.)*.

4. For a description of such a system, see Lynda Applegate, "Lockheed-Georgia Company," Harvard Business School Case 187-135, 1987. See also references in Note 5. For problems of implanting an expert system, see the case "Planpower: The Financial Planning Expert System" (Harvard Business School 186-293, 1986), written by John J. Sviokla.

5. For a bibliography on Expert Systems and Decision Support Systems, see Germain Böer, *Decision Support Systems for Management Accountants* (Montvale, N.J.: National Association of Accountants, 1987). Some useful publications: Paul Harmon and David King, *Expert Systems* (New York: Wiley, 1985); P. Keen, P. and M. S. Scott Morton, *Decision Support Systems: An Organizational Perspective* (Reading, Mass.: Addison-Wesley, 1978); F. Warren McFarlan, ed., *The Information Systems Research Challenge* (Boston: Harvard Business School Press, 1984); F. Warren McFarlan and James L. McKenney, *Corporate Information Systems Management* (Homewood, Ill.: Irwin, 1983); R. H. Sprague, Jr., and E. D. Carlson, *Building Effective Decision Support Systems* (Englewood Cliffs, N.J.: Prentice-Hall, 1982); John Sviokla, "Business Implications of Knowledge-Based Systems," *Data Base*, part I (Summer 1986), pp. 5–19; part II (Fall 1986); pp. 5–16. D. A. Waterman, *A Guide to Expert Systems* (Reading, Mass.: Addison-Wesley, 1985).

6. As is to be expected with ground-breaking developments, the experience with expert systems has not been entirely favorable. For example, a financial planning firm purchased for $50,000 "PlanPower," which is an expert system with over 6,000 rules. Initially, individual professionals spent as much time finding out why PlanPower arrived at its recommendations as they previously had spent in making their own recommendations. (See Harvard Business School Case 168-293, "PlanPower.")

7. In its early years, the Soviet Union attempted to develop a system in which equivalent units of

labor were the common denominator. The idea was to implement Marx's edict that all values emanated from human labor. The system failed. A few overall planning models use a nonmonetary common denominator. Models forecasting the sources and uses of energy use quads of energy. Some agricultural models use calories of heat and others use horsepower as a common denominator. These models are not used for management control, however.

8. Public Law 81-784 of 1965 required agencies to shift to a cost basis of accounting as soon as practicable. As of 1988, few have done so.

9. On the basis of experimental evidence, Miller has concluded that most individuals can deal simultaneously with no more than seven "chunks," or qualitatively different items, of information (George A. Miller, *The Psychology of Information* [Baltimore: Penguin Books, 1969]).

10. The American Accounting Association publications listed in Note 1 describe these concerns in depth.

11. This point is developed, with striking examples, in F. Warren McFarlan and William J. Bruns, Jr., "Information Technology Puts Power in Control Systems," *Harvard Business Review* (September–October 1987), pp. 89–94.

12. This example is described in the article listed in note 11.

13. Henry Petroski, "Superbrain, Super Risk," *Across The Board* (December 1985), pp. 51–52.

14. For a social scientist's observations on the subject of this section, see Richard E. Walton, "Social Choice in the Development of Advanced Information Technology," *Technology and Society*, vol. 4 (1982), pp. 41–49.

The best information on the techniques of systems design and installation is that developed by consulting companies based on their own experiences. This information is proprietary; the companies publish only enough to awaken the interest of possible clients. For a recent and useful symposium, see F. Warren McFarlan, ed., *The Information Systems Research Challenge*.

15. The problem of management resistance is not unique to the United States. Margaret K. Chandler describes an attempt to install a huge national information system for Poland. Managers opposed it, and the effort failed. The attitudes described in the article are essentially the same as those in this section (Margaret K. Chandler, "Project Management in the Soviet Bloc," *Columbia Journal of World Business* [Summer 1978], pp. 71–86).

Chapter 7

1. Hofer lists 54 variables; Hambrick and Lei list 10. See C. W. Hofer, "Toward a Contingency Theory of Business Strategy," *Academy of Management Journal*, no. 18 (1985), pp. 784–810. Donald C. Hambrick and David Lei, "Toward an Empirical Prioritization of Contingency Variables for Business Strategy," *Academy of Management Journal* (December 1985), pp. 763–768.

2. For example, I do not list size as an important variable, in the belief that, beyond a modest lower limit, size does not have an important effect on the management control function. However, Kenneth A. Merchant, in "Design of the Corporate Budgeting System" *(The Accounting Review,* [October 1981], pp. 813–829), reports that "larger, more diverse, decentralized firms tend to use budgeting in an administrative manner with greater importance placed on achieving budget plans, greater middle-management participation in budget-related activities, more formal patterns of communication, and use of more sophisticated budgeting supports. Smaller, more centralized firms tend to rely more highly on direct supervision and more frequent personal interactions and less on formal budget."

3. The classic study is Alfred Chandler, Jr., *Strategy and Structure: Chapters in the History of the Industrial Enterprise* (Cambridge, Mass.: MIT Press, 1962). The relationship between strategy and organization behavior is usually referred to as "contingency theory"; see Joan Woodward, *Industrial Organization: Theory and Practice* (London: Oxford University Press, 1965); James Thompson, *Organizations in Action: Social Science Bases of Administrative Theory* (New York: McGraw-Hill, 1967); Paul R. Lawrence and Jay W. Lorsch, *Organization and Environment* (Homewood, Ill.: Irwin, 1967); Jay W.

Lorsch and Stephen A. Allen III, *Managing Diversity and Interdependence* (Cambridge, Mass.: Harvard University Press, 1975); and Selwyn W. Becker and Duncan Neuhauser, *The Efficient Organization* (New York: Elsevier, 1975).

For a description of strategy formulation, see Kenneth A. Andrews, *The Concept of Corporate Strategy* (Homewood, Ill.: Dow Jones–Irwin, 1986).

4. Michael E. Porter, *Competitive Strategy* (New York: Free Press, 1980); and *Competitive Advantage* (New York: Free Press, 1985). For Arthur D. Little's classification scheme, see Robert L. Wright, *A System for Managing Diversity* (Cambridge, Mass.: Arthur D. Little, Inc., 1975). For Boston Consulting Group, see Bruce D. Henderson, *The Logic of Business Strategy* (Boston: Ballinger, 1985).

5. Anil K. Gupta and V. Govindarajan, "Build, Hold, Harvest: Converting Strategic Intentions into Reality," *Journal of Business Strategy* (March 1984), pp. 34–47; Anil K. Gupta and V. Govindarajan, "Business Unit Strategy, Managerial Characteristics, and Business Unit Effectiveness at Strategy Implementation," *Academy of Management Journal* (March 1984), pp. 25–41; V. Govindarajan and Anil K. Gupta, "Linking Control Systems to Business Unit Strategy: Impact on Performance," *Accounting, Organizations and Society,* vol. 10, no. 1 (1985), pp. 51–66.

6. Hofstede suggests the following questions for assessing the degree of uncertainty. (1) Are the objectives unambiguous or ambiguous? (2) Are the outputs measurable or nonmeasurable? (3) Are effects of management intervention known or unknown? and (4) Is the activity repetitive or nonrepetitive? He goes on to suggest types of control that are appropriate for activities that have different combinations of these characteristics. Geert Hofstede, "Management Control of Public and Not-for-Profit Organizations," *Accounting, Organizations and Society,* vol. 6, no. 3 (1981) pp. 193–211.

Gordon and Miller combine the idea of uncertainty with that of differences in management style in developing a model of control systems. They describe types of organizations based on the styles of their managers: (1) the *adaptive firm,* which is successful because it adapts its organization structure and its management control process to its environment; (2) the *running blind firm,* which attempts to react to uncertainties by intuitive judgments rather than by an analysis based on good information, and which is generally unsuccessful; and (3) the *stagnant bureaucracy,* which is unsuccessful because it doesn't respond to changes in its environment (L. A. Gordon and D. A. Miller, "Contingency Framework for the Design of Accounting Information Systems," *Accounting, Organizations, and Society* [1976], pp. 59–69). I believe this classification is simplistic.

7. Simons used essentially the same classification with different names. One category is *interactive control,* which he defines as "situations in which business managers actively use planning and control procedures to monitor and intervene in ongoing decision activities." The other category is *programmed control,* which he defines as "process where business managers direct their attention primarily to ensuring that predetermined control procedures are established and maintained by designated subordinates," (Robert Simons, "The Process of Planning and Control in Uncertain Environments" [*working paper,* Harvard Business School, June 1986]).

8. The management control problems associated with internal consistency are described in depth in Richard F. Vancil, *Decentralization: Managerial Ambiguity by Design* (Homewood, Ill.: Dow Jones–Irwin, 1979). See also Jay W. Lorsch and Stephen A. Allen III, *Managing Diversity and Interdependence.*

9. See F. J. Roethlisberger and W. J. Dickson, *Management and the Worker* (Cambridge, Mass.: Harvard University Press, 1939); Douglas McGregor, *The Human Side of Enterprise* (New York: McGraw-Hill, 1960); Joseph G. San Miguel, "The Behavioral Sciences and Concepts and Standards for Management Planning and Control," *Accounting, Organization, and Society,* vol. 2, no. 2 (1977), pp. 177–186; V. Govindarajan, "Budget Evaluative Style and Organizational Effectiveness: A Situational Approach" (Ohio State University Working Paper No. 178, 1985); Kenneth A. Merchant, "Design of the Corporate Budgeting System"; and Robert W. Zmud, "Individual Differences and MIS Success: A Review of the Empirical Literature," *Management Science* (October 1979), pp. 966–975.

10. Harold Geneen and Lee Iacocca are successful managers whose style is vastly different. See

Harold Geneen, *Managing* (Garden City, N.Y.: Doubleday, 1984); and Lee Iacocca and William Novak, *Iacocca: An Autobiography* (New York: Bantam, 1984).

11. Mitch Kapor, founder of the highly successful Lotus Development Corporation, resigned as its chief executive officer in July 1986, indicating that he no longer found the challenges that he was seeking. He sold some of his stock for $74 million, but kept 653,750 shares. For an excellent description of the entrepreneur, see Larry E. Greiner, "Evolution and Revolution as Organizations Grow," *Harvard Business Review* (July–August, 1972), pp. 37ff.

12. Geert Hofstede, *Culture's Consequences* (Beverly Hills, Cal.: Sage Publications, 1980).

Appendix

1. Charles Frankel, "Explanation and Interpretation in History," *Philosophy of Science*, vol. 24 (1927), p. 142.

2. Kenneth Boulding, "General Systems Theory—The Skeleton of Science," *General Systems, Yearbook of the Society for the Advancement of General Systems Theory*, vol. 1 (1956), p. 11.

3. John B. Miner asked 100 knowledgeable scholars for a list of established organizational theories, and from their responses identified 32 generally accepted theories. He then asked which of these theories was useful. The consensus was that 13 of them had a low degree of practical use, 12 had a questionable degree, and only 7 had a high degree. John B. Miner, "The Validity and Usefulness of Theories in an Emerging Organizational Science," *Academy of Management Review*, vol. 9, no. 2 (April 1984), pp. 296–306.

4. See James G. Miller, "Living Systems: Basic Concepts," *Behavior*, vol. 10, no. 4 (1965), pp. 192–236. Cybernetics is a similar subject. For an explanation, see Stafford Beer, *Cybernetics and Management* (New York: Wiley, 1959).

5. When I went to college, the term was "social science." Some people had the impression that there was a connection between this subject and socialism, which they hated, so the term was changed to "behavioral."

Following is an example of the difficulty of using research from the behavioral sciences. It is based on the paper by Katherine I. Miller and Peter R. Monge, "Participation, Satisfaction, and Productivity: A Meta-Analytic Review," *Academy of Management Journal* (December 1986), pp. 727–749. That paper reported on a careful analysis of 106 articles and book chapters on the relation of participation to productivity and satisfaction. The authors eliminated 59 of these for a number of reasons such as they contained no data, did not clearly measure participation, or had serious methodological problems. After analyzing the remaining 47 studies, they concluded that "participation has an effect on both productivity and satisfaction," but that "participation in goal setting does not have a strong effect on productivity." In Chapter 4, I state, on the basis of experience and common sense, that participation in the budget formulation process (which is goal setting) is a good thing. A person who relied on research findings prior to the publication of the Miller-Monge paper presumably would at least skim these 106 papers, and, having done so, would reach the equivocal conclusion quoted above. The research required to write my paragraph would have taken many months. I am satisfied with my conclusion, even though it is not based on research.

For further discussion of the problems of doing research in the behavioral sciences, see Paul R. Lawrence, "Historical Development of Organizational Behavior" (Harvard Business School working paper HBS 83-75 [1983]).

6. For a review of agency literature, see S. Baiman, "Agency Research in Management Accounting: A Survey," *Journal of Accounting Literature* (Spring 1982), pp. 154–213.

7. Recent studies showing the prevalence of full-cost pricing are Thomas M. Brueggelmann, et al., *The Use of Variable Costing in Pricing Decisions* (Montvale, N.J.: National Association of Accountants, 1986). (Despite the title, the conclusion is that full-cost pricing is dominant); and Vijay Govindarajan and Robert N. Anthony, "How Firms Use Cost Data in Pricing Decisions," *Management Accounting* (July 1983), pp. 30–34. The firms predominantly used full-cost pricing.

8. F. S. Roethlisberger and W. J. Dickson, *Management and the Worker.* For a critique, see H. M. Parsons, "What Happened at Hawthorne?" *Science* (March 8, 1974), pp. 922–932.

9. The experiment is reported in Andrew C. Stedry, *Budget Control and Cost Behavior* (Englewood Cliffs, N. J.: Prentice-Hall, 1960).

For further discussion, see Kenneth W. Thomas and Walter G. Tymon, Jr., "Necessary Properties of Relevant Research: Lessons from Recent Criticisms of the Organizational Sciences," *Academy of Management Review*, vol. 7, no. 3 (1982), pp. 345–352; and Michael E. Gordon, L. Allen Slade, and Neal Schmitt, "The 'Science of the Sophomore' Revisited," *Academy of Management Review*, vol. 11, no. 1 (1986), pp. 191–207.

See also *Studying Organizations: Innovations in Methodology*, a series of six books published by Sage Publications, Beverly Hills, Cal., 1982 and 1983.

10. See Robert D. Buzzell and Bradley T. Gale, *The PIMS Principles: Linking Strategy to Performance* (New York: Free Press, 1987).

11. An excellent source is the series of "technology transfer papers" issued by the Program Evaluation and Methodology Division of the U.S. General Accounting Office, Washington, D.C. Titles include *Designing Evaluations, Causal Analysis, Content Analysis, Using Statistical Sampling*, and *Using Structured Interview Techniques.*

An example of a deficient survey is James B. Edwards, *The Use of Performance Measures* (Montvale, N.J.: National Association of Accountants, 1986). The topic is important, and a well-conducted survey could shed light on it. This one consisted of two mail questionnaires. The first had 19 responses. The second was a shorter survey (5 items), with 39 responses. (The shorter questionnaire may have gone to those who found the first one too time-consuming, but we are not told anything about the rationale for the two surveys.) We are not told how the sample was selected, what the response rate was, or given any other information that would help us judge the validity of the responses. In any event, 19 or 39 responses are too few. The report contains 12 pages of data from the 19 responses (over one–half page per response!). It contains an 11-page listing of individual responses to the short questionnaire, with no attempt to summarize, and respondents are identified only by industry. No attempt is made to draw generalizations or conclusions (which is probably a good thing). The responses do suggest ideas for performance measurement in an anecdotal way, but the study would not qualify as useful research under any reasonable standards.

12. Thomas J. Peters and Robert Waterman, *In Search of Excellence* (New York: Harper & Row, 1982). An excellent analysis is Daniel Carroll, "A Disappointing Search for Excellence," *Harvard Business Review* (November–December 1983), pp. 78–88.

Michael Hitt and Duane Ireland compared the performance of the Peters and Waterman "excellent" firms with the *average* performance of *Fortune* 1000 companies, using the same criteria that Peters and Waterman used. They found very few differences that were statistically significant (Michael A. Hitt and R. Duane Ireland, "Peters and Waterman Revisited: The Unended Quest for Excellence," *Academy of Management Executive* [May 1987], pp. 91–98).

Michelle Clayman reported that 29 of the "excellent" companies experienced declines in financial health in the five years following their selection, using the Peters and Waterman criteria. Also, although the portfolio of "excellent" companies outperformed the market by 1 percent per year in the years 1981–85, the portfolio of "unexcellent" companies outperformed the market by over 12 percent per year. [Michelle Clayman, "In Search of Excellence: The Investor's Viewpoint," *Financial Analysts Journal* (May–June 1987), pp. 54–63.]

13. A book about ITT written by an outsider is Vijay Sathe, *Controller Involvement in Management* (Englewood Cliffs, N.J.: Prentice-Hall, 1982). I regard it as more reliable than books by ITT people.

14. Chester I. Barnard, *The Function of the Executive* (Cambridge, Mass.: Harvard University Press, 1938); Alfred P. Sloan, *My Years with General Motors* (Garden City, N.Y.: Doubleday, 1964).

15. For a review article, but unfortunately not recent, see R. Kaplan, "Application of Quantitative Models in Managerial Accounting: A State of the Art Survey," in *Management Accounting—State of the Art*, Robert Beyer Lecture Series (Madison: University of Wisconsin, 1977).

16. Charles T. Horngren, *Cost Accounting, A Managerial Emphasis* (Englewood Cliffs, N.J.: Prentice-Hall, 1981), p. 689.

For references on agency theory, see Note 6.

17. For a concise listing of recent literature of this type, see "Business Fads: What's In—and Out," *Business Week* (January 20, 1986), pp. 52–61.

18. Chris Argyris, "Human Problems with Budgets," *Harvard Business Review* (January–February 1953), pp. 97–110. This article was cited as recently as February 1983, in *Management Accounting*, p. 45.

19. This was reported by Roger H. Hermanson and George S. Minier in *Atlantic Economic Review*, vol. 26, no. 4 (1975). In the federal government, agencies were permitted to reexamine their programs starting at a base that was higher than zero. The Department of Defense started with a "zero base" that was 98 percent of the current year!

SELECTED SOURCES

B IBLIOGRAPHIES on the topic discussed in this book contain hundreds of references. I see no point in providing a long list here. References relating to specific topics are given in notes for those topics. Authors are listed in the Index. Following are three short lists of general works:

1. annotated bibliographies and literature surveys containing descriptions of books and articles on the subject.

2. books of readings, which tend to include the most interesting articles.

3. a short list of relevant books that have been especially useful to me. Included are both "classics" and relatively recent works.

BIBLIOGRAPHIES

Clancy, Donald K. *Annotated Management Accounting Readings.* Houston: Dame Publications, 1986. An annotated and carefully cross-referenced list of 425 articles published from 1962 through 1984.

Daniels, Lorna. *Business Intelligence and Strategic Planning.* Boston: Baker Library, Harvard Business School, 1982. A selected, annotated bibliography.

————. *Business Information Sources.* Boston: Baker Library, Harvard Business School, 1985. See Chapter 12.

Klemstine, C. F., and M. W. Maher. *Management Accounting Research: 1926–83.* Sarasota, Fla.: American Accounting Association, 1984. Similar to Clancy, but with earlier articles.

Marquette, Penny, et al., eds. *Bibliography of Articles on Governmental Accounting, Auditing, and Municipal Finance: 1971–85.* Sarasota, Fla.: American Accounting Association, 1987. Abstracts over 1,000 articles from 31 journals.

Merchant, Kenneth A. and Robert Simons. "Research and Control in Complex Organizations: An Overview," *Journal of Accounting Literature*, vol. 5 (1986), pp. 183–203.

BOOKS OF READINGS

NOTE: The edition listed is the latest known to me in 1988. Successful readings books are revised every four years or so. This note applies also to texts listed in the next section.

Bell, J. *Accounting Control Systems: A Behavioral and Technical Integration.* New York: Markus Wiener Publishing Co., 1983.

Ramanathan, Kavasseri V., and Larry P. Hegstead. *Readings in Management Control in Nonprofit Organizations.* New York: Wiley, 1982.

Rappaport, A. *Information for Decision Making.* 3rd ed. Englewood Cliffs, N.J.: Prentice-Hall, 1982.

Rosen, L. S. *Topics in Managerial Accounting,* 3rd ed. Toronto: McGraw-Hill Ryerson, 1984.

Thomas, William E., Jr. *Readings in Cost Accounting, Budgeting, and Control,* 6th ed. Cincinnati: South-Western, 1983.

SELECTED BOOKS

Anthony, R. N., J. Dearden, and N. Bedford. *Management Control Systems,* 6th ed. Homewood, Ill.: Irwin, 1988.

Anthony, R. N., and W. W. Young, *Management Control in Nonprofit Organizations,* 4th ed. Homewood, Ill.: Irwin, 1988.

Barnard, Chester I. *The Functions of the Executive.* Cambridge, Mass.: Harvard University Press, 1938.

Cyert, R. M., and J. G. March. *A Behavioral Theory of the Firm.* Englewood Cliffs, N.J.: Prentice-Hall, 1963.

Hofstede, G. H. *The Game of Budget Control.* Assen, The Netherlands: Van Gorcum, 1967.

Lawrence, Paul R., and Jay W. Lorsch. *Organization and Environment.* Homewood, Ill.: Irwin, 1969.

Lorange, Peter, *Corporate Planning: An Executive Viewpoint.* Englewood Cliffs, N.J.: Prentice-Hall, 1986.

Lorsch, Jay W., and Stephen A. Allen. *Managing Diversity and Interdependence.* Boston: Harvard Business School, Division of Research, 1973.

March, James G., and Herbert A. Simon. *Organizations.* New York: Wiley, 1958.

McGregor, Douglas. *The Human Side of Enterprise.* New York: McGraw-Hill, 1960.

Merchant, Kenneth A. *Control in Business Organizations.* Marshfield, Mass.: Pitman, 1985.

Odioiorne, George. *Management by Objectives: A System of Management Leadership.* Belmont, Cal.: Pitman Learning, 1965.

Roethlisberger, F. J., and William J. Dickson. *Management and the Worker.* Cambridge, Mass.: Harvard University Press, 1942.

Sathe, Vijay. *Controller Involvement in Management.* Englewood Cliffs, N.J.: Prentice-Hall, 1982.

Simon, Herbert A. *Administrative Behavior*. New York: Free Press, 1945.

Simon, Herbert A. *The New Science of Management Decision*. Englewood Cliffs, N.J.: Prentice-Hall, 1960.

Skinner, B. F. *Beyond Freedom and Dignity*. New York: Alfred A. Knopf, 1974.

Sloan, Alfred P., Jr. *My Years with General Motors*. Garden City, N.Y.: Doubleday, 1964.

Solomons, David. *Divisional Performance: Measurement and Control*. New York: Financial Executives Institute, 1965.

Steiner, George A. *Strategic Planning*. New York: Free Press, 1979. (Despite the title, the book is primarily about management control.)

Vancil, Richard F. *Decentralization: Managerial Ambiguity by Design*. Homewood, Ill.: Dow Jones–Irwin, 1978 and 1979.

Wiener, Norbert. *Cybernetics: Or Control and Communication in the Animal and Machine*. New York: Wiley, 1948.

Woodward, Joan. *Industrial Organization: Behaviour and Control*. London: Oxford University Press, 1970.

AUTHOR INDEX

SUBJECT INDEX